ON TOP
OF THE
WORLD

HarperCollins*Publishers*

TOM BARBASH

ON TOP
OF THE
WORLD

Cantor Fitzgerald,
Howard Lutnick, and 9/11:
A Story of Loss and Renewal

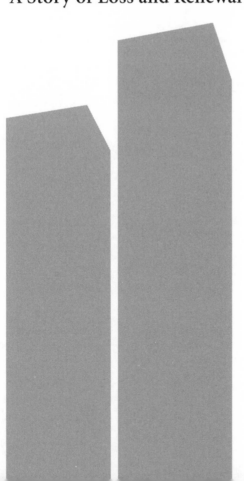

In consideration for its contributions to the preparation of this book, Cantor Fitzgerald has arranged for a significant portion of the royalties from the sale of *On Top of the World* to be donated to the Cantor Fitzgerald Relief Fund, set up on September 14, 2001, to aid the families of those associated with the company who died on September 11.

HarperCollins books may be purchased for educational, business, or sales promotional use. For information, please write: Special Markets Department, HarperCollins Publishers Inc., 10 East 53rd Street, New York, NY 10022.

Grateful acknowledgment is made for permission to reprint "Masters of War," words and music by Bob Dylan, copyright © 1963 by Warner Bros. Inc., copyright renewed © 1991 by Special Rider Music. All rights reserved. International copyright secured. Reprinted by permission.

All photographs courtesy of Howard Lutnick unless otherwise noted.

Photo insert errata: Page 5 top: The Shea Brothers are pictured from right to left. Page 15, top: Harry Fry is the senior managing director for Cantor Fitzgerald.

FIRST EDITION

Designed by Elliott Beard

Printed on acid-free paper

Library of Congress Cataloging-in-Publication Data
Barbash, Tom.
     On top of the world: Cantor Fitzgerald, Howard Lutnick, and 9/11: a story of loss and renewal / Tom Barbash.—1st ed.
        p.   cm.
     ISBN 0-06-051029-3
     1. Cantor Fitzgerald (Firm)—History. 2. Stockbrokers—New York (State)—New York—History. 3. September 11 Terrorist Attacks, 2001. 4. World Trade Center (New York, N.Y.) I. Barbash, Thomas. II. Title.
HG4928.5.L886 2002
332.6'2'097471—dc21   2002027550

03 04 05 06 07 ❖/RRD 10 9 8 7 6 5 4 3 2 1

Editor's Note

A FEW DAYS AFTER September 11, Howard Lutnick received a call from a college friend, Tom Barbash, who was phoning to express his condolences. Lutnick had lost his brother, his best friend, and 658 of his employees when Tower One of the World Trade Center, which housed the offices of his firm, Cantor Fitzgerald, was struck by a hijacked plane.

Lutnick and Barbash had played on the tennis team together at Haverford College and over the years had maintained their friendship while living vastly different lives—Lutnick on Wall Street, Barbash in San Francisco, where he was writing short stories and finishing his novel.

As the two men talked, Lutnick described the nightmare his life had become. There were funerals to attend, a crisis center to manage, a relief fund to set up for the spouses and children left behind, a media clamoring for information, and, finally, a business on the brink of collapse.

Lutnick asked Barbash, a former newspaper reporter, to come to New York. He said he wanted a record of what was happening, that he was in the middle of an extraordinary time, both in his own life and in the country's history, and was afraid that when it was over it would all be a blur. Although Lutnick's original intent was to serve as co-author, over the following weeks and months his responsibilities and obligations multiplied beyond all possible expectation. He was too immersed in the events to write about them. Barbash, who'd been involved since the beginning, took over the role of sole author.

Because of the constantly evolving nature of the events at the heart of this story, the narrative unfolds in real time, with shifting perspectives and firsthand testimony from survivors. Lutnick's accounts are set off in italics. It is a book of many voices, but it is told primarily from the point of view of two men—one at the center of the maelstrom, the other given complete access to observe and record what he sees, as he sees it.

This book is dedicated to the men and women of Cantor Fitzgerald, eSpeed, and TradeSpark who died on September 11.

In Memoriam

Andrew A. Abate
Vincent P. Abate
Laurence Abel
Paul Acquaviva
Donald L. Adams
Shannon Adams
Lee Adler
Daniel Thomas Afflitto Jr.
Alok Agarwal
David S. Agnes
Joanne Ahladiotis
Andrew Alameno
Edward L. Allegretto
Joseph R. Allen
Christopher Allingham
Michael Rourke Andrews
Laura Angilletta
Lorraine D. Antigua

Peter Paul Apollo
Frank Thomas Aquilino
Michael Armstrong
Joshua Todd Aron
Michael Asher
John Badagliacca
Jane Ellen Baeszler
Paul Barbaro
Ivan Barbosa
Colleen Ann Meehan Barkow
Renée L. Barrett-Arjune
Carlton William Bartels
Guy Barzvi
Inna Basina
Alysia Basmajian
W. David Bauer
Lawrence Beck
Maria A. Behr
Debbie Bellows

Bryan Bennett
Dominick Berardi
Alvin Bergsohn
William H. Bernstein
Timothy Betterly
Bella Bhukhan
Joshua Birnbaum
Balewa Albert Blackman
Craig Michael Blass
John Bocchi
Bruce D. Boehm
Martin Boryczewski
Thomas H. Bowden Jr.
Kimberly Bowers
Shawn E. Bowman Jr.
Alfred Braca
Michelle Bratton
Edward A. Brennan III
Frank Brennan

IN MEMORIAM

Mark Broderick
Lloyd Stanford Brown
Brandon J. Buchanan
Dennis Buckley
Patrick Buhse
John Bulaga Jr.
Stephen Bunin
Matthew Burke
Thomas Burke
Keith Burns
Milton Bustillo
Brian Cachia
Richard Michael
Caggiano
Scott Cahill
Thomas Cahill
Dominick E. Calia
Gene Calvi
Sandra Campbell
John A. Candela
Vincent A. Cangelosi
Stephen Cangialosi
Louis A. Caporicci
Jonathan Cappello
Jeremy Carrington
James Carson
John F. Casazza
Leonard Castrianno
Christopher Sean Caton
Jason Cayne
Jason Cefalu
Charles Chan
Delrose Eunice
Cheatham
Stephen Patrick Cherry

Nestor Chevalier
Swede Chevalier
Catherine Chirls
Abul K. Chowdhury
Pamela Chu
Frances Cilente
Nestor A. Cintron
Juan Cisneros
Gregory Clark
Suria Clarke
Geoffrey Cloud
Kevin S. Cohen
Anthony J. Coladonato
Mark J. Colaio
Stephen J. Colaio
Christopher Colasanti
Michel Colbert
Keith Coleman
Scott Coleman
Michael Collins
Margaret Conner
Jonathan M. Connors
Dennis M. Cook
Joseph Coppo Jr.
Joseph A. Corbett
Michael S. Costello
Timothy Coughlin
James Crawford Jr.
Joanne Cregan
Helen P. Crossin
John Cruz
Richard Cudina
Brian T. Cummins
Laurence D. Curia
Beverly Curry

Gavin Cushny
Vincent D'Amadeo
Thomas Damaskinos
Jack D'Ambrosi
Jeannine Damiani-Jones
Michael A. Davidson
Paul De Cola
Azucena de la Torre
Anna DeBin
James DeBlase
Jason C. DeFazio
Monique E. Dejesus
Joseph A. Della Pietra
Kevin Dennis
Thomas Dennis
Michael DeRienzo
Edward DeSimone III
Robert Patrick Devitt, Jr.
Michael Diagostino
Joseph Dickey Jr.
John Difato
Vincent Difazio
Stephen P. Dimino
Marisa Dinardo
Anthony Dionisio Jr.
Doug Distefano
Neil M. Dollard
Thomas Dowd
Joseph Michael Doyle
Patrick Thomas Dwyer
Joseph Eacobacci
Robert Eaton
Paul Robert Eckna
Dennis Edwards
Lisa Egan

IN MEMORIAM

Samantha Egan
Albert Elmarry
William J. Erwin
Fanny G. Espinoza
William Esposito
William Fallon
Anthony Fallone
John Farrell
Christopher E. Faughnan
Shannon Fava
Bernard Favuzza
Edward Fergus
Judy Fernandez
David Ferrugio
Louis V. Fersini Jr.
Michael Bradley Finnegan
Timothy J. Finnerty
Paul Fiori
John Fiorito
Carl M. Flickinger
Stephen Fogel
Christopher Hugh Forsythe
Claudia Foster
Morton Frank
Arlene Fried
Clement A. Fumando
Steven Furman
Paul J. Furmato
Fredric Gabler
James Gadiel
Deanna Galante
Grace Galante
Anthony Gallagher

Daniel J. Gallagher
John Gallagher
Lourdes Galletti
Thomas Galvin
Giovanna Gambale
Douglas B. Gardner
William A. Gardner
Francesco Garfi
Rocco Nino Gargano
Donald Gavagan Jr.
Terence Gazzani
Paul Geier
Peter Gerard Gelinas
Steven Geller
Peter Genco
Steven G. Genovese
Suzanne Geraty
Ralph Gerhardt
Marina Gertsberg
James Geyer
Joseph Giaccone
Andrew Gilbert
Timothy Gilbert
Ronald Gilligan
Laura Gilly
John Gnazzo
Michael Gogliormella
Jeffrey Goldflam
Monica Goldstein
Steven Goldstein
Andrew Golkin
Calvin J. Gooding
Michael E. Gould
Christopher Grady
Edwin John Graf III

Christopher Gray
John Grazioso
Timothy G. Grazioso
Donald Gregory
Pedro Grehan
Matthew J. Grzymalski
Steve Hagis
Frederic Han
Kevin Hannaford
James Haran
Timothy J. Hargrave
Stewart D. Harris
Joseph Hasson
Anthony Hawkins
William Haynes
Scott Hazelcorn
Charles Francis Heeran
Brian Hennessey
John Henwood
Raul Hernandez
Jeffrey Hersch
Mark David Hindy
Thomas Hobbs
Robert Hobson
Marcia Hoffman
Stephen G. Hoffman
Frederick Hoffmann
Michele Hoffmann
James Hopper
Montgomery M. Hord
Michael Horn
Robert L. Horohoe Jr.
Aaron Horwitz
Timothy Hughes
Zuhtu Ibis

IN MEMORIAM

Daniel Ilkanayev
Christopher Ingrassia
Paul W. Innella
Todd Isaac
Erik Isbrandtsen
Aram Iskenderian
John F. Iskyan
Aleksandr Ivantsov
Brooke Jackman
Aaron Jacobs
Jake Jagoda
Dr. Yudh V. Jain
Paul Jeffers
Hweidar Jian
Christopher Jones
Donald T. Jones
Donald W. Jones
Robert T. Jordan
Karen S. Juday
Shari Kandell
Joon Koo Kang
Sheldon Kanter
Andrew Kates
John Katsimatides
Peter R. Kellerman
Frederick Robert Kelley
James Kelly
Joseph A. Kelly
Timothy Kelly
Douglas D. Ketcham
Mary Jo Kimelman
Andrew King
Glenn Kirwin
Alan David Kleinberg
Karen Klitzman

Thomas Knox
Frank Koestner
Ryan Kohart
Bojan Kostic
Danielle Kousoulis
Shekhar Kumar
Kui Fai Kwok
Ganesh Ladkat
James P. Ladley
Joseph A. LaFalce
Michael LaForte
Stephen Lamantia
Rosanne P. Lang
Robin Blair Larkey
Christopher Larrabee
Nicholas Lassman
Eugen G. Lazar
Gary Lee
Richard Y. C. Lee
David Leistman
Jorge L. Leon
Matthew Leonard
Jeffery E. LeVeen
Robert Levine
Shai Levinhar
Edward Lichtschein
Steven Lillianthal
Craig Lilore
Vincent Litto
Elizabeth Logler
Catherine Lisa
Loguidice
Chet Louie
Edward Luckett
Marie Lukas

Michael P. Lunden
Christopher E. Lunder
Gary Lutnick
Linda Luzzicone
Alexander Lygin
Farrell Lynch
Michael Lynch
Sean Patrick Lynch
Sean Patrick Lynch
Robert F. Mace
Thomas Mahon
Joseph Maio
Alfred Maler
Edward Maloney
Christian H. Maltby
James Martello
Michael Marti
William J. Martin
Betsy Martinez
Edward Martinez
Stephen Masi
Michael Massaroli
Philip Mastrandrea
Marcello Matricciano
Edward Mazzella Jr.
Jennifer L. Mazzotta
Kaaria W. Mbaya
Michael J. McCabe
Justin McCarthy
Kevin M. McCarthy
Robert McCarthy
Joan McConnell
Matthew McDermott
Joseph P. McDonald
Eamon McEneaney

IN MEMORIAM

John T. McErlean Jr.

Francis Noel McGuinn

Thomas Michael McHale

Keith D. McHeffey

Michael McHugh

Darryl McKinney

Robert McLaughlin Jr.

Sean Peter McNulty

William J. Meehan

Alok Mehta

Stuart Meltzer

Diarelia Mena

Ralph Mercurio

Alan Merdinger

David R. Meyer

William Micciulli

Peter Teague Milano

Corey Miller

Michael M. Miller

William G. Minardi

Wilbert Miraille

Franklyn Monahan

John Monahan

Craig Montano

Carlos M. Morales

George Morell

Nancy Morgenstern

Dennis G. Moroney

Lynne I. Morris

Seth Morris

Jude Moussa

Peter Mulligan

Michael Mullin

Robert M. Murach

Cesar A. Murillo

Marc A. Murolo

Brian Murphy

Charles Murphy

Edward Charles Murphy

James Murphy

John J. Murray

Richard Myhre

Frank Naples

Manika Narula

Francis J. Nazario

Luke G. Nee

Ann Nelson

Michele Ann Nelson

Jody Nichilo

Martin Stewart Niederer

Troy Nilsen

Paul Nimbley

Robert Noonan

Brian Novotny

Brian F. Nuñez

Michael P. O'Brien

Timothy M. O'Brien

James Patrick O'Brien Jr.

Dennis James O'Connor Jr.

Amy O'Doherty

Matthew O'Mahony

Seamus Oneal

Sean Gordon Corbett O'Neill

Ronald Orsini

James Ostrowski

Jason Douglas Oswald

Todd Ouida

Peter J. Owens Jr.

Angel M. Pabon

Thomas Palazzo

Richard A. Palazzolo

Alan Palumbo

Christopher Panatier

Edward J. Papa

Vinod Parakat

George Paris

Robert Parks

Hashmukhrai C. Parmar

Dipti Patel

Steven Paterson

James Patrick

Bernard Patterson

Stacey Peak

Thomas E. Pedicini

Todd Pelino

Michel Pelletier

Carl Peralta

Robert D. Peraza

Jon A. Perconti

Angel Perez

Angela Susan Perez

Anthony Perez

Joseph Perroncino

Edward Perrotta

Danny Pesce

Davin Peterson

Kaleen Pezzuti

Matthew M. Picerno

Bernard Pietronico

Nicholas Pietrunti

Susan Pinto

IN MEMORIAM

Christopher Todd
Pitman

Joshua Piver

Joseph Plumitallo

John Pocher

Laurence Polatsch

Steve Pollicino

Richard Poulos

Gregory M. Preziose

Everett M. Proctor III

Beth A. Quigley

James F. Quinn

Christopher A.
Racaniello

Harry A. Raines

William R. Raub

Gregg Reidy

Joseph Reina

Thomas Barnes Reinig

Frank Reisman

Joshua Reiss

John Armand Reo

Rudolph Riccio

Gregory Richards

Joseph R. Riverso

Stephen L. Roach

Leo Roberts

Donald Robertson

Donald Robson

Antonio Rocha

Raymond Rocha

Gregory E. Rodriguez

Scott William Rohner

Elvin Romero

Eric Ropiteau

Angela Rosario

Brooke Rosenbaum

Sheryl Rosenbaum

Lloyd Rosenberg

Andrew I. Rosenblum

Joshua M. Rosenblum

Richard D. Rosenthal

Michael Rothberg

Bart Ruggiere

Adam Ruhalter

Steven Russin

Christina S. Ryook

Thierry Saada

Joseph F. Sacerdote

Jude Safi

John P. Salamone

John Salerno

Anne Marie Sallerin
Ferreira

Wayne J. Saloman

Carlos A. Samaniego

Jacquelyn Sanchez

Eric Sand

James Sands Jr.

Maria T. Santillan

Rafael Santos

Paul F. Sarle

Vladimir Savinkin

John Sbarbaro

Robert Scandole

Scott Schertzer

Sean Schielke

Steven F. Schlag

Ian Schneider

Jeffrey Schreier

Edward Schunk

John B. Schwartz

Adriane Scibetta

Michael Seaman

Jason M. Sekzer

Matthew C. Sellitto

Adele Sessa

Jayesh Shah

Khalid M. Shahid

Gary Shamay

Robert Shay

Daniel Shea

Joseph Shea

Atsushi Shiratori

Thomas Shubert

Allan Shwartzstein

David Silver

Valerie Silver Ellis

Kenneth A. Simon

Michael Simon

Marianne Simone

Thomas Sinton

Peter Siracuse

Paul Albert Skrzypek

Christopher Slattery

Vincent R. Slavin

Robert F. Sliwak

Wendy L. Small

James G. Smith

Karl T. Smith

Sushil Solanki

Ruben Solares

Daniel W. Song

Timothy Soulas

Donald Spampinato Jr.

IN MEMORIAM

Robert A. Spencer
Frank J. Spinelli
William E. Spitz
Saranya Srinuan
Eric Adam Stahlman
Corina Stan
Anthony Starita
Alex Steinman
Andrew Stergiopoulos
Andrew Stern
Richard H. Stewart Jr.
Timothy Stout
Thomas Strada
James J. Straine Jr.
Steven Frank Strobert
William Sugra
Patrick Sullivan
James Suozzo
Claudia Suzette Sutton
John Swaine
Kristine Swearson
Kenneth Swensen
Joann Tabeek
Robert Talhami
Michael Anthony Tanner
Kenneth Joseph
Tarantino
Michael Taylor
Anthony Tempesta
Brian Terrenzi
Lesley A. Thomas

Glenn Thompson
Nigel Bruce Thompson
William R. Tieste
Stephen Tighe
Robert Tipaldi
Michelle Lee Titolo
Luis Eduardo Torres
Daniel P. Trant
Walter Travers
Michael A. Trinidad
William Tselepis
Michael P. Tucker
Michael A. Uliano
Jonathan Uman
Allen Upton
John Damien Vaccacio
Felix Vale
Ivan Vale
Carl Valvo
Kenneth W. Van Auken
Frederick Varacchi
Gopal Akrishnan
Varadhan
Santos Vazquez
Matthew G. Vianna
Frank J. Vignola Jr.
Joseph B. Vilardo
Joshua S. Vitale
Alfred Vukosa
Wendy Wakeford
Glen Wall

Roy Wallace
Matthew Blake Wallens
John Wallice
James Walsh
Weibin Wang
Stephen Ward
James Waring
Brian Patrick Warner
Charles Waters
Scott J. Weingard
David T. Weiss
Vincent Wells
Ssu-Hui Wen
Peter West
Whitfield West
Adam S. White
James White
John Charles Willett
Brian Patrick Williams
Frank T. Wisniewski
Michael Robert
Wittenstein
Christopher Wodenshek
James J. Woods
Martin Wortley
Neil Robin Wright
Edward York
Joseph C. Zaccoli
Marc Scott Zeplin
Charles Zion

May our love help you heal—

Lauren Manning

Harry Waizer

Virginia DiChiria

DUST

W HEN I WALKED UPTOWN, *before I saw Jimmy Maio, I thought, It's over. Over and done. Everyone was dead. Every single person. All my friends. My brother. Everything I'd put together. I would liquidate Cantor Fitzgerald. There was nothing left of it, no people, no building.*

I had the patents. They were worth something. And there'd be the insurance. Montana, I thought. I would get out of the city and move my wife and three kids to Montana and we would figure out a life there.

I was caked from head to foot in ash and dust, and who knows what else. In those hours, whatever cord had attached me to my life had been severed. I was floating free. There was dust, and hailstorms of debris, three feet of soot. I still had trouble breathing.

The buildings, where I'd spent half my life, had fallen. I wasn't even thinking that I still had my London office or any of the other offices. I kept thinking everyone was dead.

I go to a deli to get water and I have to wait on line. When I get to the front I can't even speak. I give the cashier a five dollar bill and take the water.

We're walking with arrows coming out of us.

That's how they're looking at us. As though we're from another planet, and I look at them the same way. It's like the movies where someone dies and then they walk around like ghosts. Jimmy and I were walking ghosts.

It was as though we were in slow motion and they were standing still. We were moving uptown, we knew, because everything awful was downtown. I was dazed, but I can't really say I was sad.

Sadness is losing one person you love. But to lose your brother, and your best friend, and several hundred people who work for you is just too much to handle. You shut down.

I was trying to call Allison on my cell phone and it wasn't working. I just kept hitting the redial, hitting the phone.

We kept walking and wiping our faces, and cleaning our mouths and our eyes. In the middle of the street. There were no cars. It was so strange, like the end of the world.

At a corner pay phone there was a line, and a woman on the phone. And I just took the phone from her and hung it up. Then I called my wife.

She'd known I was with Jimmy, my driver, and she knew he could get me to the building, because he was a retired police officer. Then she hadn't heard from me for hours, and in her mind I was dead. So I took the phone from this woman, who was completely clean. We looked at each other. I was like all the people who came from the buildings, covered in dust, the ash and cement caked across my scalp and on my skin. When Allison picked up the phone I said, "Hello."

And she just let out a sound. It wasn't a yell or a cry. She said, "Oh my . . . oh Howard, thank God, thank God, thank God." And she started crying hysterically.

I told her I was all right, that I'd been standing at the doorway of the building and that Jimmy and I had run for our lives.

She told me then that Stephen Merkel, my general counsel, and David Kravette, one of our managing directors and my childhood friend, were alive, and they were at Stephen's house in Greenwich Village. I told her how it had been down there, what it was like when the buildings collapsed, and how I didn't think there was any way people could have made it out.

I remember wanting to help the families, but I didn't know yet how I could. I was fairly sure I was broke, that in fact I owed the bank 30 million dollars. I couldn't imagine looking for a job on Wall Street. I mean, who cares? I wasn't thinking I'd take care of these families because that would assume I had something left to take care of someone with.

I just thought, I've got to help them. I've got to survive. All my guys and women are dead. And I'm alive. Since I'm not dead, I've got to help them.

When I walked into Stephen's apartment he was covered in blood. I asked him, "Whose blood is that?" He said, "I don't know." The blood was all down his shirt.

He told me he had just gotten into the elevator in the lobby and heard this crashing sound. The elevator dropped to ground level. The doors flew open and a fireball raged by them.

"There was an explosion of glass," he said, and somehow he got splattered with blood.

Stephen's wife, Robin, and their sons, David and Gabriel, were there. They were running around, and Stephen was trying to be with them. The phone was ringing with people wanting to know if Stephen was in the building, and the conversations Robin had with everyone were the conversations all the wives wished they'd had.

"He's fine," she'd say. "He's right here."

I finally said, "Stephen, we need to talk. Because we have to figure out what we're going to do here. We've still got our minds now, but I don't how long I can hold it together."

So we went into his bedroom away from the kids and Robin.

His bed was white and clean, and I didn't want to sit there, I told him, with all the grime and dust still on me. So he spread out a picnic blanket on the bed, and we just started talking. The television was on, and Jimmy was watching it on the other side of the room.

He said, "You've got to look at this. You've got to look at this."

And then I look over and I see what must have been the second plane hitting Tower Two, that fierce, fierce explosion coming out the other side.

I thought then that if we'd seen that plane crashing there's no way we would have gone down there, and we definitely wouldn't have been standing at the foot of the building.

I called Lee Amaitis in London. In London they'd shifted into crisis mode, assigning tasks and weighing options. It was light-years from where we were. We were right up against it, and from where we stood it was all gone. We weren't thinking about going back to work. There wasn't anything to go back to.

But they'd been hard at it from the moment the buildings came down. Lee was trying to get the system working from London. Two of my top technology guys, Joe Noviello and Matt Claus, were alive, he said. They'd been about to leave on a fishing trip, and Matt Claus was already at the Rochelle Park, New Jersey, offices with a team of technology people, and they were all working.

We started talking about our back office, and how we could get it up and running again. Lee wasn't talking about liquidation. He's sitting in an office in London with seven hundred people. Why should he liquidate anything? He did what he was supposed to do, which is that if I die, Lee runs the brokerage business, and Fred Varacchi runs eSpeed, and Phil Marber runs equities. And I have a note in my safe that says exactly that. Allison would tell Lee, "You run the show."

So Lee is running the show, though he was as sad as anyone. He'd lost his two best friends, both of whom he'd hired.

When I talked to him I started crying. Or we'd say other things about business and he'd break down. I told Stephen we have to do this now, use our brains now, because it'll sink in soon and we won't be cogent. We're going to go to a thousand funerals. So we need to do this now. The conversations I was having were like the ones you have with a funeral director, when you're picking out the casket and the room for the memorial. You see the options, but you're numb. You don't really care about this casket or that. But this was how I felt then about the company.

We'd do what we could, but it was hard to imagine our getting through this, really. We were going to need lawyers to wind down the partnership. Because I had seen what Lee hadn't seen. And from my viewpoint, we were dead.

IF THEY SET OUT to bomb American capitalism—to hit at the heart of the American economy—the terrorists could not have done better than to kill off Cantor Fitzgerald. The international brokerage firm is responsible for transacting 200 billion dollars of securities a day, or 50 trillion dollars a year, more than the American and New York Stock Exchanges and Nasdaq combined. It is a wholesaler for bonds and third-market equities, a place where financial institutions can do business anonymously and efficiently. It is essentially the New York Stock Exchange for bonds.

The firm's founder, Bernie Cantor, was one of the world's greatest collectors of Rodin sculptures, and there had been as many as eighty pieces on display at the Cantor offices, *The Thinker* and *The Three Shades* among them. It was a firm with its own art curator.

Its brokers and traders were, for the most part, young and extremely successful, an abundance of alpha males and females working high in the sky, a hundred floors above Wall Street. Many of them met when they were single and then passed all the milestones together. They went to each other's weddings, the christenings of their children. They rented summer houses together. They hired siblings and friends. Nepotism wasn't frowned on—it was encouraged. Brothers hired brothers and brothers-in-law, and second cousins. Friends hired friends. There were over thirty sets of siblings at the firm. More than that hired childhood friends.

At 8:46 A.M. on September 11, American Airlines Flight 11, bound for Los Angeles from Boston's Logan Airport, tore through the clear Manhattan sky and struck the north side of Tower One of the World Trade Center. The twenty thousand gallons of fuel the Boeing 767 was carrying for the cross-country flight ignited on impact, causing fires that burned at more than two thousand degrees.

The plane, which was carrying a crew of 11 and 81 passengers, hit at the 93rd floor. Everyone on Cantor's floors above impact—more than 700 people, including food service workers, electricians, and several teams of consultants—died.

Cantor Fitzgerald operated out of the 101st through 105th floors. Of the firm's 1,000 New York employees, 658 were lost. A large number were hired by Howard Lutnick, the company's chairman, who lived only because he was taking his oldest son, Kyle, to his first day of kindergarten when the plane hit. He arrived at the Trade Center site moments before the first building fell, and he was then lost in the rubble for hours. What he had learned when he emerged was that his brother, Gary, his best friend, Doug Gardner, and an unknown number of his other coworkers and partners had been in the building and were now missing.

In the coming days the number of dead and missing will be staggering. Of the wives, thirty-eight were pregnant, fourteen of them for the first time. Forty-six of the lost were engaged to be married; there were at least two weddings planned for the following weekend. Worst of all, these were young people with young families, some with three and four children. Nine hundred and fifty-five sons and daughters lost a father or a mother.

Business on Wall Street begins way before eight o'clock, and by eight thirty the phones are ringing, the squawk box is blaring, markets are moving, and money is changing hands at a speed unmatched anywhere in the world. Because of this, 658 Cantor Fitzgerald traders and brokers, salespeople and secretaries, accountants and lawyers were on site.

Most of those who survived did so by random chance, and so will replay their movements and decisions on that day over and over.

If Howard hadn't taken his son to school, if Stephen Merkel hadn't stopped to ask about an exercise plan at a gym, if David Kravette hadn't gone downstairs to clear a client through security, if Maryann Burns hadn't missed her train, if Harry Fry hadn't taken a business trip he'd put off several times, if Phil Marber hadn't taken a day off to visit a client in Ohio, if Ted Smith hadn't gone to the doctor's, if John Law hadn't gone to a wedding, if Chris Sorenson hadn't fallen in love and taken his girlfriend to an exotic island, if Joe Noviello and Matt Claus hadn't had a fishing trip—they would have been at work and they would have died along with their colleagues.

Before heading home to see his wife and three children, Howard goes, exactly as he is, covered in dust, to Doug Gardner's house on Central Park West. Howard hired Doug eight years earlier, a move that improved his work life immeasurably. Doug, who would become chief administrative officer and head of strategy, was his sounding board, his muse. All the big decisions he made were discussed for hours—or days—with Doug. They spent weekends and vacations together; they were godfathers to each other's children.

Doug was in the building that morning. After the first plane hit, and Stephen Merkel had escaped the falling elevator, and the fireball, he'd called Doug.

"Something just hit us, but we're okay. No one's hurt," Doug said.

Merkel saw the fire raging, smoke choking the outside of the building. He saw the gaping hole where the plane had entered.

"It looks really bad from here," Merkel said.

Doug told him he was leaving. He was worried and felt responsible for getting people out of the building. He didn't sound scared. He also spoke to his father to say he was all right. His father told him just to get out.

Doug has two children—Michael, who in a month will break his front teeth on his fifth birthday, and Julia, who is two.

Howard knows Doug is dead, and he knows that Doug's wife, Jennifer, knows. And he understands now that the fact that he wasn't in the building, even if it was to bring his son to his first day of kindergarten, will be a complicated thing for some people to accept. He needs for her to see him this way—not when he's cleaned up, and not when his mind is occupied with saving the company. It will be days before he can see her again with all the work he'll have to do, and he wants her to know that Doug's death is a singular event for him, not one in a thousand—though it is that too.

When Howard, Stephen, and Jimmy reach Doug's apartment on Central Park West, Doug's parents, Joe and Charlotte, and his filmmaker sister, Danielle, are there. Doug had gone to work early that morning because September 11 was his father's birthday. The family had made five o'clock dinner reservations so the kids could come, and Doug was planning on leaving work early. Danielle had been walking to her gym when she saw the first plane hit. She'd tried to call Doug, then stood watching and calling whomever she could as the second plane struck.

She had for a moment thought the plane was pulling close to help—though in retrospect how could it have at that speed, and at that terrifying angle? Soon she will be unable to watch television, or enter a store for fear of hearing a radio report about September 11 or about the war in Afghanistan. She will sleep only a few hours each night. Theirs is a close family, and their love for Doug extreme.

Howard is still caked in dust, the sight of him is a dreadful confirmation of all they'd feared.

Danielle runs from the room.

Howard embraces Jennifer now and they hold on to one another for a while. "He's *gone*," each remembers saying to the other. He tells her to call him past one in the morning, because he won't be sleeping. He wants to be there to support her, but won't be able to for a while.

His life as he knew it before is gone, and ominous trials lie in wait. He knows that now, but he can't really see what's ahead, how difficult and public his choices will be in the coming months, how much resentment he will invoke, how much strength he will need to summon.

He has little right now, and he hasn't yet spoken to his sister, Edie, about his brother, Gary, though he knows Gary called Edie to say good-bye.

When Gary phoned, Edie had told him how relieved she was that he wasn't in the building, and he had to tell her, "But I *am* in the building, Edie."

One thing at a time, Howard tells himself. And he heads home.

I N THE HOUSES AND APARTMENTS of the men and women who worked at Cantor Fitzgerald, the phones are ringing; friends are arriving to offer support. The world knows two jumbo jets struck each of the twin towers of the World Trade Center—as much as anyone can comprehend something like that. Everything else is still in question. They call one another for information, any information—at this point, as for most of the world, they share rumors. While they wait, they check e-mail, or watch the horror unfold on television screens. Many of them talked to their spouses and were told—*It's all right. We're getting out of here.*

It is a disaster movie with their lives at the center. And in disaster movies doesn't the hero usually make it home?

They tell their parents and children and their friends—*He'll make it home.* He has to make it home.

S TUART FRASER had a nine o'clock meeting that morning at the Ramada Inn about three miles and a few minutes' drive from his home, so he woke up late, got dressed casually—no tie, no jacket. There was a chance that he and his visitor, an Australian investor, would meet the previous day, Monday, but the Australian investor had moved the appointment back. Ordinarily Stuart was in the Cantor Fitzgerald offices on Tuesdays, Wednesdays, and Thursdays.

After nineteen years at the firm, Fraser, vice chairman and nephew of its founder, was in semiretirement. He had bought a ski house in Vermont on Mount Snow, and at age forty, was spending more time with his kids.

He drinks his coffee now and reads the paper in his kitchen, with the TV on as background noise. At around eight fifty or so he sees the World Trade Center on fire.

Then his mobile phone beeps. There's a message from his secretary,

Lourdes Galletti, calling from his office, telling him about the smoke, and that they can't get down—*Could he send help? They needed help.* Her breathing is labored. In her voice he can hear the thickness of the smoke.

He tries several times to call her back, then tries calling his brother-in-law, Eric Sand. He keeps dialing numbers, but reaches no one. It's now nine A.M.

He begins pacing and slamming his fist down on his table. He learns from someone at Howard's house that Howard had been dropping Kyle off for his first day of kindergarten and was headed downtown with Jimmy to the building.

He looks at the buildings on his TV and yells, "Get down! Get down!"

The bridges into Manhattan are closed and public transportation is shut down. So he is stuck in his kitchen in Armonk with a useless phone.

For nineteen years he'd been getting in at around seven fifteen. He knows all the quirks of the building—the stairwells, the exits, all the places to go, and he wants to be there now. He can help people get out, he thinks.

On the TV someone yells, "Oh my god!" and a plane smashes into Tower Two at a horrific speed.

He should do something, organize something, help out somehow—how ridiculous was it to be out here in Westchester?

When he sees Number Two go down, he is stunned and silent. He imagines their movements, pictures them barricaded inside a conference room, never thinking the whole building would go down—who could imagine that.

"Then my phone rings and it's my sister-in-law saying my brother-in-law, Eric Sand, had called their house. He said he was on his way down, that he was on 106.

"I'm thinking, *Why's he on 106 when he works on 104? Why isn't he heading* down? Then Number One came down. And I was just . . . My feeling was that they all were up there, and they were all dead. There wasn't enough time to get out. I knew that because in '93 it took longer for everyone to get out. And then the smoke, and the call from my secretary, and Eric's calling from 106, rather than from a lower floor. I just thought, *Everybody's gone.*"

M ARYANN BURNS, Howard's thirty-four-year-old administrative assistant, had left her house in Bayside, Queens, before eight o'clock that morning, but there were no parking spots outside the train station. She ended up parking five blocks away and walking, a bit annoyed, to her train, which she missed by a minute. For the past three years, Maryann has kept Howard on course. She makes his appointments, listens to him, teases him, knows his foibles and moods, and navigates them with the right balance of respect and humor. She tells great dirty jokes.

She catches the next train ten minutes later. When she climbs the steps from the subway her cell phone starts ringing. It's a friend calling to say a plane had hit the tower.

"Which tower, One or Two?"

"I don't know. Which is which?" her friend said.

"Antenna or no antenna?"

Maryann looks up and sees Tower One on fire.

"Oh my god, I gotta go," she says.

The first person she dials is one of the traders, Gregg Reidy, whom she'd just started dating. The traders usually arrived at six thirty or seven in the morning, she knew.

"I was standing there looking up. And then everyone was *freaking out*. There was this huge sound. You know how you can feel the sound of a jet in your chest, the rumbling? Well you could feel that. People were screaming at the top of their lungs—men, women. It was just crazy. We knew it was terrorists at that point and I couldn't move. I was in the middle of the street with hundreds of other people. I didn't know anybody.

"After the second plane hit, people started jumping. They were holding hands on their way down. And I knew it was our people. Because it was us, and two floors of Windows on the World above us. So the first thing you do is you gauge—well, the plane must have hit in the 90s somewhere, and you try and figure out where we were.

"I couldn't do anything but stand there and cry. There was scream-ing. It's still like a wound in your head.

"When the buildings came down, I thought it was bombs going off around us. I remember seeing a cab drive straight into a building. Cars were swerving, cops yelling *'Ruuuun!'* Everyone was running for their lives. Someone standing next to me must have spilled their coffee. My ankle suddenly burned and I didn't know what it was. I thought for a moment it was chemical warfare, and then saw it was coffee. I said, *Relax, you're getting a little crazy.*

"We kept running, running, running. Someone yelled, 'It's coming down!' When I turned around, there was a mushroom cloud coming at me. I kept running. I thought I was dead; there was no way I was get-ting out of it. I had work shoes on—heels.

"When the air cleared, I walked into a shoe store on Chambers or something and bought myself a pair of sneakers. I still have the receipt."

A MONTH LATER, Howard's driver, Jimmy Maio, will tell me his version of the day. Maio, forty-two, Brooklyn-born, has been driving Howard for five years and was with him when the buildings came down.

He's a big man, who wears jackets over thin wool sweaters. He still carries a gun—his privilege as a former police officer. He says most of the CEOs in New York have ex-cops as drivers. His close-cropped dark hair is flecked with the first signs of gray, and he speaks with a thick New York accent.

He begins by describing the moment when Tower Two fell. "I ran right along the building line," he says. "My thought was if it *is* another jet, you can't outrun it. You just try and get behind cover, something big to block whatever it is that's going to be flying at you.

"Mr. Lutnick peeled off to the right. He didn't follow me. And so I got around the corner of the building. I think it was Five World Trade Center. There's an eaves that sticks out around six feet, or *was* one. I thought, *I've got something above me, I've got a wall to the side of me*, and I just balled up." He pulls his head down and covers it with his arms to demonstrate.

"Mr. Lutnick had run to the right. I definitely thought he was dead, because at this point I still thought it was a plane that came in. I didn't know the building was coming down. So I'm balled up, this crap is coming down, falling all over, nothing big, but it's *black*, black as night, *darker* than night. You couldn't see your hand in front of your face. It was the darkest black I've ever been in, and I couldn't breathe. It seemed like with every breath I got less air, or oxygen. My lungs were filling up with this stuff, and I was starting to panic, trying to get oxygen.

"A lot of things run through your mind. At first I was terrified, because I hear this noise and I'm saying it's a plane that's just about to *wipe me out.* I'm dead meat. And then I get behind the thing and the stuff is falling and nothing's hitting me. And I have no idea what the hell is going on. There's a lot of loud noise and it lasted . . . I don't know how long, minutes maybe, and I couldn't breathe. After it stopped falling, it was totally silent. There wasn't a sound.

"I guess the stuff in the air had muffled everything, so that even if there was noise you couldn't hear anything. It was like I went *deaf.* No sound. So I'm struggling for a breath and every time I open my eyes it's still black, and you can't keep them open long because all this stuff is like cinder in the air—it really hurts your eyes. So you have to close your eyes, clean them out. I'm struggling to breathe and it's still black, and I'm saying, *I know it's a* beautiful day out, *and I know I'm outside.* I didn't know why it was so black. What *happened?* I didn't know what happened."

This is a common thread from the people who were down there. None of them knew what had taken place. Most of them saw the planes for the first time on television that afternoon or night. Jimmy seems exhausted in the telling of the story. He takes two deep breaths and then looks ahead through the windshield, up Madison Avenue again.

"Then I'm saying I'm not even supposed to *be here.* The planes have already hit, we're not supposed to be—I'm gonna leave my kids orphans and we weren't even supposed to *be here.* We had escaped the thing and now . . . Anyway, I don't know how long it took, but one of the times when I opened my eyes, it wasn't black anymore—it was gray. I couldn't see anything, but *it wasn't black.* That's when I first said, *Maybe I'm gonna live.* So I got up. I'm hacking up this *crap.* It was thick, like a log coming out of your throat. I'm spitting it up, cleaning my eyes, trying to clean my mouth out because it was very thick stuff I was breathing in. I started walking. I still thought it was a third jet that came in. I had no idea what had happened.

"When I first told Mr. Lutnick, I thought it was a mistake that an airplane had hit, but as we were making our way downtown the second jet hit. We heard it on the radio, so it was clear it was terrorists. There was no question about that. And as I was driving down Fifth Avenue and saw the buildings, I knew our people weren't going to live. We had a clear shot from the Forties down, on Fifth Avenue, right at the World Trade Center, and they were just two *chimney stacks,* two gigantic chimneys. I knew that all our people were above where that smoke was coming out of and would have no shot of getting out. I never thought the buildings would come down, though. I thought everyone was going to die of fire and smoke."

Jimmy was friends with dozens of people in the building. He waited for Howard in the office sometimes and gossiped with the secretaries. He has gone to more than ten funerals himself, on his days off.

"Mr. Lutnick was consumed by getting to the building. I felt it was my job to get him there, because he felt so strongly about it. But there was nothing we could do. I wasn't so concerned for our safety because I thought the deed had been done. He felt strongly about seeing if his people were coming out, and I had a lot of people I knew. So we were going to get there, and we did.

"Eventually the ash and smoke started to clear. I could breathe again. I walked past Church Street, up Fulton. Then I was actually accosted by a police officer in plain clothes, because my gun was showing."

He tilts his head in amazement.

"I had my jacket over my head still, shielding myself from the debris that was falling. He grabs me and he says, 'Hey buddy, what are you doing?' My first thought is this *asshole* is trying to make a *gun collar* in the middle of this disaster. Who gives a *shit* about someone walking around with a gun? But I told him, 'Look, I'm a retired police officer,' and he says, 'Go up to Broadway, you can identify yourself, there's some people there.' On the way up Fulton I was looking for Mr. Lutnick. I didn't see anybody and I'm thinking he's dead. But when I get up to Broadway, there he is. I grabbed him and I hugged him. I said, 'God am I glad to see you alive.' When he turned around and looked at me, he had a bottle of water in his hand, and a roll of toilet paper. And I said to him, 'You are one *resourceful* son of a gun.' He said, 'Here, Jimmy, wash your mouth out.' We cleaned our mouths and eyes out.

We tried to clean each other up. Tower One was still standing. That's where our people are. And we're still very close to it. We're still on Broadway and Fulton, which means we haven't walked uptown at any point. We're only a block from where we were trapped in that dark stuff. And now he's *hemming and hawing* about leaving. He doesn't want to go, and he asks me, 'What should we do?' I said, 'Listen, there's nothing for us to do. There's nothing we can do.'

"'*What am I going to do?*' he says again.

"I've never talked to him this way—I said, 'I'll tell you what I'm going to do. I'm going to escort you home and I'm getting the fuck out of here. There's nothing else for us to do here but get away from this.' And we started walking, and as we were walking people were trying to interview us, reporters, because we looked like we'd just gotten out of this thing. I don't know how far away we'd gotten, but then Tower One came down.

"You know the terror of it all—after I lived through this—the terror was gone. I was numb, *past* horror. Normally, Tower One comes down, and the people you know are in there, you would feel great pain, but it was all matter-of-fact by that time: The buildings just fell."

T OM TRILLO, forty-five-year-old head of operations for Cantor Fitzgerald, had been driving from his home near Danbury, Connecticut, when the first plane hit. He was stopped at a light just off the exit of the West Side Highway, and out of the corner of his eye he saw something fly into the building. He steered the car to the side of the road. When he registered what had happened, he pulled the car up onto the sidewalk before running toward the building.

Police and security kept him from getting close. From behind the police barricades he watched the fires spreading, then left to make his way uptown to a friend's office in Midtown, where he was told the towers had collapsed. An hour later he called Howard at Stephen Merkel's apartment and was told to join everyone else at Howard's.

On his walk over, he'd realized that Howard hadn't mentioned Gary in his conversation.

"Did Gary make it out?" he asks when he gets there.

"I'm not optimistic," Howard answers. "Gary was on the phone with Edie, and he didn't think he was going to make it. He basically told Edie good-bye."

They are each given a copy of a year-old company phone list, and they start the difficult job of calling households, talking to wives and husbands to see if the name on the list somehow made it out—or if the person was home sick, or away on vacation. They call their direct reports first, the faces they look at every day.

Trillo knows that one of his charges, Vincent D'Amadeo, who runs domestic operations, was in the building, because they'd talked on Trillo's way into the office. So D'Amadeo is likely dead. Trillo doesn't call D'Amadeo's wife, Raquel. He calls instead the home of Charlie Waters, the young man who ran facilities and office services. He speaks to Waters's wife, Barbara, and asks her has she heard anything.

She says she hasn't yet, and they both begin crying.

He tries calling Jason Sekzer, who heads trade support for Cantor. Can't get through. Sekzer died as well. Then he tries the home of the head of human resources, Ed York, who had joined the firm only that year. York was at the office too. For two horrendous hours he calls home after home, and does not hear of a single person who was not in the office, anyone who for sure is alive.

In each instance a wife answers the phone (there were mostly men in his division) and has not heard a word. Trillo tries to veil his own fears and promises he will give them whatever information he can find. Someone from Cantor will be searching the hospitals and gathering lists of the wounded.

Stephen Merkel calls the homes of the lawyers they hadn't heard from; Joe Noviello, those of the missing technology staff; Peter DaPuzzo and Phil Ginsberg, senior partners of the company, call the families of people from all across the firm.

Their calls yielded false moments of hope. It was someone from Cantor. Maybe they'd found him, they thought. Even if they'd been hurt or burned severely, they'd be alive. They were all waiting to hear a voice tell them *He's okay. He's at NYU Hospital. You can see him whenever you get there.*

F OR MANY of the firms on Wall Street, Tuesday, September 11, was a series of miraculous escape stories. But Cantor had only a handful.

There were more rumors that evening: the Javits Center was a triage unit, or several Cantor employees had wound up burned and unconscious in a hospital across the Hudson in New Jersey. Family members clung to these possibilities no matter how tenuous they seemed.

* * *

Joe Asher, a young attorney for Skadden, Arps, who has worked with Cantor Fitzgerald for years, darts around Manhattan on his mountain bike that first night carrying the list of names of employees to all the hospitals. For Manhattan, it is unusually, eerily, quiet. The streets are mostly empty and the air smells like burning steel. He hopes to find a hundred or so, and perhaps that will be just the beginning. If even a dozen escaped there was every likelihood there'd be more.

The hospitals had been bracing for thousands; the blood banks were packed with donors. But the wounded never materialize. With few exceptions, people either made it out and were fine, or they were trapped in the building.

At each hospital, Asher calls Howard's apartment. He's seen scrub-suited doctors and nurses, but no patients.

By the fifth hospital, NYU, he's heartsick. Police and National Guard patrol outside. A morgue is opened but the medical examiners there have as little to do as the doctors. The awful truth is becoming clear. In all, Asher will find four people from Cantor Fitzgerald alive at local hospitals, but none, as far as he can tell, from the Cantor floors.

Nancy Shea spent most of September 11 at her home in Pelham, New York, a suburb north of Manhattan, making phone calls and waiting to hear again from either her husband, Joe, or Joe's brother Danny, both of whom worked for Cantor Fitzgerald.

She'd spoken to Joe twice after the plane hit. The first time, at around 8:50, he said he'd heard a huge sound, and saw smoke rising from below. Joe Shea's office was on the north side on the 105th floor, the side where the plane entered.

He said, "You're not going to believe it. Some *plane* just crashed into the building." He sounded aggravated more than frightened, because he'd been through this in 1993, when a bomb exploded in a parking garage beneath the building.

It had not occurred to him that the crash wasn't an accident. "You're going to see this on the news, but I don't want you to worry," he told her. "We're going to get out of here. We're *fine*."

Nancy walked toward her television, then picked up another phone and tried calling back. No answer. She assumed he'd left the building.

Then the phone rang again.

"It sounded noisy in the background," Nancy Shea says. "It was Joe. He said, 'Was that you?' I said, 'Yeah. Listen, how far beneath you did the plane hit, because Amy and Dan are below you?"

Amy O'Doherty was a former family baby-sitter, recently hired to work in the zero coupon division at Cantor. She was twenty-three. Dan was Joe Shea's younger brother. He was thirty-seven.

"'I don't know,' he said. 'The doors are stuck and the place is getting a little smoky. We're going to find a stairway that's open and I'll go find them right now.'

"'Okay, be careful,' I said. And that was that. Then I turned on the television and realized how absolutely dreadful it was. I wasn't worried, either, because he'd come through '93 unscathed. I was just so confident of his immortality.'"

By late evening, Nancy Shea began to grow increasingly restless. She couldn't just stay in the house waiting. She had to look for her husband, had to find him. The roads into Manhattan were closed off. The trains weren't running. She and Tom Shea, one of two other Shea brothers, decided to drive through the Bronx to the Third Avenue Bridge and ride their bikes across into Manhattan, to 125th Street on the East Side. Like Joe Asher, they'd check all the hospitals and comb the emergency rooms. They wouldn't go home until they found Danny and Joe. Because she sensed within herself that they weren't dead, that they were somewhere unconscious from their fall, or stuck in an air pocket beneath the fallen steel and concrete.

Every hour was essential, but at the hospitals they saw what Joe Asher had seen—doctors and nurses and EMTs, but very few patients. They looked over the lists, but the names were the same at each place. They were master lists gathered from all the hospitals, and she didn't know any of the names. She saw other Cantor family members, but they knew just as little as she.

They rode from location to location, for hours. At two A.M. they gave up on the hospitals and rode downtown toward Ground Zero.

They met what Nancy would describe as the "wall of blue." The police and armed National Guard turned them away.

"What would you have done?" I asked Nancy a few months later.

"Anything. I was going to find him. I would have looked everywhere, dug through concrete. If they'd let me in then I might still be there."

H OWARD SPENDS the night fielding calls from Joe Asher, and Nancy Shea, and other wives and husbands and parents. He talks several times with Lee Amaitis, Dan LaVecchia, and Shaun Lynn in London, and forms strategies with Stuart Fraser, Joe Noviello, Stephen Merkel, Tom Trillo, Peter DaPuzzo, and Phil Ginsberg. He doesn't go to bed until four A.M., and when he finally closes his eyes he finds not rest, but a nightmare, far too close to what he had lived through when the buildings fell all around him.

He sees a foot or two above him a spiderweb, and then another, and then a third. Before long there are a thousand webs thickening, until it's all black, and the web slips over him, and holds him in its grasp.

*T*HERE WERE SO FEW WOUNDED. *Harry Waizer and Lauren Man-ning were two of them, and they'd been badly burned.*

Harry was our tax counsel and a crucial part of our legal team. When we did our taxes, or started a new division, or contemplated buying a company, Harry was someone I talked with at great length.

Harry was in a coma, on life support, terribly burned on his face, his arms, and his knee. Physically, he was unrecognizable. Lauren was a beautiful woman, very smart, direct, and hard-charging. She ran data sales, which means she sold our market data to money managers, pension funds, and Wall Street investment banks. If you think of the stock ticker, Cantor's market data is the stock ticker for bonds.

Renée Barrett-Arjune, from accounting, was also in the hospital, having suffered perhaps the worst burns of all. She died in October. And then Virginia DiChiria, who was on the elevator at the 78th floor. When the doors opened, flames jumped at her. She decided to run through them. She kept thinking, "Drop and roll, drop and roll," like they tell you in safety class. She ran through the fire and dropped and rolled, badly burning her arms. It saved her life. She saw Ari Schonbrun there, and he said, "C'mon, I'll help you downstairs, c'mon, we'll be okay," and he carried her down seventy-eight flights of stairs.

Harry was also on the 78th floor. He was burned while in the elevator. He took a breath near the flames, and as he inhaled, they scorched his throat and lungs. I can't even imagine that pain. He had lung damage and was burned over thirty-five percent of his body. His head, ears, *hands—are terribly scarred. Lauren was burned over four-fifths of her body. But her face was mostly spared—from the worst, anyhow—because she kept her hands over her face.*

There's a question people raise about whether you suffer more if you live through burns like that or if it would be better to die. I have difficulty understanding that. I think of the moment before you die as infinite, never ending. You would always choose to live. I would, anyway, no matter what. I told Lauren she had to get through this because she was the hope of seven hundred families. And that if seven hundred families could trade places with Greg Manning they would. Because they'd all been so desperately longing for a chance, even the smallest one. Hers was the only chance left, and so they shared in it.

I told them at the crisis center that each of us had one lottery ticket. One in a million that our loved one might be alive. What if we could pool them together and ensure that one person got to live. I would gladly give up my one-in-a-million ticket for Gary to improve the chance of someone living. So I asked for everyone's ticket, to give to Lauren. I don't know what they made of it—because so many of them still had hope. But this was our chance, I believed, and I wanted us to work collectively and feel as though we could actually save someone.

I talked only of Lauren then, because I didn't yet know about Harry or Renée. The next time I visited Lauren I found out the others had been at the same hospital, right down the hall.

Recently Harry came to the office. It had been six months since the attacks. The people who hadn't seen him were shocked, but I'd seen him so much worse. I thought, My god, he looks great. He looks like Harry. He looks like Harry Waizer.

I mean, you could tell what had happened, and there were scars and scabs. He lost not only his hair but a great deal of his scalp. But he was clearly Harry, wearing his glasses, joking, smiling.

He was asking whether we could still use his assistance, and I joked, "Enough of this already. So you have physical issues. I gotta tell you, Harry, we didn't hire you for your physical attributes to begin with."

Since he can't use his hands now, I engage his expertise over the phone, while he continues to convalesce. It's therapeutic for us both, but it's also good business, because the man is supersmart and he knows our needs and issues.

 I'm not calling him to make him feel better. I do what I've always done, which is to challenge him. He says something and I push back. He tells me why he thinks he's right, and I agree or disagree. But it's not unlike a talk we might have had on September 7th. At the end of every conversation, he says, "You know, Howard, I love it. I just love it." We both do, of course.

Ten years ago, Greg Richards was twenty and headed for his senior year at the University of Michigan when he spent the summer working for Cantor Fitzgerald. In his three months with the company, he'd impressed everyone with his quickness, drive, and wit. Howard took an interest in Richards, much the same way Bernie Cantor had taken an interest in Howard. He simply had a hunch. When Richards asked if he could return to the firm after graduating, Howard instead thought of possible mentors for him who might teach him the skills necessary to run a brokerage business someday.

Howard sent him to work for Mike Reger, a partner in a billion-dollar hedge fund, in Boca Raton, Florida, which did sophisticated bond arbitrage and bond trading. Go down and work for him, Howard said. If he tries to keep you, that's a good thing. Shadow him. Don't leave until you know everything that he knows.

Richards did more than that; he lived in a spare room in Mike Reger's house. After eighteen months he called Howard and said, I got it. I understand the business. I know what he knows.

"At the grand age of twenty-four he starts working for us," Howard says. "His first year he earns three hundred fifty thousand dollars. Second year, seven hundred thousand dollars. Then he's making a million. In three years. Fantastic kid. Then he says he's a little bored so he gets a job at Goldman Sachs, learns structured finance, and complex fixed-income transactions.

Eventually, after marrying and having a baby, he returned to Cantor. Howard gave him assignments that would necessitate their talking on into the evening. He wanted to teach Greg everything he could.

The guy was a superstar, Howard loved to say. The future.

Now Stephen Merkel is at Greg Richards's house, waiting for Greg's wife, Erin, to return. Greg and Stephen are cousins. Erin had been up all night, and now she's out gathering bagels and coffee. Stephen talks with her mother. They are all waiting for news. Greg is still missing, but they are holding out hope. Stephen is fairly certain by now that there will be no survivors, that Greg is, in fact, dead, but he cannot bring himself to tell them that. He stays for an hour or two and then leaves. They will find out another way.

He had been proud of his cousin, how gentle and kind he was while rising as swiftly as he did. Worked hard, played hard, loved his family. Just because the same has been said of hundreds of the men and women trapped in the towers that morning doesn't make it any less true for Greg Richards.

So much of Stephen Merkel's day is spent this way—talking to families, responding to rumors, answering questions without knowing anything or having any good news. They are long conversations, and even as the families hold out hope, some are starting to panic: *What am I going to do? What do I tell my kids? Will I have to sell my home?*

D URING THIS TIME details begin to emerge about the hijackers: that they were likely disciples of Osama bin Laden, the Islamic militant who has pledged Holy War against the United States. They used box cutters and knives, and there were between three and six of them on each of four planes. This does not interest Howard or Stephen or most of the others. For months afterward, few will talk about the terrorists or the war.

There is nothing they can do now to change what has happened, and the pit of sadness is so deep they have no energy yet for rage.

*   *   *

S OMEWHERE IN all this devastation, they begin to think of the business, however; because while Wall Street has shut down for a couple of days, it will soon be up and running again, as a "show of strength." And so with all that has happened, the survivors of Cantor Fitzgerald and eSpeed will have to pull double or triple shifts, or the firm itself will go under.

Indeed, most of them *want* to work, if for no reason other than to keep from feeling as helpless as so many felt watching the towers fall. They need to do something, to *save* something, though it's not clear what is left to be saved.

In the eyes of many on Wall Street, Cantor Fitzgerald is through, killed, destroyed—seven hundred people are missing, the offices are gone, the systems wrecked.

Wednesday morning, September 12, will be the Bond Market Association conference call to determine when to open again. The U.S. Treasury is pushing for both stocks and bonds to begin trading. The stock market will remain closed until Monday the 17th, but despite Cantor's condition, the Bond Market Association pushes for Thursday the 13th. If there'd been no deaths and only the Trade Center was gone, simply trading on Thursday would be a long shot. But without so many of their frontline forces—programmers, brokers, technicians, accountants, and salesmen, and all of their bosses, and their bosses' bosses—it doesn't seem possible.

Equally daunting, perhaps, as the prospect of *opening* on the 13th—and doing business under such crippled circumstances—is the imminent task of settling the trades, billions of dollars of them, that took place on Monday the 10th and on the morning of the 11th. The records of those trades are gone as well as the people who might retrieve them from their backup computer files.

Howard asks Noviello and Trillo and the London team if they can open, because it's not at all a given. At the time of the conference call, fewer than 150 New York employees out of a thousand are alive and accounted for. "We gotta," Lee Amaitis says, without hesitation. "If BrokerTec (an upstart company attempting to challenge Cantor for market share) opens and publicly proclaims themselves the bond market of America, we'll never get back there. We're through."

They know he's right. Wall Street is already jittery about Cantor. The firm's competition and some bank heads talk publicly of the need for *stability* in the bond market, meaning trading with a company at full-strength.

Cantor and eSpeed will need to open and function in all areas. If they lose their place in the market, it will be impossible to help any of the families.

When the members of the Bond Market Association decide the market will open Thursday, Howard does not say they are callous or that his best friend and his only brother are dead. He listens in amazement to their plans and thinks of all he needs to do to keep the firm from going under.

Maybe because he is in London, where there are no casualties, Lee Amaitis, Cantor's European CEO, is hopeful. His most pressing concern is about the technology. Will the backup systems work when the bond market opens? If so, the bond side of the business will survive, because Cantor was already doing most of their trading of U.S. Treasuries through their electronic system, eSpeed.

They need to know what's lost and what's left. The branch offices for equities are untouched. Phil Marber, who runs Cantor's equities division, was on a business trip in Ohio, a huge break, Amaitis knows. The fact that he's alive may mean the business will pull through.

When he returns, Marber will jump in, and from across the Atlantic Amaitis's staff will contact customers, trade stocks, call families, whatever Marber needs them to do.

They pool resources, take on teams of volunteers, stay at their offices by their phones night and day, talking to one another like soldiers from scattered bunkers. What previously would have taken months to do, they now do in hours. In a normal world the operations people tell the Treasury people how much money the firm has taken in, what they'll need to settle, and what they'll need from the bank. Now a handful of sleep-deprived employees must do the job of forty. Trillo and his London counterpart, Clive Triance, head of European and Asian operations, speak thirty times a day to each other.

The London staff takes over hundreds of jobs from their missing

New York colleagues. And on their customer calls, Dan LaVecchia, Phil Norton, and their charges try not to let on that they are most likely in over their heads.

It is soon apparent that the New York office won't be able to restore their in-house backup system—the one that receives trades from eSpeed and creates the firm's books and records—in time to open for Thursday's trading. In London they used a subsidiary processing system of ADP called Wilco.

Clive and his team are improvising ways of connecting New York to ADP so that eSpeed can feed the trades through the new London network, on their way to the primary clearing organizations and banks. It amounts to an entirely new way of doing business, conducted in large part by Brits who know little about the U.S. bond market.

The amount of money to be cleared is overwhelming. On Tuesday morning alone, Cantor had already conducted nearly twenty-five hundred trades, worth billions of dollars.

Joe Noviello, chief information officer, Jim Johnson, head of technology in London, and Matt Claus, head of software development, pore over whatever records they can retrieve. Whenever they think they're getting somewhere, another roadblock appears.

"I remember thinking it was impossible that we were where we were," Jim Johnson will say later. "And finding our way out seemed equally impossible. But we gave ourselves these small goals, and we got them done. Matt and I were on the phone constantly. If I was up eighteen hours, I was on the phone with him for eight, talking and trying to work through the technical issues. At the time, I remember you almost felt guilty about the high. Because there was an incredible rush associated with doing that much work in that little time. The only thing that mattered—or rather, the only thing we could control—was getting our U.S. Treasury trading system up and working."

What Lee Amaitis requested on Wednesday was, on the face of it, absurd. He was asking his London operations staff to build a U.S. Treasuries clearing system to support eSpeed and have it ready within twenty-four hours.

Clive Triance calls his contact, Terry Williams, over at Wilco, and tells him what he needs.

"We can do that for you. We can definitely do that," Williams tells him, then adds that they'll need three to four weeks to implement it properly. Given the complexity of the current system for clearing securities, three to four weeks is an extraordinarily fast turnaround.

"We've got twenty-two hours," Triance tells him.

In an hour Williams calls him back and says, "We'll get it done."

The teams under Tom Trillo and Joe Noviello are living in Cantor's Rochelle Park, New Jersey, disaster-recovery site, sleeping in chairs or in corners or in their cars, eating take-out pizza and Chinese food, as they try to implement the systems the London team is building. The pressure is unrelenting. They guzzle coffee and Coca-Cola, pace rooms to stretch their legs. Then they get back to it. They tell their families they don't know when they'll be home.

Phil Marber is mustering his own troops, hiring new traders, attempting to equip the too small Darien office with enough desks, computers, and phones for all the additional staff until there's at least an interim Manhattan office to go to. Several former employees have returned to help out. Steven Bliss, who had risen to number two in Cantor's Nasdaq trading business before taking a leave of absence, began building a proxy version of the Nasdaq trading desk the afternoon of September 13. Heidi Olson, who'd left when the firm downsized last spring, also showed up, and was put to work supervising all the logistics.

Cantor's equity division is connected by a system of speakers and radio mikes, called the "squawk box," or the "hoot 'n' holler." Traders talk into the microphone and their voices go out to all the squawk boxes in all the Cantor equities desks, all the trading rooms around the country and in England.

They bark what it is they're doing as they're entering the trade into the system. They'll shout out, *I'm a seller of Microsoft. I'm a buyer of*

Adobe. I'm a seller of Herman Miller. I'm a buyer of Cisco. As a result, sales traders on the phone with a client don't have to see a transaction move on their screen. They can simply listen.

This system unites the groups and energizes them. It's a comforting sound, and most traders say it would be depressing to work without it. There are usually several people talking at once. But for the traders— who are as accustomed to it as they are to the sounds of their parents' voices—they can pick out instantly what's important to them.

On Thursday, from Cantor's emergency space at the law offices of Morgan Lewis, Howard speaks over the squawk box with all nine of his remaining equity offices and asks the same question he had asked earlier about bonds: *Can we open?*

If not, they can wait until they're ready, he says. No need for bravado, and no need to place any more pressure on themselves.

"But if you think we can, we'll do it. Just tell me," he says.

The answer is unanimous. Everyone who responds over the hoot that afternoon tells him, *Yes, we can open Monday.*

On Friday, at the end of the day, Howard asks Marber again.

"We'll do the best we can," Marber tells him.

Nobody sleeps more than an hour or two. There are those camping out in New Jersey and Connecticut, or over in London getting the business up and running, and then those who spend all day and night at the crisis center at the Pierre Hotel. Some travel between these worlds.

On the afternoon of the 11th, Arthur Bacall, an executive at the Pierre, called Howard and asked if there was anything he could do. Bacall and Howard grew up together on Long Island. At five thirty the next morning, after Allison came up with the idea of a central meeting place for the families, Howard called Arthur to say there *was* something. Could Cantor use the hotel for a few days?

"As long as I can cancel the parties booked," Bacall says.

"I don't think anyone's having a party for a while," Howard says.

Within hours, the main ballroom, hallways, and reception rooms of the Pierre Hotel have been turned over to the Cantor families. Volunteers carry in tables and chairs, phones and computers. By one o'clock, all the rooms are packed. Anyone calling a Cantor office or the 800 number hotline is told to head to the Pierre, and the majority do just that—wives and husbands, parents and siblings. The mood Wednesday is more anxious than sad at first because of how little anyone knows.

Kent Karosen, Howard's assistant, and Joe Asher have lined up grief counselors, who arrive by the dozen, and clergy too—priests, rabbis, ministers. A bulletin board is placed against a wall for the families to post information about their loved ones. To watch only that process is to understand the rapidly widening nature of the tragedy. First a few sheets with information and small photos are posted. Then, by two in the afternoon, the board is entirely covered. Another board is brought in, and then a third. Each fills up within an hour. It continues that way through the night and the following days. On the signs the families write MISSING. These are the "missing boards," and the posters and shrines spread outside to streetlamps, doors, bus stops, then all through the city. Because no one knows if the person they're looking for might be alive somewhere—or they don't want to know that they're not.

So many employees from the other companies with offices in the Trade Center have survived—thousands. How can it be that these hundreds upon hundreds of people in these cavernous rooms can all come up empty, that no one from Cantor made it out?

In the photos posted, the missing men and women are shown having fun, in T-shirts, out at the beach, at a restaurant, arms around two or three children.

That first day, people are searching for husbands and wives, brothers and daughters. In a few days they begin asking about insurance and death certificates, bonuses and salaries.

Kent Karosen has the task of dispensing information, of telling the families what he knows, and what he doesn't. He tells them about the need to submit DNA samples, how to file a missing-persons report, and other details. He lists the religious gatherings and ceremonies planned, and tells them there are counselors waiting to help just outside the main room.

Eventually, on Wednesday, people ask for Howard. And not so patiently. If he's alive they want to know why, and what he knows, what he's doing to find their loved ones.

Kent calls Howard and tells him—*You better get here; they're growing angry.*

*   *   *

T HEY RETURN each day wearing name tags and holding pictures—and new families join them. When they leave the crisis center, many spend panicky hours canvassing the city, posting more "missing" notices. No one wants to plan a funeral, file for death certificates, or fill out the forms the Red Cross is passing out. How can they think that way? There are no bodies. There's no *proof.* And there is so much chaos in the city—Lower Manhattan is still closed and the smoke is still rising from the wreckage.

Some public faces turn up at the crisis center. Upper East Side Congresswoman Carolyn Maloney stops by. The woman with her has curly gray-streaked hair, an angular face. Many recognize her, though with everything on their minds, they would be forgiven if they couldn't place her. She sits down at the piano and begins playing, and then they realize, it's Carole King. She's singing "You've Got a Friend."

T WICE A DAY Howard speaks to the families. He gives out information, and while others avoid putting their grief into words, Howard talks frankly about what he went through when the buildings fell and about his brother's phone call to his sister. The dozens who line up to speak with him afterward ask the same questions, even if they've just been answered. They show him photographs of their missing family member and ask if he knows them or has a story he can tell.

He obliges them as best he can. But for all the comfort it provided, there are some who leave the crisis center at the end of the day resentful for what it hadn't provided. They had come, after all, expecting answers, expecting to be either closer to finding their loved one or to confirming their deaths.

What they hadn't prepared themselves for was the reality of learning nothing, or of learning only that it did not look good. Dread without release. Grief without closure.

There were moments of relief, when they would see someone they had assumed was dead. But too often they encountered families they had taken trips with, kids whose birthday parties they'd attended, who were now, like their own children, missing one of their parents.

There is too little information they want to hear, and too much that they can't possibly accept; accounts from rescue squads or other eye-witnesses of the body parts, the incomprehensible carnage.

Dozens of Cantor employees jumped—all those guys in the creased white shirts and khakis. It was worse then anything in any war, people are saying.

It isn't only—that phrase could be used a hundred times, because *it isn't only* losing your friends. And *it isn't only* losing your brother, or husband, or wife. Or your brother and your best friend. It isn't only losing your place of work. It isn't only how many died. *It is also* the gruesome way they died, and the amount of time they had to contemplate their death. Something truly horrific has happened to Cantor Fitzgerald—although no one yet knows the extent of it. The papers mention the firm's substantial losses with no substantiated numbers, and the more hours that pass, the more desperate the thousands of family members and friends become. They wait for phone calls, from someone at Cantor, or from a hospital, or from the coroner. At least then they'll have something.

The news from Ground Zero is worsening by the hour, no survivors and few bodies. Dental records and DNA samples will be needed to confirm identities.

On TV, the chief of Morgan Stanley says that more than 90 percent of his employees are now accounted for. More than half of Marsh and McLennan's initial estimate of seven hundred dead will turn out to be alive. As the total death toll dropped, it was understandable that those connected to Cantor hoped for the best.

But if anyone had bothered to really think about it—to see the pictures and video footage of Tower One, of the Cantor floors billowing smoke, if they had seen the men and women perched outside the windows, if they had heard the phone calls, the pledges of love—they would have known that no one made it down. That not one person from above where the plane hit had made it out of the building alive.

Documents

JOE ASHER

"I remember the day of the death certificates. Typically, if your spouse dies without a body, you have to wait a number of years before the city will give you a death certificate. But people needed them to begin taking care of their spouse's estate matters—life insurance and the rest. The city set up a system where a death certificate could now be obtained with an affidavit from the next of kin and an affidavit from the employer.

"The employer's affidavit said essentially: name, Social Security number, date of birth, et cetera, worked for Cantor Fitzgerald at One World Trade Center, and to the best of our knowledge was in the building on September 11, and hasn't been seen since—something like that. The city had asked us to provide one affidavit to cover everybody. But there was no way then to make a definitive list. There were too many people who were alive but still hadn't called in.

"So we did individual affidavits. We got the list created at Howard's house and Paul Schnell confirmed it. A team of us cranked out these affidavits. Stephen Merkel came over to sign them, at around midnight. He had them all piled up in a conference room on the 38th floor at Skadden, Arps, with three or four notaries present, because they had to be notarized."

"The stack of affidavits was a foot high. Each one was two pages. Stephen sits down to start signing, and for each one, he would look at it, and if he knew the person, he would say something about the person. 'Vinnie Abate, Amaitis's best friend, worked on the mortgage desk.' When he'd get to the lawyers, he'd tell you about the lawyer, the name of their wife and kids. I remember standing over his shoulder when he got to Doug. And he said just, 'Doug'—you know. Just like that, just 'Doug.'

"And I remember, I was there when he got to Matt Leonard's. And when he got to Arlene Fried's, Steve Fogel's, Dave Weiss's. And then I remember when he got to Fred Varacchi's. This went on for hours. It was just awful. One by one and he was reading the name of each and every one. It ended in the wee hours of the morning. And then we finally went home."

MATT CLAUS
"One of our technology workers, a guy named Shekhar Kumar, had just gotten married. He and his wife were from India. He'd gone back to India for the wedding, spent two months there, and then returned with his wife, who'd never been out of her very rural hometown. On September 11 he was going to bring all their documents in to the INS to get her a passport and then a visa. He had every document they owned with him in the building when the planes hit. So when he didn't come home that night, she was left with no identification or driver's license. She wasn't a citizen. She was just here with him. Nothing, right? And both their families are in India. His family needed to get here. And there was no way at first that they could.

"Eventually we worked it out. We helped get them temporary visas from some contacts we have down in Washington. But his wife was all alone in those first days, with no one here she knew, and no identification. Think of how scary that is on top of everything. And plus she wouldn't accept that he was dead, either. She was one of the people who went down to Ground Zero and just camped there. She had dreams that she knew where he was, in very specific places. She would just go down there and walk around in her sari and look for him. It was tough. That was really tough.

"And see, Kumar is a common name. There's a guy who works here whose name is Kumara. Same spelling, but with an *a*. And people saw his name among the survivors, and that got back to her. She was so happy. She went to the website and saw 'Kumara,' and said, 'That's him. You spelled the name wrong.'

"And I had to say, 'No, that's not him. That's someone else.'"

Thursday, September 13

As the Cantor survivors struggle to keep their firm alive, questions ripple through Wall Street—who's hurt, who made it out, and what did that mean for stockholders and the businesses connected to the Street?

If Cantor couldn't make it back, what did it augur for the bond market? It wasn't as though the economy was in great shape to begin with.

On September 13 Morgan Stanley Dean Witter runs a full-page ad, signed by its chairman, Philip Purcell, in the *Wall Street Journal,* stating that many of its employees had made it home but a few had not.

> *Thanks to our network of over 60,000 people throughout the world, including those in New York City, our assets and all of our clients' assets are completely safe. And we are ready to begin again as soon as the markets reopen.*

In the ad, they stress that this is a human tragedy and not a financial one, but the ad is placed to tell the world that it should do business with Morgan Stanley. Because the fact is, that for all the sympathy the financial community has—and there is plenty—people will want to do business with a company that is functioning on all cylinders. There is a limit to how long people will stick with a company, if it has suffered. It is in this context—and in the context of the conversation Howard has had with the Bond Market Association, and with others who doubt that Cantor can make it back, and it is in the context of all the it-could-have-been-far-worse stories he's seen, and in the context of the lack of information out there about Cantor—that Howard decides to go on television, because he wants the world to know what happened to the men and women who went to work that morning, and because he needs his customers to know Cantor Fitzgerald is still in business.

During those days, desks and computers and phones were added to the Darien, Connecticut, office. The operations group worked around the clock to ensure that it could input the coming Monday's transactions.

As with bonds, processing the trades will be a major obstacle. eSpeed had opened on Thursday, September 13, and in Wall Street's view had functioned admirably, and the same way on Friday. But the new deadline date was the following Tuesday, September 18, when the firm would receive the tens of billions of dollars of securities it had bought. Not a problem on a normal pre–September 11 day, because there was always an equal amount flowing in and out. That was the nature of the business.

But now with the back-office systems in pieces, and the Bank of New York knocked out of both their primary and secondary locations, clearing anything was an ordeal.

The major investment banks complicated matters by holding on to their cash in many instances and closing their doors to the securities they'd agreed to purchase. Cantor's bank, J.P. Morgan Chase, decided to go ahead and pay for the securities Cantor had bought. And so money was traveling out faster than it was coming in. The stocks and bonds were piling up, trades couldn't settle, and Cantor's money was flying out the door.

With all these questions looming, the bank came by that Friday to discuss Cantor's loans. It wasn't that they were unsympathetic. But the loans had been soaring, and Doug Anderson, Chase's head of Wall Street lending and a longtime friend of Cantor, told Howard they'd need to come down, or at least stabilize. While he didn't spell out what would happen if they didn't, the message was clear: The firm was in danger of going under.

IN THE BEGINNING, when it happened, I saw the world clearly. I saw my own role, what it was I had to do. But I could also read people more easily. At least it felt that way. I could tell my allies from my adversaries the moment someone walked into the room, or shook my hand.

The morning after the worst terrorist attacks in the history of the Unites States decimated my firm, I had a conference call with the members of the Bond Market Association. Now everything is still as raw as it could be. The southern tip of Manhattan still smells of scorched steel, and who knows what else. There are fewer than 150 names on our safe list.

The monitor introduces me. There were twenty people on the phone and only one of them says, "I'm sorry, Howard."

These are guys I do business with regularly. Spoken to on countless occasions. Had dinner with. You would expect—"I'm so glad to hear your voice, Howard." Or, "I'm so very, very sorry." But they couldn't say those things because they had these long-standing agendas. If they said, "I'm sorry," then the next thing out of their mouth would have to be—"Is there anything I can do for you?"

What they did was eliminate the personal. How else can you explain it? They made it just business. Essentially they said, Howard, I understand bad things have happened to you, but this is a business conversation. And in this business conversation you're screwed.

They actually wanted to open the bond market the night of September 12. Think about it. No one knew who was alive and who wasn't. The banks were pushed out of their buildings. Mail wasn't being delivered.

We opened on Thursday the 13th because we had to, and our trading customers from around the world immediately came to our aid. Our competitors in the bond business, however, were as brutal and rough as you could imagine. One of our competitors was closed the first week and they leaked to the press that they'd taken market share from us. They were closed. Their computer systems weren't even operating. People bought it because they saw us as wounded, and maybe on our way out. And with all we lost, 658 people, how could it not be true? It just wasn't.

All this time there were new rumors of rescues. That Sunday someone handed me a safe list with six new names, and I was ecstatic. I saw names of people I'd been sure were dead—Beth Logler, who ran our investor relations; Frank Vignola, who prepared our regulatory reports for the SEC. It was exhilarating. But the problem with this list was it wasn't right. They weren't alive.

I realized that when I walked into the crisis center that night and I saw Beth's family. It tore your heart out—it was like losing them for a second time. But that's how it was in those days. You'd be sure someone was dead, and then they'd walk in the crisis center or call on the phone—but really there were far too few of those.

So many things were going on at the same time. And I needed to treat each issue separately, to segment each hour so that I could be in as many places as possible, so that at each moment I could be on top of what was happening.

Each time I spoke to someone, I needed to say to myself, This is what I'm doing now. And if that took a half hour, then when the time was up I gave the same attention to the next subject. There were emotional issues, and business issues, and some that touched both areas, and I couldn't be emotional with the banks, and I couldn't even think about business when I was talking to the widows of my closest friends. I shifted from extremes, sometimes from minute to minute.

If people wanted to talk about the friends they lost, we just would. I didn't limit them to what they talked about any more than I limited myself. We had enormous amounts of work to do. But we were grieving, and you *couldn't tell when it would hit you full-force. I mean grown men like Lee Amaitis and Phil Marber—guys you don't associate with tears—are crying often in those days.*

It wasn't up to us. It simply depended on what you talked about. In the first weeks, if someone mentioned my brother or my best friend, Doug, I would break down. I'd start seeing so many other faces. I mean, what could be more sad than knowing I'd never see all these people again, that that entire part of my life, working with people whom I enjoyed immeasurably and spent most of my time with, was gone.

But then someone would say, "Okay, let's talk about clearing and settling securities," and we'd actually have a conversation about securities and I'd answer the person's question. There's nothing sad about settling stocks, and there's nothing emotional about how we're going to process them.

We were struggling through the most complex and difficult scenarios, and we needed all our energy and focus. Now it seems crazy that we could have done this all at the same time—grieved and saved the company. But they were at once different processes and the same. And that's still the case—we all worked together, and now that so many of us are gone there is nothing more natural than to honor them and their families in our work, through our work.

There were so many moving parts. So many issues. And as your mind starts solving one then new ones crop up. Always we were thinking which way do we go now, where do we move? Like chess. And other people's hands are coming in moving their pieces and ours. You're staring at the table while everything is in flux, and it's your move.

That's the business side, but there's also the relief fund, and there's also the plan for the families, and there were the funerals that my guys wanted to go to, and there's your own family. Lots of guys didn't see much of their families in those days.

It was twenty issues in twenty hours with every emotion shot through it all and the only way to deal with it was to focus intensely on the words you're saying or the crisis at hand. That's what I did. Focus on survival. Address the issues. Resolve the issues.

*   *   *

And at the center of this were the families. We were supporting each other, sharing information. Maybe I was helping them, but certainly it was helping me to talk with the families. Every time I left the crisis center I was energized. And I would describe it at the time as physical. Hugging, holding, and crying with the families energized me. I didn't need to sleep.

The unthinkable: When the plane hit, everyone on the top floors
of the North Tower above impact was trapped. The Cantor Fitzgerald offices
were on the 101st, 103rd, 104th, and 105th floors, where nearly
seven hundred employees were at their desks and ultimately perished.

With frightening speed, the building collapses:
"There was no 'I love you, take care,' because I don't think for one
second he thought that he wasn't going to make it out."

Without information and without a body, the families remained hopeful in the early days, posting pictures of their loved ones at the Cantor Fitzgerald crisis center and around the city. Eventually these "missing" posters became powerful shrines and underscored the extent of the loss.

Left to right: Fred Varacchi, president of eSpeed; Andrew Kates, senior managing director of administration; and Jeff Goldflam, CFO of Cantor/eSpeed—three of Cantor's stars, all died on September 11.

At Varacchi's service, Lutnick said he was worried once that Fred (shown here with his son, Thomas) had died in a motorcycle accident. When he realized he hadn't, he hugged and kissed Fred and told him, "I'm glad you're alive."

The Shea brothers. *Left to right:* Tom, Dan, Frank, and Joe. Joe, a Cantor executive managing director and head of North American Brokerage, and Dan, a partner, died on September 11.
Nearly twenty sets of siblings at Cantor were killed in the attacks.

Joe and Nancy Shea on a recent vacation with their children, Patrick, Peter, Casey, and Dan. The Cantor tragedy includes 955 children who lost a parent on September 11.

Left to right: Michael Tucker, Barry McTiernan, Tim Grazioso, and Pat Dwyer, members of Cantor's equities team. All but McTiernan perished. The equities team was an unusually close group of men and women who spent nearly as much time together outside of work as they did in the office.

Left to right: Stephen Colaio, Mark Colaio, and Tom Pedicini. June Colaio, whose husband, Mark, ran Cantor's agencies division, suffered one of the greatest losses: her husband, her brother-in-law, and her brother.

John Grazioso, younger brother of Tim.

Jonathan Uman, eSpeed's head of corporate development, and Paul Acquaviva, a deal maker for that department, at a company party. Acquaviva had been let go on September 10 because of downsizing and had returned to the Cantor offices the morning of September 11 to discuss his severance agreement.

Cantor's pro-am golf tournament at Pebble Beach. *Left to right:* Bill Rice, head of the firm's Los Angeles office; Phil Marber, head of equities; a local golf pro; Chuck Zion, one of Wall Street's top equities salesmen; and Ed Farr, Marber's friend and a Cantor client. Zion died in the attacks.

Members of Cantor's equities desk at an office party. *Back row, left to right:* Alex Steinman, Will Raub, Valeri Silver, Nicholas Pietrunti, Vincent Slavin, Thomas Pedicini, Craig Cummings, John Caudela, Stephen Cherry, Peter Kellerman, and Casey Knoll. *Front row, left to right:* Jerry Sullivan, Patrick Dwyer, Chuck Zion, Marion Bear, and Michael Tucker. Of the 114 in the division, 110 perished.

Greg Richards, a Lutnick protégé, who Howard said would one day lead a company on Wall Street.

Tim O'Brien, head of mortgage-backed securities, with wife, Lisa. O'Brien was the best friend of former NFL quarterback Boomer Esiason, who had an office at Cantor Fitzgerald for his cystic fibrosis charity.

Tim Coughlin *(left),* a legend in U.S. Treasuries, was one of Wall Street's most popular brokers. His was one of the few bodies found in the first weeks. His funeral at Saint Patrick's was attended by more than one thousand mourners.

Cantor's international desk. *Top row, left to right:* Paul Nibley, Jay Ludovico, Elvin Romero, John Halliday, Aaron Jacobs, Roger Hughes, and Paul Eckna. *Bottom row, left to right:* Steven Downham, Tom Shubert, William Micciulli, Chiqui Pabon, and John Wallis. All but Ludovico and Hughes were killed in the terror attacks.

Cantor's government securities trading desk in action before eSpeed and 9/11.

Left to right: Vice Chairman of Equities Peter DaPuzzo, Chuck Zion, and Steve Larrabee. Larrabee, who works in the Los Angeles offices, lost his son, Chris, in the attacks. Chris had just been hired by Cantor in June 2001.

Cantor's senior managing partner Harry Fry *(middle)* at the baptism of his goddaughter, Dante Valvo, pictured with Carl Valvo *(left)* and his wife, Lori. Fry hired Valvo, a friend from middle school who died in the attacks, to work at the firm. "Talk about survivor's guilt. He was there because I brought him in."

Glenn Kirwin, a product-development whiz, one of the rising stars Howard courted and eventually signed on. "We were like the Yankees. We saw someone we liked and we went after him."

Ian Schneider, head of Cantor's repo desk, was known as a major player on Wall Street.

Howard Lutnick with his best friends and vice chairmen, Doug Gardner and Stu Fraser. Fraser is Iris Cantor's nephew. The three, Howard says, were like brothers.

Calvin and LaChanze Gooding, out on the town with Howard and
Allison Lutnick. LaChanze was eight months' pregnant when Calvin,
a friend of Howard's from Haverford College, died.

The Lutnicks and Gardners on vacation. The couples were
inseparable and godparents to each others' children.

The Fishing Five. *Back row, left to right:* Chris Crosby and Jim Coffey. *Front row, left to right:* Tim Jones, Joe Noviello, and Matt Claus. Members of eSpeed's technology team, all survived because of an annual fishing trip. Together with Jim Johnson in London, they opened the bond markets on September 13.

Stephen Merkel *(left),* Lutnick's friend and Cantor's general counsel, was in the elevator when the first plane hit, and missed being engulfed by a fireball by only seconds.

Jimmy Maio, Howard's driver and a former New York City police officer. Jimmy and Howard ran from the Trade Center as the South Tower fell and were lost separately in the rubble for an hour before finding each other again and walking uptown to safety.

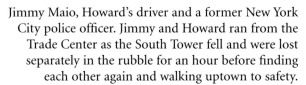

Frank Walczak, a broker on the FX forwards desk, was surfing at the Jersey shore on the morning of September 11. "I looked at the skyline and thought, 'Oh my god, there's smoke coming out of the Trade Center.' I rode the next wave in."

Maryann Burns, Howard's indispensable administrative assistant, survived because she missed her usual train and, as a result, arrived at the Trade Center just after the first plane struck.

This is my friend, Uncle Gary. He was in the explo- sion and he died. And Daddy was safe, he was here at school.

Howard's five-year-old son, Kyle, reacted strongly
to the death of his uncle Gary.

In Memory:
Gary Lutnick
&
all of our
friends
at
CANTOR
FITZGER

Members of the military sent a
photograph of this personally
inscribed warhead to Cantor's
interim office on Park Avenue.

Peter Jennings is speaking to a national audience about the terror attacks.

"There is no company, to the best of our knowledge, which has been more profoundly affected than the company of Cantor Fitzgerald, which does a huge amount of the bond trading in the United States. A huge number of its employees have been lost and are still missing. And earlier today Connie Chung sat down and talked with the CEO of that company, and we wanted very much for her to come back live and review her reporting."

Connie Chung is at a table to the right of Jennings.

"Peter," she says, "to some on Wall Street, Cantor Fitzgerald sort of symbolizes the devastation of the terrorist attack. When American Airlines Flight 11 hit the North Tower, it cut off hope for almost all of the Cantor employees."

Connie Chung interviews Jennifer Gardner, who is composed and sorrowful. She talks about Doug and how he was the center of everyone's life, the shoulder his friends leaned on.

The story soon switches to Howard. There's a photograph of Howard and Allison on vacation with the Gardners, arms around one another. It was a happy time for Howard, for all of them.

Chung asks, "You have suffered such great professional and personal loss. What is the fate of your brother?"

The screen shows Gary healthy and roguish-looking, stifling a laugh.

"My brother was on the 103rd floor," he says. "He called my sister just after the plane hit."

Howard talks about the phone call, and how Gary told Edie he wouldn't make it out.

"So while I'm head of the company, I'm trying to help my seven hundred employees who are missing their loved ones. I'm just another one of them . . . another one of them."

This is what he's said over and over at the crisis center meetings because he's wanted to dispel the notion that he survived unscathed. He's the boss, but his family has been devastated just as theirs have been. *I'll tell you everything I know, I'll stay all night, I'll answer every question, but you can't be mad at me. Because I can't take it,* he told them. *I'm no different than you.*

"You weren't at the building, because of a critical decision you made."

His face brightens for a moment as he talks about taking five-year-old Kyle to his first day of "big-boy school." Then he describes the drive down Fifth Avenue to the Trade Center.

"I saw the buildings on fire, so I didn't go in."

On the screen the second plane has struck. A massive cauliflower of flame and smoke billows around the upper floors of the South Tower, while the North Tower continues to burn.

Howard's voice races: "I stood at the door of Five World Trade Center and people were running out. I would ask them what floor are you coming from, and someone would say 41, another 55, and I kept wanting to get higher up the building."

"How high did you get?" Connie Chung asks.

"I got as high as the 91st floor, and I knew if I got one employee, *one* employee, then there had to be more; there'd be others behind them, coming out other doors, but I got to 91 and then I heard this *sound.* It was so unbelievably *loud* and someone yelled out, 'There's another one coming.' So I turned around and *ran.*"

"What was it?" Connie Chung asks.

"It was Two World Trade Center collapsing."

Three separate shots show the towers falling, the wave of rubble and dust building.

He describes how the clouds of debris overtook him, how he couldn't breathe or see, before he finally made his way out.

"I don't know of a single one of my employees that got down. Zero. It's really sad. But I think we're all pulling together with the view that we want to make things happen for them. We need to take care of them. We need to figure out how to take care of them, to give them more. It's going to be a different kind *of drive* than I've ever had before, without a doubt. It's not about my family. I can kiss my kids. But other people can't . . . And I think it's amazing that three hundred people, they lost all their friends. They lost the person to their left, the person to their right. They come in and they say, 'I want to go to work.' And I say, 'Why do you want to go to work? Let's go to funerals.'"

His voice breaks and he begins sobbing.

"They say, 'I *can't* stay home. I can't stay home. I have to work. I have to do *something.*' We have to stay in business. But the reason we want to stay in business—and there's only one reason—is because we have to make the company be able to take care of my seven hundred families. *Seven hundred families . . . seven hundred families.*" His face is puffy and wrecked. After days of grim-faced spokespersons, here was someone of authority weeping uncontrollably for the loss of family and friends, for everything.

At the news desk Chung recounts to Jennings, "Many of the Cantor families we spoke with said he's truly a remarkable man, and Peter, he literally doesn't fit the image of a typical CEO on Wall Street."

"No kidding," Peter Jennings says in grave agreement.

"Thanks, Connie, very much. Howard Lutnick. A personality . . . from Cantor Fitzgerald, the CEO, a man with seven hundred families. And a much *expanded* family now that we have seen him and shared his tragedy with him. Howard Lutnick, a personality this country will never forget. Period.

"Now as we take a deep breath . . . "

HOWARD DID two more network interviews shortly after his appearance on ABC. He became the face of the tragedy that evening, and Cantor Fitzgerald its epicenter.

On Friday a group of surviving Cantor executives gathered around Howard's dining room table and went through the divisions—who was alive, what businesses they'd be able to salvage. They each worked from a list of survivors, having decided earlier it would be too difficult to face all the names of the missing and likely dead.

In municipal bonds only the boss was accounted for—1 out of 36. In corporate bonds, 4 out of 86. Equities, 16 out of 140. Mortgage-backed securities, 2 out of 36. FX (foreign exchange) forwards, 1 out of 8. TradeSpark, 4 out of 44. Human resources, 1 out of 9. Of Cantor's and eSpeed's management—Doug Gardner; Fred Varacchi; Joe Shea; Jeff Goldflam, the CFO; Jonathan Uman, the corporate development director; Dave Bauer, national sales manager; Tim Grazioso, head of Nasdaq trading; Mark Colaio, head of agencies; Tim O'Brien, head of mortgages; Glenn Kirwin, head of product development—all were missing.

Repos, they hadn't heard of anyone who lived—an entire desk wiped out—a business that borrowed and then lent 20 billion dollars a day. Virtually all its members had been promoted from the accounting staff. Ian Schneider ran the desk. He'd hired most of them, including Paul Jeffers, his friend's brother. Shaun Lynn and John Banks had to re-create the business out of London—the entire U.S.-based borrowing-and-lending business. New loans were coming due each day. But every single person associated with the business was dead.

"We're sitting around the table determining whether this person is alive, or that one," Howard says. "But then the names come up—Dan Afflitto or Rich Lee—and you'd start thinking of others; this one had a wife who was four months pregnant, that one eight months pregnant. A voice in my head kept saying, *This can't be happening. This* can't *be happening.* It was the most intense business crisis, and sadness beyond comprehension."

They couldn't process the enormity and brutality of what had happened, and certainly not in a work context. This was a war room—a general with his surviving officers after a historic massacre. But a general would have had some training for this. These were guys fresh from their Labor Day barbecues, in shock, and the issues they were tackling were as foreign to their minds as a language whose words they could neither understand nor pronounce.

Each person in the group gathered up a small list of names and began to think about what they needed to do next.

Tom Trillo would pull together a staff to begin clearing trades, Stephen Merkel, a new, stripped-down legal team; and Lee Amaitis in London would patch together whatever he could to keep many of the other businesses running until they could rebuild their U.S. staff.

"We were only going to stay in the businesses in which we were absolutely certain we could succeed," Howard said. "I was fighting my ego, because a part of me wanted to keep it all and show that we could turn it all around—save everything. But I knew what the risks were—that if we tried to save everything, we could lose the whole company."

They begin cutting divisions, core businesses on whose efforts they had created their reputation: corporate bonds, forward foreign exchange, mortgage-backed securities, zero coupons.

David Kravette remembers the meeting as the low point, after the sight of watching Tower One fall. "The numbers were so depressingly small. It was horrible going through each group like that. It was sickening. I wanted to puke at one point. It was like a war."

O VER THE WEEKEND, Marber doesn't know what will happen, whether they will make it through the next week. The direct lines to the customers are gone. Cantor sales traders, like others on Wall

Street, have a system of phone lines from their desks to the desks of their clients. Their phone stations, called turrets, have dozens of buttons on them that, when pushed, connect them directly to their client, say, Fidelity, or Oppenheimer. You touch the button and it flashes CANTOR on the other end—no ringing, you're put right through.

On the 11th they lost all those lines, and their line to the New York Stock Exchange. Verizon is battered and months away from functioning at full-strength. So now when the surviving traders and new hires call customers or the stock exchange itself, they do now on regular phones. They haven't yet reconnected to the Nasdaq system. The technicians at Verizon are too busy trying to bring power back to the devastated areas of downtown Manhattan to help the equities department of Cantor Fitzgerald string new lines to the stock exchange.

The Connecticut office is a sales branch, not normally a trading room. Last week it was a support center. Traders and salespeople were thrust into the role of grief counselors. They fielded calls while they helped bring in additional desks and computers and new staff. The phone lines were lit up from early in the morning until well past midnight. They did their best to tell callers what they knew. By Friday there was anger directed at them, and they tried to remind themselves that it wasn't their fault.

But sometimes that was hard to do. One older trader had arranged to retire when his younger colleague returned from vacation.

The older man died a week before his last scheduled day at Cantor Fitzgerald.

Several people were let go on Monday, September 10. One had come back that Tuesday morning to clear out his desk. He died. A young woman who had been hired on Monday arrived early Tuesday to fill out her paperwork so she could start working as soon as possible. She, too, was killed. All the small choices people made—when to go on vacation, or take a long weekend, or come in early to get a jump on the next day—became life-or-death determinations, because of the actions of a bunch of men from across the world who hated Americans—especially, in the words of Osama bin Laden, the most prosperous ones who worked at the very top of the World Trade Center.

*   *   *

Everyone is at full-throttle, filling three roles at once, and answering phone calls from families, or returning calls from their own friends to say, I'm all right, but I won't be able to talk to you or see you for a while.

Help comes from a variety of places. Microsoft sends in technicians and computers; Cisco Systems CFO Larry Carter, a board member of eSpeed, sends in new data lines to connect New York and London, along with teams of technology personnel, and other equipment. UBS Warburg offers office space and volunteers to build a trading floor. The law firm Fish and Neave takes in the relief fund.

Cantor's data lines had been duplicated at Verizon's hub, which was a few blocks from the Trade Center and now ruined, but they were also backed up in a Rochelle Park, New Jersey, disaster-recovery site, which was a saving grace. Soon the volunteers are working side by side with the surviving staff and new hires, everyone recognizing the magnitude of what it is they're doing. There's no time for egos or petty allegiances, not with Monday and the opening of the stock market hours away.

If the back-office systems don't work, Marber has a contingency plan of sorts. They'll open in equities, but not at full-force. They'll do a few trades to check that the pipes work, to show the Street they've survived. But they'll keep the volumes small; a hundred transactions, no more than one per customer, to reduce pressure on the patchwork back office. These are Marber's and Howard's instructions, because if the systems fail on a hundred transactions, then they can still process the trades by hand. A giant pain for sure, but at least their bank loans won't climb.

Opening small has its own risks. The more trades a firm transacts, the easier it is to find a buyer for each seller and vice versa. With a hundred trades, you risk not finding the other side. On balance, though, it's far better to settle the trades on time, because if you don't get paid for the stocks you've sold and your own cash is flying out the door, the bank can shut you down, and then you're through. And you won't just lose money then. Even the most loyal workers need to make house payments. All those firms that watched Cantor grab their best brokers and traders over the years will hardly feel guilty about taking a few of them back.

I F WE WAITED," Marber tells me weeks later, "I thought the perception would be worse—They're out and now they're going to try and get back, and who knows if they're going to be okay; maybe we should stay away from them for right now. And I didn't want that. I wanted to be *right there*. And I know it was the right decision, because our customers just showered us with business that first week, probably two times the normal volume.

"That first Monday, we were bombarded, and in the old days that sort of load would have been managed by professionals who would have known how to handle it. It would have been me and Patty and Greg and Danny and the group around us, and now it was just *me*. And the kid on the desk next to me, instead of helping is yelling phone numbers because he doesn't know how to help. He's never done this before. Luckily we had the people in Connecticut pitching in—all of them—executing orders, doing things outside their normal jobs. We had a couple of traders in L.A. helping too. So some orders went to Los Angeles, some to Darien.

"One major problem was the phone system. You'd get busy signals all day. You'd have fourteen orders, hundreds of thousands of shares you needed to execute, and along with being shorthanded, you'd pick up the phone, dial over to the stock exchange—we used to have a direct wire to the stock exchange, now you had to dial the number—and you couldn't get through, and L.A. was having the same problems so they couldn't get the orders in. It was controlled mayhem—you knew what you needed to do, but you couldn't get it done.

"And when you finally got it through, everything was delayed. The reports that the customers got back from the exchange were terrible— sell the stock at the market and you were selling it fifteen minutes later and half a point lower. But they understood, and we weren't the only ones in that boat. Everyone on Wall Street had the same problems."

Jennifer Gardner knew what would happen, that soon others would acknowledge the deaths of their spouses and they'd want to plan funerals. And then they'd all happen at once over the same crowded weekends and each service would overlap the last. She wanted Doug's to be the first.

On Sunday, September 16, friends came from across the country and from along the East Coast, even with the flights grounded until the weekend. At the service, Jennifer speaks first and manages to give a loving and funny and perceptive eulogy about the father of her children, about their courtship, and about the blizzardy night she'd been working late and he'd come bounding over snowbanks in her law firm's parking lot to pick her up. "He carried me over the snow. I thought to myself afterward, 'I'm keeping this one.'" Her ability to talk to a packed synagogue of his friends and family this way, just five days after their lives were destroyed, is nothing short of valiant.

Joe Gardner speaks second and describes how his son had become his confidant and friend. "I always thought it would be Doug doing this for me," he says. Doug's friend Neil Kornfeld then talks of how Doug took care of his friends, his parents, his sister, Danielle, of Doug's Super Bowl and New Year's parties, and how he was a "psycho on the basketball court." He pokes fun at Doug's jump shot and his loud Hawaiian shirts. He tells a story about Doug, away on a weekend, just after getting engaged to Jennifer, and losing his prescription glasses while out on one of Howard's jet skis.

"And for the rest of the weekend, which really was Doug's happiest weekend that he ever experienced, he couldn't see a thing."

That it begins to resemble a wedding toast is understandable. Most of the people in the room are far more used to weddings than to memorials, although that will change over the coming weeks. Friends laugh at the stories; they are meant to be a celebration of Doug's life. But the stories are all too contemporary—it's hard to think of someone who is thirty-nine as a memory. Most of the people present likely talked to Doug in the last two months.

Howard asks everyone to close their eyes and visualize Doug. Before they'd arrived at Haverford, he'd heard Doug was a tennis player, but when practices started he was nowhere to be found.

"Then crossing the campus one day, I see this tall guy wearing one of those lime green Adidas warm-ups, and I thought that must be Doug Gardner."

He continues in this way for close to half an hour. It is an extemporaneous biopic of his intense bond with Doug, written on the drive over from the crisis center.

He tells about having his first expense account during one of his summer jobs in college and using it to take out his friend Doug; Doug making chicken parmesan for every meal; Doug unwittingly bringing a girl he just met to his surprise birthday party.

When he speaks of Doug, one has the feeling he's mourning the loss of the understanding that Doug has for him, that Howard has been able to know himself better with Doug as his friend and partner. Every choice Howard has made was filtered through Doug, and after every speech he suffered Doug's critique.

He wipes his eyes. He ends by talking about Jennifer, about the four of them—Doug and Jen, Howard and Allison—how they spent every Friday and Saturday night together. How they never tired of each other's company.

Danielle, Doug's sister, is the last up, and the hardest to watch. She has so much to say, and her brain runs too fast and in too many directions. She is pretty, and by nature a bit high-strung. She pulls her long blond hair back continuously as she speaks.

She talks about how she and Doug were in many ways two halves of the same whole. He was the one person with whom she could be herself. She's afraid of the world now and is worried she won't be able to do anything right anymore. With Doug she could do no wrong. "He was the only completely peaceful place I could go."

She says she's realized when she looks at her life that she can't find a story that she wouldn't end with the words, "And then I called Doug." As her speech goes on, her mother, Charlotte, motions that it's time. It's too painful, but she has so much more to say. It's difficult for everyone in the room to witness. The world wants a well-formed grief—but this one isn't. At these times the focus is both outward to the one lost and intensely inward—mourners think of their own lives, and deficiencies and fears. Danielle's are laid open, seemingly in penance.

Maybe it's appropriate the service ends with her eulogy because it does nothing to wrap things up, to create more of an understanding. There's nothing healed about her emotions.

Only five days have passed. They are a gaping wound.

On Monday evening it is clear that Cantor's equity division—on the day it needed to open slowly—has instead had one of its biggest days ever.

While Howard and Phil Marber appreciate all the support and kindness this flood of business represents; they are also convinced that the massive amount of transactions will crush their fragile back-office systems.

In their minds there's no way these trades will settle on time. There will be mistakes, they know, because it's only this makeshift group of traders trying to service their branches and a handful of people in the back office. London will do its part, but the likelihood is that Cantor's bank loans will skyrocket.

Getting the loans down means receiving money for the stocks and bonds sold. The challenge now is to prove who bought the securities and at what price. With the stock market down drastically, those who'd bought at last week's higher prices are likely to try and get out of those prices if they can.

"Monday was an amazing thing to witness," Howard says. "All of the accounts—money managers, mutual funds, hedge funds—they reached out to help us. They pumped us up with so much business, and we had one of the busiest days ever. And when I went home that night, I told Allison, 'I think we're done.'"

"Because we can't process the trades, and we've got no margin of error here. We were crushed with kindness, I thought."

Wednesday morning Howard heads to the emergency office at Morgan Lewis, on Park Avenue and Fortieth Street—his temporary headquarters, a bland conference room with phones and a few computers and a tray of sandwiches and coffee outside.

He does what work he can, but his mind is on the call he'll be getting from J.P. Morgan Chase, the one that will tell him if he has a business or not.

"Since it's out of my control, all the stress is gone," Howard says. "We are done. We have to be. We couldn't possibly process all the business we executed on Monday. So I'm waiting, staring at the phone. It was a good try, I was thinking. At least we went down swinging. And then the call comes through and they tell me our loans hadn't gone up. We had delivered out just enough stocks and bonds. We can remain open. It was absolutely unbelievable. In the saddest time of my life, I was jumping for joy as if I'd just won the lottery. Cantor could survive—would survive. It was a miracle, and now we could start to take care of the families. It was a new beginning."

I T'S HARD TO SAY what was the right or wrong way to act in the aftermath of the terrorist attacks. But from the perspective of the surviving Cantor Fitzgerald employees, the response of their competitor BrokerTec could have been a tad more gracious.

A Bloomberg news article issued within weeks of the attacks declares:

BrokerTec Gains Bond Market Share as Tragedy Begets Opportunity

BrokerTec LLC Chief Executive W. H. "Hal" Hinkle was spared the devastation the Sept. 11 terrorist attacks inflicted on its largest competitor, Cantor Fitzgerald LP. Cantor lost more than 700 employees and its New York offices were destroyed.

The article says that BrokerTec, because it is situated in New Jersey, was largely unaffected by the events of September 11.

As a result, BrokerTec has taken business from Cantor, long the dominant broker of U.S. government securities, and gained prominence it may not surrender.

"They are doing a ton of business; they really stepped in and doubled their market share," said John Santoro, head government trader at SG Cowen Securities Corp., who predicted "some" of BrokerTec's gains will be permanent. Santoro traded mostly through Cantor before the attacks and now splits his business between the firms.

The trend has put Hinkle, a 48-year-old former mortgage trader and son of a grocery clerk, in the uncomfortable position of profiting from a rival's tragedy.

"You don't want to take advantage of your competitor when his leg is cut off," said Hinkle, who declined to disclose how much BrokerTec's business has grown over the past two weeks.

The article then offers a quirky portrait of Hinkle, tells how he's tacked twenty fortunes from Chinese restaurants on his office wall "beside his desk, which is oval and bare except for a black phone with 40 speed-dial buttons marked with first names."

"You notice I'm on the ground floor of the oldest building in Jersey City," he said. "I was offered space up in the World Trade Center and I didn't want it. I'm very superstitious."

The rest of the article consists of quotes praising BrokerTec, by head government bond traders, many of whom are BrokerTec board members. The kicker is a tacit endorsement from the chief executive of the Bond Market Association itself, Micah Green.

It was as though the benchwarmer had been thrust into the starting lineup due to an injury to the first-string quarterback. But what had actually happened was that the quarterback's two brothers, and all his friends and several of the coaches, had been murdered on national TV. Might it have been better, in a chirpy article about your success, to avoid referring to Cantor Fitzgerald as a competitor whose "leg is cut off," when so many spouses of Cantor employees were still waiting to find out what was left of their loved one's bodies?

Poor word choice wouldn't be confined to BrokerTec. In a few weeks, Connie Chung will ask Howard how he could have "cut the families off at the knees." And most inappropriately, e-mails from Michael Spencer of ICAP, a British brokerage firm, will be quoted in newspapers, saying, "Oh, I would love to put one up their bottom," and "This is the time I have been waiting for," in reference to Cantor's post-attack vulnerability. There are rumors that even worse things have been said. Cantor employees have heard such comments as, "They're grave dancing" over the Cantor news, and that some have referred to Howard as "The Grim Weeper."

* * *

*W*E HAD TO STRIKE *a delicate balance, which meant we were committed to helping the families, but the surviving staff needed to believe there were still opportunities for them to do well by their own families. After all, it was on the shoulders of the survivors that we were rebuilding our company.*

I knew that 25 percent of this company would end up being infinitely more money than any number of paychecks. I talked about it with Stuart, Lee, and Stephen and the other partners, but I wasn't going to announce it until I knew that we'd have a company and significant profits from which to draw that 25 percent.

I knew it was a lot of money, but it was still coming from me and my partners, and it had to be something we could live with, and be proud of.

I had to act both benevolently and responsibly. If Cantor Fitzgerald no longer made money, our partners would walk, and we couldn't continue to attract the best from other firms.

The Cantor Fitzgerald partnership had never lost money. The partnership itself was created on that premise. The flaw in its structure was that if we ever lost money, then we'd start losing partners. And without them there would be no company.

We came out of the gate Monday, September 17th, with the kind of volume that stunned us. And while we were at risk the first week, that enormous amount of business produced the revenues with which we'd later be able to pay out cash to the families.

That morning when I learned from the bank that our loans didn't go up, that Tom Trillo, Clive Triance, and their team had managed to deliver enough of our 70 billion dollars' worth of securities to pay down our loans, I was ecstatic, but then I had to figure out how to get the news out to the families—we would be making profits and they would get a sizeable percentage of them.

Stuart, Peter, Phil, and I figured 25 percent was the most we could give and still maintain our business. I spoke to Bill Rice in Los Angeles and he agreed.

But now that we had a course of action we needed to get the message out. We still didn't have many of the phone numbers and addresses we'd lost when the buildings were destroyed. And certainly it would be a while before we'd get the numbers of their parents and siblings. I asked Amy Nauiokas, our marketing director, to set something up and Larry King seemed like the right place, and one where I could reach a wide audience of my families, and customers.

So I WAS FEELING pretty good. We'd been under such unbelievable pressure, but we'd pulled through. And now I was heading into St. Ignatius Loyola Church on upper Park Avenue, with fifteen hundred other mourners to honor my great friend, Joe Shea—number four guy in our company, head of all our North American bond brokerages. I loved his family too—Nancy, and their four children. Allison and I arrived just as the service was beginning. We walked all the way to the front, to the second row where seats were saved for us, and we sat down.

Now my favorite Joe Shea story is the one about him at the West Hampton Country Club, where a lot of our competitors play golf and tennis. A group of three asked him one day, "How could you work for them?" Joe is an impressive person, a four-sport athlete, my customer guy. Really well liked. He leans into them—gets so close that he's invaded their personal space. He says, "I am them."

The word "pillar" is overused. But Joe really was the pillar of his community. This was a huge Catholic church and there were a hundred mourners outside unable to get in.

I was engrossed in the service, singing the psalms. During a pause I picked up the Mass card to see who would be giving the eulogies. On the front was a picture of Joe, in suspenders and tie, smiling. But what I wasn't ready for was the other photo on the card of his little brother Danny, who also worked for us. I'd somehow managed to forget that Danny was gone too.

Something collapsed within me. And maybe it was a lot of things arriving all at once but the sight of Danny Shea's picture next to Joe's was too much to bear.

I started sobbing then, shaking and hyperventilating. My shirt was *drenched. I got up to leave, because I just couldn't stay. I walked out of the church and sat on the steps outside still shaking and crying. My car pulled up and Amy was inside, and she says, "C'mon Howard, we've got to head over to Larry King."*

Now it wasn't really the most brilliant time to be interviewed on live television. When it was done, some of my guys hated the interview. One told me it had nearly given him a heart attack. A lot of people later said they were moved by it. I didn't feel good at the end of it. I'd had a clear message I wanted to get across, that we'd be taking care of the families, but it got buried under all that emotion and stress.

In the coming months, no decision would affect the company more—and Howard in particular—than the one made to discontinue salaries following the September 15 paychecks. Some were opposed to it and had urged Howard to keep paying them for another month or two.

He made the decision after he'd guaranteed that company-provided life insurance could be paid without the need for death certificates and after Cantor executives had gotten the Red Cross to agree to begin making sizeable cash distributions to the families. In Howard's mind there was no choice—if he continued paying the salaries, they'd lose the company.

What he hadn't anticipated was the visceral reaction people would have when the paychecks stopped. Many didn't want to proceed on the assumption that their husband or wife or daughter or son was dead. They were holding out hope, and in their minds stopping the bi-monthly paychecks denied them that hope.

He is on the Larry King show now to try to put the families at peace, to let them know that while they won't be getting paychecks, they will soon receive far more than that. The firm will pay out 25 percent of its profits for the next five years.

He tells King about Kyle's first day of kindergarten and about the drive down to the Trade Center, essentially the same story he told Connie Chung six days earlier. He starts to explain the 25 percent plan, but before he finishes, King asks about Gary and what Howard told his sons about the fate of their uncle.

"My wife has a brother named Gary too. So they always had two Uncle Garys. I told them they now only had one." Howard starts crying but continues speaking. "The other Uncle Gary got hurt at work and can't come over anymore." He describes how his days have been filled with wakes and funerals, and calls from the wives of his deceased employees.

"They call me and they say, 'How come you can't pay my salary? Why can't you pay my husband's salary? Other companies *pay* their salary, why can't you?" His voice is pleading. He's still in shock from the Sheas' funeral, operating on no sleep and without having eaten all day, and he just feels jittery, emotional. "But you see, I lost everybody in the company, so I can't pay their salary. They think we're doing something wrong. I *can't* pay their salaries."

Here perhaps more than at any other moment is where Howard's trip through the media took a different course.

FALLOUT

Howard is out somewhere when I arrive at his apartment, but he'll be back soon. Two of our college friends, like most here, are hard at work answering phones and filing letters that have arrived from around the world, from churches and synagogues, middle schools, politicians and business leaders, a few celebrities.

I had expected a somber place as I walked here, but at least on the surface it isn't at all. Everyone has a role and everyone is communicating. The bosses are Allison's high school friends, Karen Weinberg, by occupation a TV and film makeup artist, and Lynne Granat, a marketing director for a culinary academy, who have been devoting their days to helping Howard and Allison set up a command center to assist the Cantor families.

Karen tells me what it's been like the last two weeks. Not all the families of those who died live in the New York area; some have come in from as far away as India, China, and Japan. And since there's no one at a Cantor office who can help them with hotels or negotiate for visas, they've been calling here and talking to Karen or Allison.

Those answering phones are equipped with information on filing for death certificates, on insurance, on funerals, and even caterers for memorial services. In addition, the surviving employees have been calling in to arrange rides from their homes to their new offices in New Jersey or Connecticut. Some workers whose divisions have since been closed have been encouraged to relocate to the London office.

"They keep calling needing things," Karen says of the families. "A woman called the other day to ask if we'd found her husband's *Producers* tickets. She wanted to sell them. Can you believe it? Her husband's dead and she's worried about theater tickets."

The calls increasingly have been about money, about what Cantor will do to take care of the families.

I flip through a copy of the *Daily News,* and amid a photo spread of the memorials is a picture of eight grim pallbearers carrying the long wooden coffin of Tim Coughlin, Howard's popular head of U.S. Treasuries, who died at forty-two.

It is a sight too rare. Not only have there been few survivors, there are few bodies. Rescue workers continue to dig through the mountains of burning steel and scorched concrete. The families are asked to bring toothbrushes and hairbrushes to the medical examiner's office for the purpose of DNA identification. The details they are given are grisly. Fingerprints can be used, but only if they can find fingers; dental records, if they can find jaws. There are all manner of body parts being recovered. Tens of thousands of tests will be conducted and the slow searching continues, and by the eighth month, fewer than a third of the missing bodies will be found.

Photographs of close friends and of Gary cover the downstairs walls. Most were taken this summer at Howard's fortieth birthday party, which took place at a castle in England. There's Doug Gardner leaning back on a bench, next to Howard, the two moguls in sunglasses away from the office. There's another of Doug swallowing up Howard's boys, Kyle and Brandon, in his huge arms. Doug was a large, big-hearted, deeply principled man, six feet four, his shoulders memorably broad, his chest cut like a weight lifter's. He liked to bang under the boards at basketball, the game his primary love interest until he met his wife.

The photographs are matted on construction paper and the words are penned in Magic Marker: WE LOVE YOU JONATHAN UMAN. WE LOVE YOU GLENN KIRWIN. WE LOVE YOU DAVE BAUER. WE LOVE YOU FRED VARACCHI. WE LOVE YOU JOE SHEA. WE LOVE YOU TIM GRAZIOSO. And on and on. It is Howard and Allison's alternative to the "missing posters" that have appeared around town.

Among those photos is one of Howard and Andy Kates, the handsome younger brother of Howard's college roommate Seth Kates. He is wearing a tweed jacket, a royal blue shirt, and a bemused expression. For Howard's fortieth, Allison asked friends to contribute a page—stories, poems, pictures for a commemorative journal. Andy created a fictional interview with an old teacher of Howard's, Mrs. Weiner, who remembered Howard's grade school business savvy.

In a week they will find Andy's body, largely intact—just broken bones. His service is scheduled for Sunday. He was thirty-seven and had three children. His wife, Emily, had just given birth to a son.

I am hardly the first to remark on this, but it is difficult to look at a wall of photographs of people in their prime, with their families and friends, and know that they're all dead. Since most of the photographs are of couples, one can look at the smiling face of the spouse left behind and have that terrible feeling that happens when watching a movie for the second time—looking at a character who is happy and hopeful, knowing that in a few moments their life will be wrecked beyond recognition.

John Swomley, a college friend who introduced Howard and Allison, has dropped his legal practice in Boston for a few days to fill in doing errands and answering phones. Close to ten friends of Allison's and Edie's have put their lives on hold in order to help out. They are not playing minor roles—they are filling human resources jobs and accounting jobs, doing public relations and office coordination. Every room serves a separate function. There are letters to sort, funerals to place on the website, and e-mails to answer. Upstairs in the dining and living rooms, Howard and his executives have been gathering to rearrange personnel, meet with bankheads, even interview prospective employees.

It has, oddly, the adrenaline-laden feel of a start-up. There's just enough time to pull all the elements together, and even then they may miss their deadline. The survival of the company, though it's seeped in history, is far from certain.

"You need any boots?" John says, and it's then that I see the office I'm in isn't an office. It's Howard and Allison's closet. Shelves run the length of the walls, and they hold a Marcosian collection of shoes and boots, leather jackets, and a half mile of suits and jeans. It's like a show-room.

But what's surprising is that the Lutnicks aren't allowing themselves to be self-conscious about it. There's a crisis going on and their house has been turned over to those who are here to help them, and to be with them. You can wander any room or dig through the fridge. There's not a scrap of privacy for Allison and Howard here. Their lives are entirely open.

In this spirit, Howard has ramped up the flow of activity by giving out his home number at the crisis center. The next day it appeared on the website. Anyone from anywhere in the world now can call in and speak to him. Not such a problem for most people, but these days it seems that everyone, everyplace, has something to say either to or about Howard. The phone rings incessantly. The fax machine churns out page after page after page. The letters arrive in tall bundles.

Upstairs in Howard's den, his childhood friend David Kravette is sitting by himself. I met Kravette around the time I met Howard, when we were kids playing eastern tennis tournaments. His is the first story I hear about that day, and it is brutal: the sound of the elevators free-falling to the ground, the sight of the fireball that came a few yards from his face and that overtook one of his colleagues, a beautiful young woman named Lauren Manning. He tells me the details in an almost matter-of-fact fashion. He says he's doing all right. He's got a new job now in Phil Marber's division. His old division is gone.

It's all about survival now, he says. Getting through to the other side of this.

"I'll tell you this," he says. "If we lost this guy [Howard] we'd be through. There's no way we'd make it. We'd have liquidated the company. That I'm sure of."

Howard arrives at around ten P.M. carrying two huge black briefcases. He kisses Allison and walks around the apartment hugging friends. At the crisis center, when Howard addressed all the families who'd lost loved ones, he requested that if anyone wanted to ask him a question, they hug him. He has always been a physical man, fond of rubbing a shoulder, slapping a back. And it fits with his personality—his pleasure in being a host, in feeding his friends, showing them a good time. Now, though, he looks as if he's aged ten years. There are deep lines in his face from not sleeping, and from crying.

The news here is that against monumental odds Cantor Fitzgerald and eSpeed are functioning smoothly again—or as smoothly as a company can without offices and three-quarters of its personnel. They still need a permanent place for the equities team. Much of Wall Street has been in chaos, layoffs everywhere, at the airlines and investment houses. The previous day, the Dow dropped 4.5 percent in one of the busiest days of trading in history. Cantor is in crisis-hiring mode. They need lawyers, accountants, a human resources team, and dozens of new brokers and traders.

Now a major concern is to specify what Howard meant when he said the company would be giving 25 percent of its profits to the families. Would there actually be profits? How would they deal with health care, bonuses, and unused vacation time?

The problems are manifold. "Our problems have problems," Allison says.

Allison, formerly a partner in a large Manhattan law firm, has been talking to families from the early morning until she can't stay awake anymore at night. "There's no one I know on earth who would do what he's doing," she says. "He's made up of parts no one has. He's got a hundred hearts. If he does this, if he pulls this company through, if all of them pull it through, it'll be the most miraculous thing anyone's heard of."

The operative word for me in that is "if." It is the first time I hear anyone in the inner circle mentioning the possibility that they won't pull through—but of course there's that chance. With all that's happened, how could there not be?

There are four of us, college friends, in Howard's living room. Howard tells us about the crisis center they set up at the Pierre Hotel.

"When we opened it, there's maybe five people there. I left to attend some meetings. During one of them, I get a call from Kent, my assistant. He says, 'Howard, you've got to get over here, it's mayhem. They're angry. They want to know where their husbands are.'

"There are people milling outside the Pierre—they're across the street, they're everywhere. And inside it's just packed. Kent is waiting outside. He says I shouldn't walk through the crowd, that I'd be beaten up for being alive. So I said, 'You got to be kidding.' I start leading people into the main room. And when I walk in front of the podium, it is like Gary is there lifting me up.

"There was so much anger in that room, but I lost Gary, and that was a shield. And I felt protected, almost unfairly. Then I realized, as I was talking, that if Gary walked in there and he was okay, or if somebody said they found my brother alive, then my ability to communicate with them would be gone.

"But I knew he was dead. He'd told Edie, 'There's no way out. I'm not going to make it. Smoke's coming in. I can't breathe.' Then he said, 'I love you.' All these people, they kept holding on to 'missing.' 'He's missing.' They weren't *missing*. There was not one second I thought my brother was missing. He was in the World Trade Center when a plane hit and took away all exits. He probably died of smoke inhalation before the building collapsed, which would have killed him anyway. The stairs . . . during the bombing in '93, it took an hour and twenty minutes to get down the stairs. So even if they had a clear path down, most of them, virtually all of them, wouldn't have been able to get down in time, especially with the traffic jams on the stairs."

His voice is hoarse and he looks exhausted. Howard and Gary were closer than most brothers. They lost their parents when Gary was fifteen and Howard was eighteen. Gary lived with Howard for a while in Ardmore, Pennsylvania, when Howard was in college and Gary in high school.

The Cantor families weren't the only ones to think their loved ones might still turn up. There were "missing" signs all around the city, on makeshift bulletin boards and on cement walls, on streetlamps and on news kiosks.

"I'm the guy who cried on TV," Howard says. "I'm famous now because everyone died. Great thing to be famous for, huh?"

*   *   *

There is among the survivors such enormous guilt that it swamps the gratitude they may feel at having escaped with their lives. You might think the first thing Howard would want to do was to spend more time with his family. That's the movie plot: the businessman, given a second chance, spends less time at business and more time with his family. But given a second chance, Howard wants to spend all of it building his business up again—honoring his brother's life, and his friend Doug's life, and Joe Shea's, and Fred Varacchi's and Glenn Kirwin's and Jonathan Uman's.

He watched it all come down—watched someone murder his friends and destroy everything he built—and he cannot let it sit this way. Rebuilding Cantor is, among other things, an act of vengeance.

At close to three, some of us who'd been working at Howard's go out in the Lower East Side of Manhattan. There is a curfew, and those of us who've grown up here, and spent our college years returning and finding the bars open until four or five, are disconcerted to see that there's only one open, a lamp-lit basement-level place in the midthirties. We do not want to turn in—we want to be together and feel alive. And we do until four A.M. when the bartender boots us out. In the taxi uptown, Karen tells us of a phone conversation she had with David Kravette the first weekend after the attacks.

"We were going over names and addresses," she says, "and we'd say alive or not. I read him names and he said, 'Not. Not. Not. Not . . .' We weren't using 'dead' those nights. That was the rule: No 'dead' or 'die' or 'dying.' After five pages or so, he says 'Alive. *Alive!*' I wasn't thinking about who the individuals were. I said, 'It's only the *K*'s we've gotten through.'

"'Is that all you have to say about that one?' he said. We'd just added his name to the list of the living.

"I said, 'Dave, we're losing it, aren't we?' And that's when we just started laughing. Because it was way too much. You couldn't cry every minute of the day, and so we just cracked up sometimes. And then we started paying attention to how many times we'd use the word 'death' or 'dying,' just as figures of speech.

"I'd say, 'I'm dying of thirst,' and then everyone would look at me."

The next day a group of us crowd into a car and head up to Riverdale to visit LaChanze Gooding, whose husband, Calvin, died during the attacks. He was thirty-eight. LaChanze is eight months pregnant with their second child, and up until the last few days, she has been holding out hope for Calvin's return. Now she has set a date for his funeral. The temperature that day is in the mid-seventies, and it's still green out, a glorious fall moment. LaChanze is an actress who has starred on Broadway in *Ragtime, The Bubbly Black Girl Sheds Her Chameleon Skin,* and *Once on This Island,* which earned her a Tony Award nomination.

There are friends and relatives at the house, and food cooking on the balcony—a wide area with a lovely view of the Hudson River. LaChanze is in the bedroom, braiding her daughter's hair.

She is very, very pregnant, and while all of the deaths are equally horrendous, there is something singularly poignant about the sight of a pregnant wife who has recently lost a husband.

The talk is not of death or of terrorism, but of Calvin and the babies. We speak in cheerful voices about whether or not the new baby will look like her father or have his personality. LaChanze tells stories about him in the present tense, and so we do too. I keep staring off at the pictures of them on vacation—Calvin looking just a little cocky in blue swim trunks, LaChanze in a bright red bathing suit, arms around each other. Self-confidence was never a problem for Calvin.

LaChanze tells us about the night she and Calvin met. The story is already legend.

"I had actually noticed him first, that night," LaChanze says. "I saw Calvin from behind and I was attracted to him."

"Everyone loved Calvin's behind," our friend John says.

"I was inside the restaurant and he was outside. I was sitting at the window with my girlfriend and he walked by. We saw him from the side and then from the back, and said, 'Whoa, look at him,' and my girlfriend said, 'I'll drink to that.' Then he ends up walking in the restaurant. And I was so *aware* of him because he was talking to everybody. I said to my girlfriend, 'He's working the room. He knows everybody in here.' He would go from this group to that group and on to the next. About an hour later, he made his way over to us. He asked me was I an actress. I said yes. He asked me was my picture up at the hair salon, and I said yes. He said, 'I've been trying to meet you for two years.'

"He asked could he buy us a drink, and we laughed, because my girlfriend was carrying a flask, and we were ordering ginger ales and topping them off with Bacardi. And we had had about three or four by the time he walked over. So he said, 'What are you drinking, ladies?' and we said, 'Ginger ales!' and he couldn't figure out why we thought it was so funny.

"There was this issue of *The New Yorker* that had just come out, and the theme was 'Blacks in America,' and it was real popular among the black bourgeoisie in New York. So we were chiming in what we thought about it for about an hour, and then my girlfriend said, 'I've got to call my boyfriend.' And this was pre–cell phones, and Calvin said to her, 'Do you need a quarter?'"

She laughs. "What I remember is that I thought he was very handsome. He had a lot of charisma. He wasn't at all intimidated by a couple of actresses at a bar."

LaChanze gave him her number. By the time she'd made it home from the bar, there were three messages on her machine, all from Calvin.

"I think the first was, 'I'm still in the bar and I just met you and you're one of the most . . . ' You know, one of those—*I just met you and I just want to make sure the number's right.* The second was making sure I got home okay, and in the last one he was asking me could we get together."

"That didn't disturb you?" another friend asks.

"I liked that he wasn't afraid to let me know how attracted he was to me." She smiles modestly. "And I went out of town, and when I got back he'd called, like, six times, wanting to know why I wasn't calling him back. And I was away for only three days—for Memorial Day weekend with my family. When I got back I felt so bad because this guy—I really liked him, but I didn't expect to talk to him again until the following week."

LaChanze called him the night she returned to the city. They went out that night to see the movie *Twister*. It was his birthday.

Within the year, they were engaged.

Calvin was rising quickly within the company. His salary had increased as his responsibilities expanded. And as a black man in a white world he had a chance to make a real impact. He was an active, if potentially demanding, father, and he was becoming more spiritual, LaChanze says.

The talk turns to Howard. She's been worried about finances, she says. She wants Howard to call her and explain her financial future to her—investments, insurance, taxes. She is considering bringing a lawyer to a meeting with Howard, and she wants to know if that would be the wrong thing to do, if that would seem too aggressive.

"Maybe," someone answers, "but that doesn't mean you shouldn't do what you feel you need to do."

"I'll call him," LaChanze says. "He's so busy now. It's so hard for him."

The next thing we do is pick up Jennifer Gardner, Doug's widow, and go to the bar at the Four Seasons Hotel. We trade stories of Doug, of which there are hundreds. Doug was the glue in a very large group of friends. He kept in touch with everyone—grade school, high school, college, and work friends. He never seemed to drop anyone. He was like someone who's built a house and can't stop adding rooms.

He was at once smart, capable, and easy to poke fun at—he over-emoted, yelled too loud when playing sports, became too enthusiastic when he was having fun.

Doug wasn't supposed to be at the building that morning, Jennifer tells us. He was supposed to be on a business trip the week of September 11. It was their son Michael's first day of preschool, but the next day would be their daughter Julia's first. So Jennifer and Doug decided Doug would postpone his trip and take both kids to school on Wednesday morning.

These are the issues so many people are dealing with: Calvin was in Martha's Vineyard and nearly spent an extra few days there; Gary was in the Hamptons on Monday and had considered coming in on Tuesday afternoon rather than that morning.

September 11 was also Doug's father Joe's birthday. "We were going to go out to dinner, with the kids, at five. So Doug wanted to get to work early. It destroys Joe thinking about it."

She remembers what he wore and how he looked—his blue shirt, his Cole Haan shoes, his khaki pants. "He looked great. I always loved him in blue shirts because it brought out his eyes. We were sitting in the kitchen, and I gave him a tiny bit of shit. I said, 'You're missing Michael's first day of school. You're missing the pictures.' But it didn't matter. I gave him a big kiss and said 'I don't care,' because I didn't. It was no big deal."

I'm not sure what a widow should look like, but somehow I suspect they shouldn't look pregnant like LaChanze Gooding, they shouldn't look as young and still in the throes of love as Jennifer Gardner when she talks of Doug. Her stories reflect an enormous amount of good fortune. Her expressions shift within a sentence; she begins a long story about Doug, about the house they built, or a vacation, something silly he did—and it's possible to hear in her voice just a little rage at him for not being there. She digs her thin frame into the banquette as she might have into Doug's side for warmth and reassurance. Her voice races and then slows. She is uncomfortable sitting.

She listens to other people's stories about Doug, confirms or corrects them. Since last weekend, the weekend of Doug's memorial, Jennifer has heard hundreds of people talk about her husband, some of whom knew Doug since he was a child, or in high school or college, and she has felt the need to articulate the fact that length of time of knowing someone isn't the best criteria for judging the depth of one's love.

"I knew him better than he knew himself," she says more than once, then grows silent. "Can we get out of here?" she says.

When we get back, Howard is upstairs in a meeting. We pile into his bedroom. There are thirteen rooms in this place, five bedrooms, six thousand square feet. His last apartment was in Trump Palace, forty-nine floors up. When my wife and I traveled to New York, we were taken home by Howard's driver. He knows it's fun for us. Howard is wealthy in a way I don't entirely understand. It's not the wealth so much as it is his standing in the world.

At twenty-nine, Howard became president of the largest bond brokerage firm in the world. The one that sat atop the World Trade Center. In the beginning a lot of us had no idea what it was that Howard Lutnick did, only that he kept making money. I knew that in a semester off from college he had been trading foreign exchange, and that the job consisted of yelling a lot and being aggressive, for which he seemed ideally suited. He was also just a little quicker than most—quick at figuring out problems, at figuring out how things worked.

But none of us really knew what Cantor Fitzgerald did any more than the country knew what the company did on September 10. Our friends who worked on Wall Street knew. But what I would soon learn was part of Cantor's appeal in the business was that it offered anonymity to firms trading through them—and the lower the profile Cantor Fitzgerald kept, the less resented they would be for essentially being the New York Stock Exchange for bonds.

What we did know was that Howard's apartments got bigger, his cars got nicer, and his parties, when he threw them, more lavish. His contributions to our college have made him their favorite son ten times over. He regularly matches our entire class gift.

There was always an element of showmanship to him. For Allison's thirty-fifth birthday he took twenty friends to Arizona. They stayed in a resort hotel and then rode all-terrain vehicles out into the desert, where a four-course meal was waiting for them on blankets.

He loves to pay for things, to take a large group out to a meal and pick up the check. I never had the sense he felt better than the rest of us—only richer, maybe luckier, or just more single-minded. His good fortune was his friends' good fortune, and their wives' good fortune, and their wives' friends' good fortune. He found jobs for people he knew were talented and underutilized elsewhere. But mostly we've been happy for him because we knew well that he'd lost his parents, that his extended family had cast the three kids out. That he'd worked unbelievably hard.

He wasn't born into a monied family—wasn't left much of anything. And we knew too that there had been personality struggles at his job, ugly turf battles that he had scraped his way through.

Howard's father, Sol, died our freshman year. We didn't know the details at the time, didn't know that someone at the hospital had accidentally given him an overdose of chemotherapy, which killed his father. We knew Howard had left school for a few weeks and that his mother, Jane, had died when he was in high school, that he was now an orphan.

I have since lost both my parents, my mother in college and my father five years ago, but at the time I hadn't known many people yet whose parents had died.

He went home for the funeral. When he returned he wasn't quite how we expected. He was distraught, sure, but he was focused, and he didn't retreat from his life. He, in fact, shot up the tennis ladder, and began pulling in A's at a college with a reputation for tough grading.

I bring this up because in some ways I think Howard has had a dry run for what he's going through now.

E IGHT OF US are sitting on the bed or leaning against it, as though we're in Howard's dorm room at college. Howard walks in and hugs his old roommate, Michael Kaminer, a dermatologist in Massachusetts. The news is on. Mullah Mohammed Omar, the Taliban leader, has refused to turn over bin Laden. Someone turns the TV off.

No one here talks of the terrorists, or Bush, or the U.S. response. Howard says if bin Laden appeared at his door he wouldn't have the strength to throw a punch.

*   *   *

Howard and Allison are discussing which funerals they can attend and which ones they can't. Each of the 658 Cantor funerals will have hundreds of mourners, in many cases more than a thousand. And while there is some duplication, it's fair to say a quarter of a million people will have attended a funeral for someone at Cantor Fitzgerald.

We look at the list and see familiar names slated for the coming weeks. The schedule is seventy-eight pages long, ten a day, running through Thanksgiving. There is a problem here for those who are grieving: It's that all their closest friends are mourning, or dead. This weekend, there are forty Cantor Fitzgerald funerals.

Rather than gaining solace from the number of others in their place, they find it depersonalizing. There is even a fear among some that their husband's, or brother's, or wife's, will be the least-attended service, and that will reflect poorly on them. They take note of who attends, and certainly of whether Howard is there.

SATURDAY–SUNDAY, SEPTEMBER 22–23

Saturday, September 22:

A Taliban spokesperson says they can't find Osama bin Laden. Refugees flee to the Pakistan border. The news show American jet fighters heading for Afghanistan.

At Ground Zero, it's been more than ten days since anyone was found alive. Bulldozers and earthmovers cart away thousands of pounds of rubble. Christian groups have set up prayer stations.

Some of the Cantor survivors make it over to the site to see the damage. The destruction is evident everywhere in Lower Manhattan. Buildings ten blocks away are coated in a thick gray layer of concrete and ash.

Funerals

PHIL MARBER

"One of those Saturdays, I got up at seven thirty, left my apartment in the city, and headed to Long Island for an eight-thirty service for Jonathan Connors. And I got a seat in the last row of the balcony. It's still half an hour before the service. J.C. was a superpopular guy. There are more than a thousand people there. When you go to these services, you could see why we were so successful—just a great quality of people—so I'm sitting in the last row, perspiring. Before it's over I gotta leave, because I have an eleven o'clock for one of my other guys, Jeff LeVeen, and it's half an hour away. J.C.'s started at nine. At ten fifteen I stand up to leave because I don't want to be late and end up in the last row again. I walk out and my car is pinned in. So I see Craig Cummings, and since he's parked in a different lot, we get in his car and we go to the next service. There must have been a thousand people there too. Enormous church, and it's standing room only, lines out the door. That one lasted until twelve thirty. We go back and get my car, then go to a reception, and there's a half-hour line to get in. I said, 'I can't do this.'

"So I drove farther east on the LIE to go to see the wife of one of my top guys and best friends. She called me on Friday ranting and raving, hollered at me for killing her husband. I let her go on, anyway. I got there and I played human punching bag. She took every shot at me, Cantor, the firm, everything. She just beat the crap out of me until she was done, until she had no more. Finally there was a silence like she had just gotten it off her chest. I gave her a big hug and a kiss.

"After that I went to his parents' house, and it was exactly the opposite. They wanted to tell stories about him. It was nice but it was extremely sad. I spent a couple of hours there.

"It was about eight thirty then, and I saw one of his clients out at a Marriott hotel, and we spent two hours for dinner. Finally, around eleven, I start driving back and I'm going about fifty, and I'm behind a car that's doing about thirty-five miles an hour, I get right behind him, I swing into the next lane. I hear *weeeeew*. There's a cop behind me, and I know I'm not speeding, so I pull over. I'm sitting in my car, seven minutes or so while he's going through the computer. It's the absolute last thing I wanted to do. He says, 'You were following too closely and you changed lanes without signaling.'

"And while I was sitting there someone passes by doing a hundred miles an hour. I said, 'I'm not speeding.'

"He said, 'This is not a debate, sir.'

"And the next day I went to two or three more."

TOM TRILLO

"Even though I've only been with the firm three years, I knew a tremendous amount of people, knew them pretty well. I could go to six hundred fifty-eight wakes. But I can't do that and also do what they're asking me to do. I'm doing the job of twenty people. We all were. So I made a decision early on that I wasn't going to attend any of the memorial services, that if I allowed myself to get caught up in the grief and emotion of what's going on, I couldn't work at the level they needed me to. And that was very hard for me, because here I am thinking about the close friends, the people I'd lost. And then I got guys coming in and saying, 'Well, I gotta go to so-and-so's memorial service today,' or, 'I gotta go to so-and-so's wake.' And I tell them, 'Okay, you have to do what you have to do.' It was an *extremely* difficult process to manage, because it didn't end. It just kept coming in waves . . . and it would just go on . . . because, you know, there's six hundred fifty-eight of these things that are going to occur in one way, shape, or form. And some people didn't give up hope for weeks. You felt like it was never going to stop. And that's why I didn't even get started."

Tracy Claus

"There were days we went to four and could have gone to six. Matt didn't sleep for a long while, so I didn't sleep. Think of it this way: I had a two-and-a-half-year-old at the time. From the chaos that was in our house, all the funerals we went to, everything we were doing—now my husband was not killed, nor was he injured, nor was he ever missing—but my daughter started to stutter. She started to have nightmares, she said that Daddy works in buildings that fall down. And nothing *happened* to my family. We only knew people who died. I simply can't fathom how hard it was for those who did lose someone."

SUNDAY, SEPTEMBER 30

I reach David Kravette at home on a Sunday evening. He's feeling a little numb these days, but other than that, he says things could be a lot worse.

Kravette has known Howard since seventh grade. In the last weeks, word has gotten out that Kravette was in the offices that morning, the last to make it out of the offices before the plane hit and therefore the last to see many of the people who died.

He's been going to four or five funerals a week. When he sees the families of his friends at these events, or when he saw them at the crisis center, they want him to tell them about what their husband or wife was doing just *before,* what they were joking about or working on. In many cases, the men and women who worked at Cantor had left so early in the morning that their spouses didn't know what they'd worn to work that day—and so that's another question.

They want to fix in their mind a last, peaceful image of their wife or husband. The questions, Kravette tells me, "were really bringing me down badly . . . you see the pain on all their faces, and there's nothing I could do to make them feel better. I had nothing for them."

We talk about his kids and his wife, Janice. Everyone's doing fine, he says. Kravette feels lucky because he lived.

I ask if he can talk about the day. He's told me the story in pieces but not yet from start to finish. He says he went to work early because of a meeting with Quick & Reilly, an online brokerage that was thinking about putting eSpeed on their website. He's speaking calmly now, as though it's a story about a fouled-up sales call. "At eight my customer calls. They're running late. No problem. 'Just make sure you remember to bring ID,' I remember saying to them. I told them the technology guys need photo ID because of the [1993] terrorist attack. Eight forty the security desk from downstairs calls. 'Are you expecting visitors?' Yes. 'Well, one of them forgot his picture ID. You'll have to come down and sign him in.' Now, it's annoying because it's a five-minute trip downstairs. So I look at my assistant who I would have sent downstairs, but she's seven and a half months pregnant, and she's on the phone chatting, personal call. I just felt guilty so I went down myself.

"I get up to go and the phone rings. I've got caller ID. I see it's Janice calling me. I pick up and she starts talking to me, telling me how the kids are running down the driveway to retrieve the newspaper there. They're running into the street. She's scared they're going to get hit by a car. I say, 'Let's discuss this later. There are people downstairs and I don't want to keep them waiting.' She says, 'Let's talk now.' I said, 'Come on, Janice. It's not a big deal. It can wait.' She says, 'Let's talk now.' I say I can't. She says, 'Fine. *Whatever.*'"

Kravette laughs now.

"We hang up and then I take the two elevators down. It's fifty feet from me to the ropes at the visiting desk. I yell to those guys, 'Which one of you knuckleheads forgot your ID?' And as soon as I say that, the building shakes. I turn around and I *hear* the elevators, at least two of them, falling, *free-falling.*

"The lobby of the Trade Center is very tall—at least five stories— and the same time these elevators come crashing down there was a huge fireball explosion. I think that's what took them down. But this fireball comes out of the middle elevator bank. The middle bank I guess has a service shaft that goes to the top of the building. The jet fuel must have come down there. All I saw was this *huge* fireball like the one you saw when the plane hit, red and smokelike veins in it, and it came billowing out the middle. It's like . . . picture a barbell coming out both ends, spreading out rounder on the West Street side. I didn't see the other side, the side toward the concourse part of the building, which was just *exploding.* This all happened in seconds, and it was coming *right* toward us. Everyone was diving somewhere, and I *just froze.* I just stood there and saw death coming. And I remember saying, 'I'm dying. I'm going to die.' I remember being really *calm* about it, like I'd given up. But as quick as it came toward me it just stopped and sucked back in on itself. This was all in, at most, four seconds. It blew out and pulled back in on itself. All the glass and everything was *blown* out. There was smoke and fire and my customer had more sense than me, he just pushed me toward the only way I saw out, which was over the overpass . . . over West Street to the World Financial Center. We got halfway over the overpass and we thought we were safe. We didn't know what was happening and then we just walked over West Street down to the other side, and we went to where the marina is and we just watched.

"I just wanted to reach Janice at that point, but none of the cell phones worked. So we're just watching the building burn. And it looks like debris is falling out the window, but it wasn't debris. It was people. And they were jumping. We saw pairs of people jumping. It was where the plane had hit. I guess they were just burning alive in there.

"I finally got Janice on the phone about an hour later. All her friends were there by then. She thought I was dead because she'd seen the building on TV. We just cried hysterically. I remember I was on the corner by a loading dock, and I just broke down the moment I heard her voice. And I got cut off. Right then this stranger, a big guy, just gives me a big bear hug and he says, 'You're okay now,' and then he walks away.

"I thought everyone was dead. We were calling around, trying to find out who was alive. I remember when I finally saw our building go down on TV, when I saw the antenna go down, I'll tell you . . . I knew they were all dead for a long time before that, but when I saw that thing go down . . . it was just so *final.* That's it. It's gone. You're never going back there . . . Everything you had in there, all your memories, people you've known for . . . it all just *collapsed.*"

Neither of us says anything then.

O NE OF BERNIE CANTOR'S earliest money-making ventures was a job selling hot dogs at Yankee games when he was a boy growing up in New York City. He made his inroads in the investment world when as a young man he settled in Los Angeles and began advising wealthy clients such as Zsa Zsa Gabor and Kirk Douglas on their portfolios. As his firm grew, Cantor established himself as a maverick, watching and plotting and moving at all the right times.

In the early 1970s, he began offering bond-pricing data over a computer screen and thereby revolutionized the country's bond markets. Before then clients and brokers relied on rumors and hunches. The Federal Reserve Bank would run day-end surveys to gauge dealer prices.

There was none of what people on Wall Street called "transparency." Outsiders had great difficulty judging bond prices. Now that Cantor was offering real quotes in real time, everyone could know the prices at which issues were bought and sold. A once hidden, inside market was now open for all to see.

Dealers would watch bond prices move across a screen on their desk. When they liked what they saw, they'd call their Cantor broker and make a trade or ask questions. Most important, they could trade without giving away their position. For example, if Merrill Lynch wanted to sell 200 million U.S. Treasury bonds, they wouldn't call up Goldman Sachs and declare their intentions. They'd enter the Cantor marketplace and no one would know it was them. Or they might put up a bid for the bonds to convince competitors there was a big buyer out there, only to sell in the bond futures' pits of Chicago. They could trade through Cantor to take a position or to get out of one.

In the old days, dealers barked numbers over the phone like radio announcers calling a horse race. It was an imperfect process, and success more often boiled down to who you had drinks with and who you knew, rather than your knowledge base.

In a sense, Bernie Cantor was leveling the playing field—and in another sense, he was growing the bond market itself—in a way that would make him a very rich man, and his brokers and traders among the most well compensated.

Not only was Cantor serving as a wholesale exchange, it was also providing the main price index—or stock ticker—for bonds, and it had become one of the main players in the area of third-market equities. This meant they weren't members of the New York Stock Exchange, or any exchange—they brought neutral buyers and sellers together, and again, as in the bond business, offered them anonymity.

The dealers didn't fuss too much about Cantor's influence over the marketplace because the new way of doing business created (or perhaps coincided with) an explosion in the trading volume of U.S. Treasuries. The story of Cantor Fitzgerald—of Bernie and Howard—is one of impeccable business timing. And not necessarily by accident.

It is also a story of quiet dominance, of flying below the radar.

"We were never—before this thing happened—well known to the general public," Stuart Fraser says. "Bernie's rule was you don't promote yourself. We're a niche business. 'Let no one know what we do, how we do it, or how much we make.' That was always fine by me.

"Our clients are professional traders, and they're the ones with the egos. We just service them, help them get their job done seamlessly. Another thing Bernie told us was, 'Don't expect people to love you, a few people might like you, but you gotta make them need you.' That's where we succeeded. Because they need us. We do the best job. We do it fairly. We don't cater only to the biggest accounts. We treated everyone fairly. If you were first, you were first whether you were the biggest firm or you were the smallest. The other shops, our competitors, did not always work that way. That hurt them."

Indeed, Cantor broke from the ranks in this respect. Other firms lowered commissions only for the bigger players who traded the highest volumes, and Cantor lowered commissions across the board. They also infuriated the banks because they offered their data to the customers, like mutual funds and money managers, who now knew the wholesale prices of bonds. Each time Bernie Cantor changed the business, people went along because he was growing the industry. The screen system, along with greater liquidity in the bond market, significantly increased the government's ability to borrow—which added bonds, lots of them—and the number of traders at Wall Street banks, like Salomon and Lehman Brothers, began to double and double again, and double once more. Bernie Cantor had created the wholesale bond marketplace, the Exchange.

"Our competitors are jealous because we run our business the way we want to, and because we make them look bad. Few ever left us," Stuart says, "and if they did . . . I don't know of anyone who was successful."

Essentially, if you were in the business, and you weren't at Cantor, you were kidding yourself. Cantor dominated the industry. If you wanted to do a big trade, to cross a billion bonds, you called Cantor.

They were, Howard and Stuart say, the Yankees of the bond business. Big payroll, great farm system, and employing their talent within the world's most recognizable and powerful home stadium. Like Yankee owner George Steinbrenner, Howard shamelessly and unapologetically recruited the top talent from other firms. "They had the best people in just about every category," a former employee told me. "Ian Schneider was famous in repos. Joe Shea was a god on corporate bonds and agencies, his brother, Danny, as well. Tim Coughlin was a monster in U.S. Treasuries, Tim O'Brien in mortgages, Tom Burke in zeros."

When an outsider impressed the executive staff, he was likely to be rewarded with a job offer impossible to turn down. After Jonathan Uman helped craft the strategy and presentations for the eSpeed road show that preceded the company's 1999 IPO, Howard and Fred Varacchi understood they could not let the then thirty-one-year-old go back to his job at UBS Warburg.

Howard says, "We looked at each other and we said, 'We have to hire him.' We were on the plane heading home, and we offered him the job right then and there. He called his wife, Julie, and they talked for about fifteen minutes. After that he was ours. He would be our deal-maker."

When people joined they brought not only their skills and their reputations in the industry, but also their clients and millions of dollars of business the firm might not have otherwise had. They also brought their friends. Success bred success, and while other firms tended to resent Howard for it, he kept grabbing talent where he could find it. He hired Glenn Kirwin, a thirty-four-year-old product-development whiz on his way up who'd been working for a competitor, designing their options business. He hired Tim Coughlin and Steve Roach from Garban, and Lee Amaitis from Patriot/Liberty.

He'd told Coughlin when he met him, "We've got the systems. We've got the best race car. Why would you want to drive their jalopy?"

He brought in dozens and dozens, people he would spend his working life with, whose wives and children he would get to know, whose friends and brothers and brothers-in-law he would end up hiring too.

MONDAY, OCTOBER 1

The day of the Cantor memorial the temperature drops and it's drizzling. Thousands—wearing raincoats over suits—assemble in folding chairs near the Central Park bandshell, near several white tents and dozens of tables. On most of the chairs are teddy bears, which have been arriving at the relief fund in droves. By Thanksgiving they'll have received more than thirty thousand of them.

Clad in red jackets, the Boys Choir of Harlem sings "God Bless America" and then "The Star-Spangled Banner." Stuart Fraser then begins guiding the proceedings. Fraser started the same summer as Howard. He had a connection. He is Iris Cantor's nephew, and now he's doing all he can to hold himself together as he introduces religious leaders and family members. He wears a black suit. His boyish face looks overwhelmed.

The Reverend Bishop Patrick J. Sheridan begins by addressing the crime: "Those shall be put to shame who heedlessly break faith in You. Guide us in truth."

New York Mayor Rudy Giuliani stands at the podium in a gray suit with a bright red tie, the Boys Choir behind him. Looking out over the crowd, he says, "Although we've been living with this for almost three weeks, I'm shocked by the number of people here . . . It's one thing to say that five thousand people are missing or that you lost seven hundred thirty-three people. It's another thing to see it."

The events of September 11, he says, brought incalculable pain to people around the world, "but they've had a *devastating* impact on a few close-knit communities of men and women who lost hundreds of friends and colleagues and family members on that darkest of days in our city's history. You can understand this feeling all too well, because you have undergone the same kind of devastating loss. The World Trade Center was first and foremost a place of *business*. And no business, *no community*, has suffered more than Cantor Fitzgerald. The hundreds of people that were taken from you—your husbands and wives, brothers and sisters, sons and daughters, mothers and fathers— were heroes." He pauses. The crowd is attentive.

"Let me tell you what I mean by that. When we think of heroes these days, we think quite naturally of the hundreds of firefighters and police officers who put themselves in danger, but there are many kinds of heroism, and one of them is the quiet heroism of working hard, supporting a family, and pursuing a dream. Our economy and our society are built on millions of men and women who engage in this kind of heroism day in and day out. Your own company has been a vital and important part of this tradition. Through your own innovation and very hard work, you've become a crucial participant in the global bond market. You represent in a very, very important way the genius and dynamism of New York City, your hometown.

"And just as your whole city has shown great determination, unity, and courage in the aftermath of the attack on the World Trade Center, Cantor Fitzgerald has shown all of these qualities in its own response. In spite of your unspeakable losses, that are still to hard to comprehend, you were able to reestablish your electronic bond trading network by the morning of *September 13th*. It was essential to the symbolism of making sure that life goes on and the terrorists don't win."

He acknowledges that some wounds, including his own, will never heal, then ends with what has become a familiar refrain:

"Remember: We're right, and they're wrong."

Nancy Shea, dressed in a black pantsuit, is the first of the Cantor widows to speak. She's tall and thin, athletic-looking, early forties, short dark hair, composed, and maybe a bit angry. Like the mayor, she speaks of the shocking breadth of the cataclysm.

"Everything about this event is oversized: the buildings themselves, the number of victims; the physical destruction, the emotional devastation, as well as the number of Cantor Fitzgerald casualties. But the size of the collective loss does not diminish the impact of the individual loss. Every victim was the center of a small universe and each will be missed. But maybe the size of this tragedy is appropriate. Our loved ones were exceptional people. They were smart, vital, charismatic. They were generous, hardworking, just as oversized as the event that took them from us, and our anger is appropriately enormous. Terrorism did not create our heroes; it took them from us."

More spouses—Maura Coughlin, Joan Kirwin, Eileen Varacchi, Sam Ellis—speak movingly. Then Judy Collins, in a dark suit, sings "America, the Beautiful," including a special verse she's written about courage in adversity.

Finally, Howard takes the stage. He speaks of the family members who took the time from their own grieving to try to comfort him, about how the survivors and others—volunteers, clients, and former employees—dropped their lives to work on behalf of the relief effort.

"They loved their friends; they were like family. They bonded together in a way no one in business will understand, because I even can't understand it. It's not about what anyone else says about us; it's not about people on the outside—it's just about us. It is an honor for me to stand here and speak for the survivors. I will never be prouder of anything in my life than being a member of the family of Cantor Fitzgerald, the family of eSpeed and TradeSpark."

Afterward people linger, exchanging numbers, making plans. It doesn't feel like an ending, or as though any aspect of this has been put to rest. There are still so few bodies. Though the war in Afghanistan has started, most, like Howard and Allison, tune it out. The mourners see on their way out of the park a Midtown Manhattan that has largely moved on, while they are, if anything, still months away from the worst. So little is understood still, and the shock of the atrocity is both pervasive and numbing. What they know is that whatever happened to them—to their family—happened as well to all these others. It is a community in mourning, an American success story buried now in unfathomable sadness.

THURSDAY, OCTOBER 4

Bill O'Reilly is ranting.

"In front of the cameras, some businesspeople were devastated by the terror at the World Trade Center. But behind the scenes, something *very disturbing* may be going on. Are the victims' families getting the benefits they're entitled to? What is the firm evidence against Osama bin Laden? We'll lay out the case for you . . . Caution: You're about to enter the No Spin Zone. *The Factor* begins in ninety seconds."

A clip is shown then of Howard talking about all the pregnant wives, and all the children—955 of them—who lost a parent, then crying while he says he's lucky to be alive, and how he now has the responsibility to take care of 700 families.

"Sounded good, didn't it?" O'Reilly says. "Another story may be unfolding."

He introduces Lynda Fiori, one of the September 11 widows, and Elizabeth MacDonald, senior editor at *Forbes* magazine, which published one of the more damaging stories to date about Howard and Cantor.

Wednesday, Fiori was pictured in the *New York Post* beneath the headline, "CANTOR KIN: BOSS BROKE BOND TO US." The paper ran a photograph of the mother of three, turned sideways to show a tattoo of a heart with her husband's name, Paul, and the date 9/11 written across.

"Howard Lutnick was a very good actor on TV. He should get an award for that," she is quoted as saying.

More striking to me than the quote from an anxious wife is the background context that the reporters provide: "Despite his grief, it was easy to doubt Lutnick's sincerity . . . The chairman of Cantor Fitzgerald has a reputation as a brash, heartless Wall Street boss."

An unnamed veteran trader (the article neglects to say where he works) refers to Howard as a "hard-ass."

"Ms. Fiori, we're very, very sorry," O'Reilly says. "We know you had the funeral yesterday. And you have two small children, a four-month-old girl and a two-year-old girl. Have you heard from Mr. Lutnick?"

"No, I haven't."

"Not a *word?*" O'Reilly says.

"No. I've called him and there's been no phone call back."

"You called his office and *no one returned the call?*"

"I called his home," she says.

The conversation progresses this way. She left a message with a woman at Howard's house and she hadn't spoken to Howard yet.

"Have you gotten any money from Cantor Fitzgerald?" O'Reilly asks.

"No."

"Not a *dime?*"

"No. I thank God for my family. If I didn't have family, I'd be out on the streets with my two kids."

"Now you just saw Mr. Lutnick on television. He also did an interview with every medium, you know, crying, you know. The whole *routine.* What did you think?"

"Well, I'm not too happy with him."

"Do you think he's a phony?"

"I think so," she says. She pauses. "You know he has his family, which is great. I mean, I don't want anybody to get hurt. But he really has to reach out to the families. Give them a phone call."

She says she was disappointed that no Cantor people attended her husband's funeral.

O'Reilly is sympathetic. "Hard to believe," he says. "Now there have been almost a billion dollars raised to help you, your family . . . Seen any of that money?"

"No. No."

"Anybody call you?"

"No."

"Red Cross? Anybody like that?"

"The Red Cross called today. I spoke with them."

"Was that before they knew you were going to be on this program or—"

"No, I don't think . . . I don't think—"

"Okay, so they just called you? What did they say?"

She explains how they offered to pay for the funeral and walked her through the forms she'd need to fill out in order to receive relief funds. The Red Cross began the process of paying out to the families in part because Howard sent his executives Bud Flanagan and Phil Ginsberg to Washington to put pressure on Bernadette Healy, the president of the Red Cross.

As Phil Marber would later say of Fiori: "Who did she think gave the Red Cross her phone number?"

"But all the other myriad agencies—nobody's gotten in touch with you," O'Reilly says. "All right. Ms. MacDonald, you're a writer for *Forbes* magazine. You know this company. What's your impression of what Ms. Fiori's going through?"

Elizabeth MacDonald, O'Reilly's Lutnick authority, replies, "Well, you know, when you see Mr. Lutnick on the air, you *want* to believe him. You want to say to yourself, 'Is this the face of compassion or capitalism, or is this the story about bereavement hitting the bottom line?'"

She brings up the stopped paychecks and voices her doubts about whether Cantor will pay bonuses. No one discusses the unlikelihood of a company that lost nearly seven hundred of a thousand employees and its offices and primary systems even staying in business. They talk as though the Cantor Fitzgerald of September 10 is still intact.

O'Reilly says that yeah, this is "being handled dreadfully," that he tried to get Lutnick on the show but that Lutnick declined. He then tries to calculate Howard's net worth—60 million dollars, he guesses—to make the point that he's hoarding his cash and leaving the families of his colleagues and friends penniless.

"What's his reputation on Wall Street?" he asks.

"He's known to be very tough, brash," Elizabeth MacDonald answers. "He seized control early on in the process. He was barred, actually, from Bernie Cantor's gravesite ceremony when Bernie Cantor, who started the firm, died back in 1996."

"Why was he barred?"

"Because he seized control of the firm while Bernie was ailing and—"

"So the guy who started the company was sick, and *this guy* did a coup d'état and took the firm *over*."

"Right."

"Oh, he's a prince. All right, I'm getting a picture on this guy." O'Reilly returns now to Fiori, tells her he'll be on top of this, that he'll get her a lawyer. He tells her she *should* be angry, what with Howard crying on television, and had she heard the worst? Had she or Mac-Donald heard that Howard had hired *a public relations firm?*

"Edelman. Yes," MacDonald says.

"It's interesting to compare it to what other companies are doing," MacDonald says. She describes how Fiduciary Trust Company International, which lost eighty-two employees, is paying salaries and benefits until they "figure out the situation."

Howard, she says, has responded to the tragedy by hiring a PR firm. There's no mention of the 25 percent, the full bonuses, the ten years of health care, or that Edelman Worldwide has been Cantor Fitzgerald's public relations firm for several years now.

"I just want this to sink in to people," O'Reilly says. "After this happened, this guy, Lutnick, went on all the programs, all right, and he hires a PR agency. To do what?" O'Reilly presses.

"To go on *Larry King*—" MacDonald says. She's got more to add, but O'Reilly interrupts her:

"Yeah. To *book him!*"

"To go on *Connie Chung*," MacDonald says.

"So he's paying these people to get him publicity while Mrs. Fiori and her two little children—he doesn't return their phone calls." O'Reilly then addresses his audience directly, "The other media, *Larry King* and *ABC News*, they won't tell you this story."

He thanks his guests, then hardens his glare into the camera, "Coming next—the case against Osama bin Laden . . . We'll be right back."

There is something between glee and uncontrolled vitriol here at the end of the interviews. O'Reilly has worked his viewers into a lather.

Karen Weinberg hands me some faxes when I come by Howard and Allison's the next day.

Mr. Howard Lutnik
CEO
Cantor Fitzgerald

Mr. Lutnik:
WHAT KIND OF PERSON ARE YOU?
HERE I AM WATCHING "THE O'REILLY FACTOR" LAST NIGHT, AND RATHER THAN HEAR OF ALL THE HELP, COMPASSION, AND SUPPORT YOU ARE GIVING THE FAMILIES OF THOSE CANTOR FITZGERALD EMPLOYEES LOST AT THE WTC, THERE IS A YOUNG WOMAN, A WOMAN WITH NO MONEY, NO SUPPORT, NO ASSISTANCE AND NO HELP FROM YOU.
I AM OUTRAGED AT YOUR PHONY ON AIR SYMPATHY AND SUPPORT FOR YOUR EMPLOYEES, YET THIS WOMAN AND HER CHILDREN ARE LIVING AND EATING ONLY DUE TO HER OWN FAMILY HELPING HER.
I REALIZE YOU LOST YOUR BROTHER IN THE TRAGEDY AND GOD BLESS HIM. BUT YOU, YOU SHOULD BE ASHAMED OF YOURSELF AND YOUR LACK OF REGARD FOR WOMEN LIKE THIS. IT SEEMS LIKE ALL YOU CAN DO IS TALK THE TALK, BUT WHEN IT COMES TO WALKING THE WALK YOU ARE A DESPICABLE PERSON.
WHY DOES BILL O'REILLY HAVE TO OFFER THIS WOMAN AN ATTORNEY TO ASSIST HER IN SEEKING SUPPORT AND HELP FROM THE COMPANY HER HUSBAND MADE A GREAT DEAL OF MONEY FOR AND

WAS LOYAL TO. SHE EVEN CALLED YOUR HOME AND
YOU NEVER EVER GAVE HER THE COURTESY OF A
PHONE CALL.
    WHAT KIND OF PERSON ARE YOU.
    YOU MAKE ME OUTRAGED AT YOUR LACK OF
REGARD FOR YOUR OWN.

And then in pen he's written "DAMN U" and underlined it three
times.

Karen hands me a second stack of letters. "Did you see the song
lyrics someone sent him?" Karen asks.

A recent fax contains the lyrics from the Bob Dylan song "Masters
of War." The sender has put two verses in bold type:

> *Let me ask you one question*
> *Is your money that good*
> *Will it buy you forgiveness*
> *Do you think that it could*
> *I think you will find*
> *When your death takes its toll*
> *All the money you made*
> *Will never buy back your soul*
>
> *And I hope that you die*
> *And your death'll come soon*
> *I will follow your casket*
> *In the pale afternoon*
> *And I'll watch while you're lowered*
> *Down to your deathbed*
> *And I'll stand o'er your grave*
> *'Till I'm sure that you're dead*

"It's sick, huh?" Karen says. "Someone took time out of their day to
send this."

The phone messages are equally disturbing:

You're a piece of trash for not helping your people. Maybe the next attack will take you.

You're nothing but a coward. What are you hiding?

At the bottom of the message slip it says, "Please note this man was also using some bad language which you can just ignore. Sorry."

"I've become a walking tabloid," Howard says.

H OWARD MISSED the Bill O'Reilly show that night. He was planning his brother's memorial and preparing his first post-9/11 conference call on eSpeed.

He doesn't seem to grasp how bad this is getting. Despite each bit of negative press, he hopes that the next person will write the real story, the one he's living daily, the one about all the men and women working twenty-hour days to support the families of their dead friends. He can't quite comprehend the story about the rich guy who faked his tears. It's this conviction that things will be made right that has rendered him surprisingly passive when it comes to presenting his case.

Meanwhile, our friends call, asking—*What the fuck is going on?* Primarily because anyone who's been around Howard these days knows that whatever faults he has, deceiving and impoverishing the families of his friends and colleagues is not one of them. Indeed, had he truly been duplicitous he would have managed the flow of information better, and wouldn't be in this mess.

Karen shows Allison the angry faxes. Allison, after reading them, looks away and blows air out of her lower lip. She goes upstairs to tend to her daughter, Casey, to change her and to put Brandon to bed. When she returns, she asks me if I've read the faxes. "I'm really starting to worry about his safety," she says.

Allison and Howard were set up on a blind date eleven years ago. As he remembers it, he called Allison and told her he could go on a date in two weeks, after he'd gotten back from visiting Bernie Cantor in California.

In the meantime, Allison continued dating someone else. "I hadn't met her yet," Howard says. "So I didn't know what I was missing." Three months later, Allison broke up with the other man and called Howard to ask *him* out.

Howard planned to take her downtown to the Vietnamese restaurant Indochine. Allison had crafted a system where if she didn't like what she saw when her blind date showed up, she'd suggest going to the Italian restaurant across the street from where she lived. The waiters there were alerted by a prearranged signal, and they'd have the meal served and cleared within the hour so Allison could end her date by nine.

"I only found out later that getting out of her neighborhood meant I'd passed the test," Howard tells me.

Allison came up with the idea of the crisis center at five in the morning on September 12. The families needed a place to gather and share information. She conceived of a meeting room with tables and phones and computers, and with a stage from which Howard could address the group.

Since then she has managed the website, answered hundreds of letters, and acted as general proxy for her overextended husband. These days there's not a ten-minute stretch when she isn't focused on helping the families.

She has been the recipient of angry phone calls and unkind remarks, about being a rich bitch who wouldn't know what it's like to lose someone she loved.

She has accompanied Howard to dozens of memorials and often gone in his stead. She traveled alone to the service of their friend Tim O'Brien and also to the one for Mark Colaio and his brother, Stephen. At Tim O'Brien's, Allison arrived during a rainstorm just before the service began. The church was too packed for her to enter. She called Howard on her cell phone. He suggested she try to push her way inside, not stand in the pouring rain, but she wouldn't because she didn't want to seem disrespectful, or entitled. She just wanted to be there for Lisa O'Brien, whom she liked very much.

It was one of the few times that Allison let her sadness and frustration get the better of her. She wept on the phone with her husband. Then gave up and drove home.

Sometimes she stops and imagines what it would be like if Howard had died. She spent several hours on September 11 convinced he had. She consciously places herself in that mind-set because she wants to understand her friends who've lost husbands and wants that empathy to be genuine. Across the tri-state area, she has put in place support groups for hundreds of Cantor families, and hosts monthly meetings for pregnant widows and for fiancées. She has come to accept that she won't see Howard most nights until one in the morning. She is always awake when he returns and ready to talk. She has had to listen as people harangue her about Howard, and she has had to learn restraint and compassion for those who have had none for her.

But she's tired of people saying her husband hasn't done enough. And she's worried about the new and threatening tone that's followed the recent press coverage.

I N THOSE FIRST WEEKS there was the rush of purposeful activity that forestalled the onslaught of grief. But many of Cantor's surviving employees had no business to return to; their divisions were gone. All of David Kravette's team was taken. Frank Walczak, broker in FX forwards, lost everyone on his desk. Teddy Smith, a top broker in U.S. Treasury notes, lost dozens of people who worked for him. Those who remained called the families and talked to them when they showed up at the crisis center.

Gary Lambert, Allison's brother, interviewed survivors and tried to gauge their psychological health and their ability to return to work. He used the safe list, the chart of all those out of the office on September 11, and phoned as many as he could. The surviving equity brokers have already returned to work, first in Darien, Connecticut, and then at 299 Park Avenue. But brokers in government bonds, munis, corporates, mortgage-backed securities, foreign exchange are largely adrift. Over the last three years, the firm had been moving increasingly toward electronic trading—eSpeed. And after the attack, few of the voice brokerage divisions can or will be rebuilt.

Gary informs these survivors that in between all the memorials, they have a desk to go to, an e-mail account and a phone to use, and voice mail to begin receiving messages from their customers and friends. They still work at a company called Cantor Fitzgerald. But when they go to the office now, it's in a new place, in a new part of the city, and the faces are mostly unfamiliar. What is more familiar these days is their seat in a pew at a church during a memorial, or the line to get into the synagogue, or the sound of a minister, or their own voice reading a eulogy that can't come close to capturing who this friend they've lost was and what his or her loss will mean.

Everything happens slowly, and at the same time everything is a blur: the funerals as well as the days themselves. Sleep is hard to come by.

Some survivors are already talking to grief counselors, though many hesitate to seek any sort of mental health care for fear of what that might mean—that it might signify weakness. So much of their identity had been wrapped up in the job, in the routine of taking the train or a ferry or a carpool, or the subway or a taxi, down to the World Trade Center and riding for what always seemed like forever up to the 101st or 103rd, 104th, or 105th floors.

It was the sort of place that fed the ego, that made you proud to have someone visit, a workplace with a computer network control center to rival something from NASA.

The offices they go to now on Park Avenue or in Darien, Connecticut, Rochelle Park or Weehawken, New Jersey, are slightly dreary, like ones they may have worked at over a summer in college before they decided what it was they wanted to do with their lives.

They've been home watching television, watching the towers go down, watching their friends die, watching the crews dig through the rubble for bodies. They've seen the cars crushed like tin cans, and all the steel beams spread out over the piles of dust and concrete.

Now they're in the office, and really for many of them work seems somehow beside the point. A few of them ended up leaving the country altogether and working over in England for Lee Amaitis.

P HIL MARBER and Tom Trillo watched *The O'Reilly Factor* from Marber's office in Darien, Connecticut. Each was getting angrier as the show progressed.

Trillo has been having a hard time with the television coverage of Cantor and Howard's media appearances. He thought the first interview with Connie Chung was moving and important, but he didn't care for the Larry King interview, and lately he's simply wanted the firm to operate outside public scrutiny. Both he and Marber spend a great deal of time on the phone with people not affiliated with the firm, and who don't hesitate at all to tell them what they think of Cantor or Howard.

When O'Reilly is done the phones are lit up. The clients are calling in, livid, about the way Cantor seems to be treating the families, about Howard breaking his promises. It simply isn't true, Marber and Trillo tell them. They're working ungodly hours in order to earn money to pay out to the families. But it's become clear to both of them that they've got to spell out more clearly what the 25 percent means, what it will encompass.

They call Howard on speakerphone. Marber explains that he talked to Lynda Fiori after the eleventh. Fiori had called Marber's house and had reached his wife. Marber, who's going through a divorce, called Lynda from his office the next night and told her that he'd help her in any way he could.

"It's just not true that no one called her," he says. "I called her."

He reminds Howard of whom Paul Fiori was, that he'd been Marber's caddy at the country club. Marber had liked him and had offered him a job. Fiori had turned it down at first and then had come back to him a year later to ask if it was still available. It wasn't, but Marber made a new position for him.

Marber had taken pleasure in changing Paul Fiori's life for the better, in making it possible for him to put a down payment on a home and to raise his two children comfortably.

More than anything, he's pissed at O'Reilly. Trillo, however, directs his ire at Howard. "No more fucking TV," he says to his boss.

But there will be plenty more TV, unfortunately. O'Reilly is just the start of a week of negative press, a frenzy of nasty, slanted reports about Howard and Cantor that neither can control. Only CNN will avoid the acrimony, eventually granting Howard and Cantor Fitzgerald the benefit of the doubt.

*   *   *

After he'd seen the article in the *Post,* Marber had called Lynda Fiori to ask why she would possibly want to hurt the company when it was struggling so hard just to survive, and doing so in order to pay more money to her and to the other families of the deceased.

"I didn't say anything bad about you or Cantor. I said bad things about *Howard.*"

"If you say something bad about Howard," Marber says, "you're saying something bad about the firm." (By the following summer, after Cantor had kept its financial promises, Fiore would express regret about her public skepticism, and she and Howard would establish a friendly relationship.)

They talked for a while, calmly, and Marber thought Fiori understood that they were on the same side. He ended the conversation with her as he had the last one: He told her whatever she needed—clothes, food, help of any kind for the kids or for herself—he'd bring his checkbook and pay her bills.

"If you have a problem, don't go to the press, okay? Call me, I'll take care of you. All right, Lynda?"

She said okay. And the next night she was on *O'Reilly.*

Marber called Fox News and spoke to O'Reilly's producers, filling them in on all the details, that he'd hired Paul Fiori personally and was his boss. He volunteered to go on the show, but they said, No thanks, they wanted Howard Lutnick.

Marber was disgusted. "That night," he says, "O'Reilly gets on his show and says, 'Ah, Howard had a couple of his flunkies call us today. When's this guy going to do the right thing?'"

A S SOON AS the media got word of discontinued paychecks and a rich boss—the one who had pledged on television to help the families—it was just too juicy to pass up. It was the perfect rise-and-fall tale, and one with a compelling back story.

A man loses his parents, becomes one of the young stars of Wall Street a decade later, then at turns is stripped of everything, becomes a hero, and then branded a villain.

The truth was, he was doing everything he said he would do, and by spring he and the surviving partners of Cantor would distribute 63 million dollars to the families.

It was a scary time for a month or two. There were so many mothers in so many states of nervousness. The breadwinner was gone. Many of the wives didn't even know where their accounts were, or the name of their phone-service provider, or mortgage company, according to Tracy Claus, an estate lawyer helping dozens of the Cantor families and the wife of Cantor survivor Matt Claus.

"It's not only that their finances aren't organized," she told me, "it's that they didn't know what *to* organize. And these are not uneducated women. It's just the way the tasks were delegated. All they know is there used to be a paycheck and there used to be a guy who paid the bills. Now there's no paycheck and the guy who pays the bills isn't here to even tell them what the bills are."

The fears surrounding the salary issue are understandable, she says. Often there are assets they aren't aware of. "They don't know what bonuses their husbands are earning or what stocks they hold. In some instances their finances are in much better shape than they know."

There are also tremendous frustrations regarding the charities— the Red Cross, the United Way, and others. The families know that already more than a billion dollars has been raised, but the steps to receive that money are intimidating and complicated—too many applications to file, too many government agencies to contact, too many rules and deadlines.

And many of them actively—or unconsciously—resist the process because filling out the forms and calling for assistance means acknowledging each time that their loved one isn't out there still. With so few of the bodies found, this is a difficult, if not impossible, thing for them to concede.

W E RIDE that evening to Howard and Allison's town house on the Upper East Side. Someday it will be their dream home, but for now it's still a ragged construction site of wires and beams, plaster board and exposed wood. It is clear after a few minutes that both Howard and Allison would like to leave. Heading down Fifth Avenue, on a perfect October night, Allison voices what the two of them might be thinking: "Let's just get a place in Connecticut, Howard."

"They just hammered you again on *O'Reilly,* sir," Jimmy says. "They said something about you not paying insurance."

"They all have insurance. We paid for it."

Allison's cell phone rings. It's her friend Nick Caiazzo, calling from the house. There have been several threatening calls, he says.

There's the feeling of an angry-mob gathering; O'Reilly and his boys waiting outside Howard's apartment building, holding clubs and torches.

B ACK AT HIS APARTMENT, Howard says to me, "A situation like this makes everything clear. Neil Cavuto doesn't know me. He says I cried *crocodile tears.*" I ask who Neil Cavuto is and learn that he's another TV news reporter, who has been criticizing Howard.

Howard walks to the pictures of Gary and all his friends, roiling with anger. "Here's what you do. Go to Neil Cavuto's house and pull out pictures of his family and everyone he knows and cross out all his friends and his brother. Everyone's dead. *Everyone.* And then let's see if he cries crocodile tears."

Howard makes asides about selling the town house and staying put. Until recently, despite all his success, Howard, like his firm, has lived largely below the radar screen. Few people outside Wall Street had heard of him. Now people know Howard Lutnick for what he's lost, and—after shows like *O'Reilly*—for how rich he is. At issue is whether wealth can insulate you from tragedy. And in the view of some, Howard has been insulated, no matter how many of his family and friends are gone.

Stephen Merkel comes by later to talk through details of the plan—to go over insurance and bonuses, unused vacation time, stock options, and the relief fund. This is where their energies are directed. First it was saving the company; now it's getting the particulars of the plan down.

They have been battling through the issues all week. Merkel, like Marber, has hated all the media attention and says he wishes Howard had never gone on television in the first place. He wants to be in on the discussions about what will and won't be said to the public.

He advises Howard to take the high road in any public statements, that he should express his sympathy for those lodging complaints, because they are grieving, after all, and he should save any harsh words for those in the media "who have been trafficking in the grief and anger of others."

"What I don't get is this idea that I could have called everyone," Howard tells me later that night, after Allison has gone to sleep and everyone else has left the house.

"You've seen what it's like. I'm calling people every night, but I'm not going to call a wife and then get off the phone after ten minutes. We talk for a half an hour, sometimes more. I'm never the one who hangs up first. But let's say I call ten, maybe twelve wives four hours a night. Then there's been how many nights, twenty-five? That's what, two hundred and fifty calls? We had seven hundred families. Seven hundred. And that's just the spouses. You have parents, mothers who lost their sons or daughters, and then there's the siblings. It just physically can't be done."

KYLE HAS BEEN running a fever and is asleep in his parents' bed. He has had a rough time lately, has been acting out in school, getting into small fights. Ordinarily, he is a good-natured, well-behaved kid, and Allison knows it's happening because of the stress in his home, and how little he's seen of his father in the last weeks.

In the room are several more poster-sized pictures of Gary leaning against the walls. After the funeral, Howard will keep the posters in his walk-in closet so he can see them each morning, and again when he comes home at night.

In spite of O'Reilly and the nasty faxes and letters, Howard is in a good mood. He will turn this around by going on television and laying out exactly how much money the 25 percent will represent—in excess of 150 million dollars. They will also provide health insurance and full bonuses.

Allison likes the plan but she's worried how it will be perceived.

"It's so much *money*. It makes you sound like a rich guy. That's what people see you as now. As a *rich* guy. I don't want someone to do anything to you. Someone sent in a Bob Dylan song to you. Did you see the words? It said something about wanting you dead."

Howard winces, irritated.

"You haven't seen it?"

"It doesn't matter. I already almost died. I'm not worried."

"Well I am."

*   *   *

O'REILLY READS LETTERS on his show, reminding viewers that Howard was the CEO who refused to return phone calls or provide any assistance for a thirty-year-old widow "with two babies and few assets."

A letter from a man in California takes up Howard's case:

Hey, Mr. O, take a deep breath. The reason the company can't help the families is that eighty percent of it is gone. There is no *there* there.

O'Reilly responds by saying the relief fund has taken in millions and Howard is paying for a public relations firm.

Most of the letters read like this:

I watched Lutnick on many talk programs and I really felt for him. Now I feel sick.

Or:

After watching a tearful Howard Lutnick on *Larry King,* I sent a check to the company's relief fund. O'Reilly, please find out where my money went.

"I will, Michele," O'Reilly says.
A man from Buckhannon, West Virginia, writes:

O'Reilly, send him to us. We'll give him some hillbilly justice.

In the morning physicians blanket the news shows talking about the threat of biological warfare. A man in Florida is dying of anthrax exposure. A California congresswoman speaks critically of the CIA and the FBI.

eSpeed's stock has fallen 32 percent, from $8.69 a share to $5.91. This is good news, Howard thinks, considering the drop in the market as a whole.

Just before eSpeed began trading again, Howard held a conference call to detail the reasons his company would defy the gloomy expectations. eSpeed, he said, "had not lost its destiny or its soul." Despite his optimism, an analyst in a *SmartMoney* article entitled "Kick 'Em When They're Down" is quoted as saying, "the uncertainty surrounding eSpeed makes the stock a risky investment."

Howard and Kent Karosen are meeting in the den with Josh Isay, a political consultant who in the spring will oversee Andrew Cuomo's New York gubernatorial campaign. Howard takes his time spelling out the public-relations disaster of the last week.

Karosen, a goateed young man in a stars-and-stripes rugby shirt, has out a big yellow note pad. Karosen is Howard's utility infielder. No one knows exactly what he does, but he fills in everywhere.

"Are you known?" Josh Isay asks Howard. "Do people know you when you walk around the city?"

Howard looks at him as if to say, *Are you kidding?* He tells the story of when he walked toward his new building the Monday after the attack.

"This older woman, she takes my arm like this"—he grabs Isay's arm—"she looks at me and then a tear rolls down her face."

Karosen then tells a story of a woman who admitted to him after the attack that she had stolen a plant from the office the week before. She thought the Cantor Fitzgerald survivors might want something from their office, so she was volunteering to return the plant.

The conversation then turns to how the public is perceiving Howard and how he sees himself. He says he's come to better understand people's resentment of the wealthy.

"I try to be a good guy. I've given an unbelievable amount to charity. But I've never done it until it really hurt. That's the difference."

He's trying to read Isay's face to see if he is with him. He means what he says. But he's become accustomed in the last week to people not taking him at his word.

Both *Dateline* and Connie Chung are doing features on discontented widows. Howard knows this because one of the widows called the night before. The thrust of the story will be that Howard is not following his words with actions.

"We need to stay ahead of the wave," Karosen says. "We have to get above it somehow."

At the end of the conversation, Isay leaves with no promise that he'll help, only that he'll give them an answer either way in twenty-four hours.

Allison enters the room. "Howard," she says, "Edie just called. She's very upset. Twenty-seven people have called her, referring to O'Reilly and now they want their checks back."

"What?"

"She's *crying,* Howard. She says she's worried someone's going to hurt you or kill you because she hasn't gotten their checks back to them fast enough."

Howard's face reddens. "She *can't* send the checks back."

"She already did."

He's fuming now.

"She can't do that! No one can do that!"

He grabs the phone and calls Edie, but when she answers he doesn't yell. She hasn't sent the checks back yet, she tells him. She shouldn't send anything back, he says, nicely. His sister, he knows, is having as hard a time as he is.

Edie has been working sixteen-hour shifts at the relief fund, which she put together back on September 14. She talks to families all day, has handwritten more than one thousand checks, and sorted and distributed truckloads of gifts—most notably the thirty thousand teddy bears sent in by schoolchildren around the country. In these first weeks she hasn't been receiving much gratitude. The bad press will only make her job more difficult.

While he's on the phone, a producer from NBC calls on another line. Howard ends his conversation with Edie and takes the NBC call. They want to interview him about the salary issue. Is he upset? they ask.

"Sure I'm angry. It isn't a *story*."

The producer is practically begging him to come on to defend himself. He'll lose his job if Howard won't agree to the interview. Stinging from the O'Reilly mess, Howard says he'll do it. They can interview him, just not tomorrow or Monday. "Monday's my brother's memorial. And Sunday people are traveling from around the country to be here for me, and I want to spend time with them. So if you want to talk on Tuesday I can talk then. Okay?"

He is becoming emotional on the phone, is pleading just a little. He can't fathom why anyone would want to go after him right now given all that happened and all that he's trying to do.

Allison's mother, Geri, calls then to check in on him. He tells her about the interview requests, how they threaten they'll do the story with or without him.

"I'll say my mother-in-law loves me, that I have the best mother-in-law. And maybe *that'll* be the story. Get *this,* the most ruthless man on Wall Street *loves* his mother-in-law."

They laugh. He is worked up, full of anxious energy.

*   *   *

Tonight is Allison's twentieth high school reunion, and Allison doesn't think they should go.

"Of course you're gonna go," Karen says.

"Why wouldn't we go?" Howard asks.

"Because everyone will be staring at us. There'll be a picture in the paper and they'll say 'Howard Lutnick was out partying last night.' You don't think so, but they will. I don't want them writing bad things about us. I think lately maybe it's better if we just stay home, or go to a movie."

This period has been particularly hard on Allison. On the night of September 12, she answered the phone when one of the wives called. The woman asked to speak to Howard, and when Allison told her she didn't know where he was, the woman responded by yelling at her, "Where the *fuck* is Howard?" Allison tried to calm her down, and the woman said she could go back to her rich-bitch life. She didn't understand—she didn't lose anyone.

The next day at the crisis center, Allison sought out the woman and ended up talking to her for an emotional hour.

"I don't want to go to a movie," Howard says.

"You want to go to the reunion?"

"Yes, I think we should go," he says. "You should be there with your friends."

SUNDAY, OCTOBER 7

The next day and night are filled with more meetings. Friends arrive to visit with Howard on the eve of his brother's memorial. Osama bin Laden is about to speak for the first time since the 11th over the Arab version of CNN, al-Jazeera. Seth Kates, whose brother, Andy, died in the attacks, sits with us in Howard's den. On TV, seated placidly in front of a pile of rocks, is bin Laden. He begins talking as subtitles roll across the screen:

"Here is America struck by Almighty God in one of its vital organs, so that its greatest buildings are destroyed. Grace and gratitude to God."

I look over at Seth. He seems more transfixed than angry. A few more friends wander into the room to watch bin Laden. One walks out in disgust.

The tape is beamed in to us from somewhere in the rugged mountains of Afghanistan, a place so remote, so entirely of a different planet, that it is impossible to conceive of a decision there creating what we are living in here.

"America has been filled with horror from north to south and east to west, and thanks be to God. What America is tasting now is only a copy of what we have tasted."

Alongside bin Laden, who is clad in a camouflage jacket over traditional Arab dress, are his henchmen, Ayman al-Zawahiri, his senior adviser, and Muhammad Mohammed Atef, al-Qaeda's military commander.

Some of Gary Lutnick's friends have arrived for his funeral. We hear their voices in the hallway. In this room are photographs of fifty people dead now because of the men we are watching on television.

Bin Laden takes the opportunity to praise the hijackers for their attack on America:

"May God bless them and allot them a supreme place in heaven, for he is the only one capable and entitled to do so."

By the end of the speech, bin Laden has left us sickened—but something else. His message is so insane, so abstract, and vile, but what stands out is his calm self-righteousness.

Howard has finished a meeting with Joe Noviello and he joins us in his den. He slips a videotape of his wedding at the Plaza Hotel into the VCR and rewinds to where Gary is giving his best-man toast. The two brothers are in matching tuxedoes with white ties and cummerbunds. Most of us in the room were there. And it is nice now to go back again if only for a few minutes.

Gary is bouncing around confidently, a master of ceremonies. It is a loving toast, concluding with a joke about power struggles between men and women:

"In heaven, there are two lines, one for women who dominate men, and one for men who dominate women. Howard was the only one in the latter. I asked him what he was doing there, and he said, 'Allison told me to stand here.'" It is the second reference to heaven in the last ten minutes—one by Gary and one by his killer.

"Nice toast," Howard says. Then he looks at us. We all nod. "*Sheesh,*" he says. "My brother." The camera pulls around and he spots others who have died, calling their names out as the shot pans the room.

Lynne, Karen, and the other bridesmaids on the wedding video sing "Will You Still Love Me Tomorrow?" and "Stop! In the Name of Love."

"'Will You Still Love Me Tomorrow?'" Howard says. "Kind of a strange choice for a wedding."

The reason we're viewing this is because Howard wants to look at his brother, see his mannerisms and hear his voice before he writes his eulogy later tonight.

At around one A.M. the guests start leaving. We will all see one another in the morning, at the funeral. For the moment, Howard doesn't look sad. He's thinking about that night at the Plaza, about how much fun he'd had.

"It was a pretty amazing wedding, wasn't it?" he says.

*A*FTER MY MOTHER DIED, *my father started a relationship with a teacher he met on one of the tours he gave from California, a woman named Joyce. She soon moved to New York and about a year later my father remarried.*

July 14th of that summer, my eighteenth birthday, he had arranged for us to go to the horse races at Belmont Park. But he had developed this recurring cough, and it wouldn't go away. After he finally had it examined, he told us he needed some tests. He had to stay in the hospital overnight. And so we canceled my birthday outing and he stayed in the hospital. He didn't look any different, and when we visited he acted as though he was fine. We jokingly called him "the walking wounded," because we thought he was perfectly healthy, but he wasn't. His X-rays revealed that he had lung cancer, and privately the doctors told him he had six months to live.

He never told us about it, never said a thing. He had scheduled his first chemotherapy treatment for the week after I had left to start college.

So I went to orientation week and signed up for classes, without having much direction. I just signed up for the courses my roommates had chosen, which were essentially along the pre-med line. I was playing on the tennis team, going to class, and meeting girls. I'd heard that a man with a big mustache was looking for me. I figured it was our tennis coach. I went to his office at the end of the day but it wasn't him. It was one of the deans, and he was trying to find me to tell me that my father had died.

My father had gone in for his first chemotherapy shot. A nurse or doctor had accidentally given him a hundred times the appropriate dose.

I didn't find out until my sister called. She was crying. At the time, my grandfather, my father's father, was terminally ill as well. It was touch-and-go with him every week, and so I asked, "Did Pop die?" That was the name we called my grandfather, and she said, "No, it's Daddy."

The room started spinning and I said, "What?"

She explained. I put the phone down and the word that came to my mind was "orphan."

I didn't have parents, and I felt cut free, like I was floating out in space. It was almost exactly how I felt walking back from the Trade Center. I left my room at the college and banged into the walls. The world was spinning.

I went up to the administration office. My RA escorted me, because I was in a daze. They told me they'd get me home, and they put me on a small commuter plane from Philadelphia to Long Island.

I went back to my house and it was just terrible. We had the funeral. My sister was a mess. She was hyperventilating, and I was worried about her. Everything about this time was surreal. One of our jobs was to call all my father's friends and tell them he'd died. I was eighteen, and each time I reached someone and told them the news, they started crying, and I'm not sure they were thinking about who was on the other end of the line.

They were sad for themselves. They were his friends and they hadn't even known he was sick.

While I was home for the next couple of weeks, both the president and the dean of Haverford College called me, and what they said was pretty incredible. They said, Look, we know you have been through a lot and you don't know what your finances will end up being. So the college will provide you with grants to cover the cost of your education. Don't worry about anything. You are effectively on a scholarship for the rest of your four years here.

It was really quite extraordinary. I'd only been there a week, so it wasn't about their liking me specifically. It was about how they treated people in general, which is why I care so much about Haverford. At a time in my life when there weren't a lot of people looking out for me, they were there unconditionally.

*   *   *

I had to make a decision then whether I wanted to take over my father's travel businesses or stay in college. Haverford had made the decision easier. I didn't want to run the businesses without my father, and so we sold some and closed others. We never got much money. What was important to me was that they continue to operate. When we closed one of the offices, I rented a van and got some of my friends together to pick up the furniture and things. We brought it back to our house and had a tag sale. Nothing in our house was worth all that much, except for one of those classic, old cigar-store Indians, a big, wood, carved statue, that we sold for two thousand dollars in cash. I gave the money to my father's lawyer, a man named Bob Frunzi, who'd grown up with him in the same neighborhood in the Bronx. They went to Columbia together, lost touch afterward for several years, but when my dad moved to Syosset, Frunzi lived around the corner, and they became friends again. He was our family lawyer.

As it turns out, maybe because he'd been relieved my father had remarried, he decided to give the money from our tag sale of the cigar-store Indian to my father's new wife, Joyce. I'd actually seen him hand her an envelope. I didn't think much of it at the time.

Sophomore year I took a course at Haverford called "Ethics in the Professions." The professor was talking about a lawyer's ethics, and after the class something clicked. I told him about our situation, that my father's lawyer friend was just giving money to my father's wife, presumably to help take care of my brother, Gary. He told me to get my own lawyer.

Frunzi was draining our account to give money to Joyce, I learned, and she wasn't necessarily using it to take care of Gary. It was a real mess. Joyce had sold our house on Long Island and moved back in with an old boyfriend in Petaluma, California, which wouldn't have mattered much except that Gary was now living across the country from Edie and me. And all this time Frunzi is still sending Joyce checks. Our lawyer demands a proper accounting for what was being done and why. We had to threaten to sue. I called Bob Frunzi's house myself to talk about what we could do about all this, and the person who answered the phone said he'd had a heart attack that morning. I said that's terrible, and I asked what hospital he was in, and they said it was too late, he'd died.

What we soon learned was that he'd put my parents' money into his own checking account. He was giving Joyce whatever she needed. She and her boyfriend hadn't really wanted Gary, anyway. He was the kid of some marriage that she'd had briefly, between stints with this other guy. But she took the money.

Her boyfriend would chase Gary around. And I found out he'd been hitting him. Edie and I flew out there to get him back. I spent part of the summer there, teaching tennis and living in a trailer—the kind you'd hitch to your car, not really for living in but for getting through a couple of nights on the road. We had to leave the trailer just to go to the bathroom. The people who let us live on their property ended up stealing virtually all of the remaining possessions my father had loved.

Maybe they thought they'd done enough for us. It was hard to tell then what was ours and what would be taken from us. Nothing was tied down, not of ours, anyway.

Edie and I were in my study on the 12th of September. We were sitting on the couch just looking at each other, talking. Earlier there'd been twenty people in the room, and now, just past daybreak, it was the two of us.

I said to her, "Do you smell it?" because there was a very particular smell to the room.

She said, "It smells just like when Daddy died." And that's when we realized it was exactly twenty-two years to the day that our father had died.

Edie managed a deep breath. I could see her eyes welling up. Suddenly she ran to the bathroom and threw up. And I think it was because the air had gone thick and heavy in the same way it had when we lost our parents.

I went into the bathroom and sat next to her, held her hair and told her that Gary would always be with us, that we would be all right. I didn't know how, only that I would do all I could to make it so.

Edie's been worried that no one will come to Gary's funeral, that there will be too many others scheduled for the day, or that everyone will be too emotionally exhausted to make the trip. But her fears are unwarranted—the room, at the 92nd Street Y on the Upper East Side of Manhattan, is packed with close to seven hundred mourners. Howard, Allison, Edie, and her boyfriend, Lewis Ameri, enter last from a side door and assemble in the first row. The posters of Gary from the house are lined across the back of the stage.

Gary's best friend Patrick Troy, from Chicago, talks of Gary's constant gift giving. He tells a story about Gary seeing a coat he liked, and deciding to buy four, and then handing them out to his brother and a couple of friends. When he bought champagne, he'd buy two cases, and give nearly all the bottles away. He drove a convertible Porsche with a "fourteen-speaker sound system" that made putting a suitcase in the trunk impossible.

Gary's other best friend, Peter Farmer, remembers Gary's prodigious cache of sunglasses, and how he placed the presents people gave him on birthdays at the center of his apartment—or if it was an item of clothing, how he'd wear it when he saw them no matter how ridiculous it looked. He liked making people feel good.

When it's Howard's turn, he talks of the brothers growing up in Syosset and Jericho, them and Edie, their enormous obstacles, and how much more difficult it must have been for Gary to face those at fifteen.

"It isn't possible that we could be any closer, and I'm prouder of what my brother accomplished in his life than what I have in mine."

The most extraordinary aspect of Edie's eulogy is that she had the strength to finish. Edie has always been the most emotional of the three siblings. And it took her perhaps longer to process the deaths of their parents. In addition, Edie a few years back lost her best friend to cancer.

It was only recently that she'd been feeling more secure and happier about her life. After a decade and a half of working on and off as a labor lawyer, she was planning to scale down her activities, go to a beach somewhere with Lewis and figure out her next move. Howard was going to give her some money to use toward buying a house.

When her brother died, Edie threw herself into her job running the Cantor Fitzgerald Relief Fund. She helped set up the fund, created the family phone lists and next-of-kin database, and assembled a staff of volunteers. In many ways, her life is like Howard's these days. She's essentially running a business—and her job is caring for the Cantor families. At the end of the night, at one or two in the morning, she goes over the day's events with her brother.

Her work has kept her going. In these last weeks her expression has been resolutely sad and focused. She talks energetically about what needs to be accomplished in order to get money and information to the families, but she is emotional whenever Gary's name is brought up. And she becomes angry when anyone talks about the media and what some of the families have been saying about Howard.

Now she's speaking of Gary and how selfless he was with her, how he made her feel special, how much they'd grown to depend on one another. She says her love for him goes beyond that of a sister. He was her brother, she says, and in other ways her son. She describes the closeness the three siblings found in the wake of their parents' deaths, and she keeps stopping and trying to find new words. She cries a few times, but in the end she holds up. She says in closing that her brother's successes sometimes made her feel like the younger sister. Now she's following their lead, finding sustenance through work, through forward momentum.

*   *   *

After the service and a reception in a first-floor wing at the Y, the family and close friends head down to Nobu, Gary's favorite sushi restaurant, one of the places for which New Yorkers will wait months to get a reservation.

We're standing near the sushi bar, which is decorated with framed photographs of the Lutnick kids as they're growing up. One black-and-white shows the three of them when Howard and Gary were toddlers, another where they all look like hippie kids, the boys with long hair, Edie in bell bottoms.

Howard is describing how Kyle and Brandon begged to go to Gary's house to play video games. "They called him 'Uncle Gary-with-the-TV-games.' He had all of them—Sega, Nintendo, PlayStation. He'd carry the kids upside down, and then throw them on his bed, and they'd grab the controls and start playing."

Gary knew how to have fun. He was an unabashed hedonist, known to drive his Porsche—with the top down and the music blaring—to Atlantic City after a long workday, he'd play the tables all night and be at his desk just after sunrise the next morning. Where Howard increasingly steered away from danger, Gary tested limits.

Howard was grooming Gary in the last months to become an executive, tutoring him the way Bernie tutored Howard. He'd given his brother a seat in the chairman's office, on the periphery of the conversations. Gary, he said, would take everything in "like a sponge."

Perhaps even more remarkable than Howard's rise to the rarified heights of Wall Street was his brother's ascent to becoming a top trader. It's one thing to become orphaned your first week of college, another altogether to lose your parents in mid-adolescence, with your older siblings away in school. An early indicator of Howard's business savvy was when he employed his brother on one of his summer breaks buying insider rights for new co-ops. Gary found the places and charmed their inhabitants. The Lutnick brothers kept turning over apartments and pocketing the difference. Howard was teaching him how to be a businessman, and learning how to delegate duties to a partner with the right skills.

A group of us talk abstractly about the news and how they haven't found Gary's or Doug's bodies yet. Seth Kates is at the table, and he tells us how when his brother Andy's body was found there were no signs of burns or smoke inhalation. Nearly every bone was broken, however, Seth's wife, Mary Jane, says. Someone asks if they think he jumped. They say they don't know.

Soon those of us around the table are discussing what we might have done, whether we would have jumped or continued searching for a way down, a place to breathe.

Morosely we ponder who would show up at our funerals, how many people would make the trip, what people would say at our service. What all the conjecture underscores is how new and unformed our thoughts are on these topics. We are trying on the fates of our friends, in an attempt to see what they might have seen.

The subject of what the last half hour or hour was like will be one everyone will visit but most will try to avoid. Months from now the *New York Times* will publish a collection of all the information gathered from the cell phone calls made from the building after the planes struck. It will become evident that a large number of Cantor employees gathered in a conference room on the 104th floor. There were acts of heroism, and friendship: brothers who searched the halls and trading floors to find one another, friends sheltering friends, running to stairwells together to search for safety, a lungful of breathable air. Little of this will ever be known.

There's a rumor going around the service that Gary's ex-girlfriend, Anne DeSollar, will play her taped answering machine message of Gary's last words on the *Larry King* show sometime this week. Edie has urged her not to, telling Anne it would deeply upset her and Howard, but Anne's decision has not been made.

Howard sits with the Gardners, walks over to his sister and gives her a kiss, and then talks with David Kravette and his wife, Janice. He's making the rounds, looking after people. Eventually he pulls up a chair and joins us at the back of the restaurant.

When Edie's name comes up he says, "I can't believe she's holding up. I really can't. What she's done in terms of the families, the relief fund, is really spectacular." There is little more Howard wants to say on the subject of his own despondency. You get the sense that he wants everyone to have a good time. We don't tell him about the subjects we've been discussing. Howard doesn't stay long. He moves off then to talk to a group of his brother's friends across the room who will next month gather at a steak house on the Lower West Side to celebrate Gary's thirty-seventh birthday with Howard and Edie. He will bring to them Gary's sunglasses and a few T-shirts and assorted other items that he imagines Gary would want them to have. He will then give Patrick Troy Gary's celebrated Porsche, which Gary had had the forethought to leave to him in his will.

B ACK AT HOWARD'S house the out-of-town friends have left. Allison is downstairs removing the photos of Gary from shopping bags. She has lost weight. Everyone, as far as I can tell, has lost weight. Especially the women. Pants hang loosely. Faces are thin. Eating hasn't been much fun lately.

Howard is upstairs with Amy Nauiokas, Diny Ajamian, Cantor's new human resources consultant, Stephen Merkel, and others who are helping him finalize the plan. Everyone is on edge. There is a feeling of resignation within the group that all they've put together is somehow playing the wrong way. O'Reilly has had a devastating effect on the business and on Howard's public persona. The angry faxes and e-mails are still coming in.

This week promises more negative media, so even if it takes all night, they will have a final version of the plan in the morning to give to the families and to release to the press.

The sticking points now are bonuses and unused vacation time. Cantor has been notoriously lax about keeping records on when people take vacations. And now virtually every family member who has contacted Cantor is claiming that the deceased employee had yet to take a vacation in 2001.

"Isn't that strange," Diny says. "You'd think some of them might have taken a week off before the end of the summer, wouldn't you?"

There is friction because they've been working for the families, and now the families want more. The issues aren't only about what to include, but how to present the various aspects of the plan. Everything is in flux.

The issue of health care is batted about as well as bonuses, a tricky matter at a Wall Street firm in normal years. Figuring these out without the divisional heads and their records will be a nightmare. The spouses who have called have each said with regard to bonuses: "He was having his best year." But in truth most of Wall Street had been fairly flat the first two-thirds of 2001.

"What do you think the chance of us having a few lawsuits from this are?" Diny asks.

Three hours into the discussion, on the night of his brother's memorial, with ten people in his dining room with papers and calculators out, and after four nights of endless circular squabbles about each issue, Howard says, "We waste so *much time* with this. This is such a huge waste of my time. Should have happened earlier. Much, much earlier."

*F*INALS WEEK, *my father's father, Isadore—"Pop," we called him— was in the hospital dying. He was in his late eighties. I guess it was his time. So they had to tell him his son had died. After they did, he never opened his eyes again. He closed his eyes because my dad, his baby boy, the most educated of his three kids, was gone. My dad took care of him. We would walk into my grandfather's carrying ten bags of groceries, and when he wasn't looking we'd fill the refrigerator. My dad would bring cash and leave it in the drawer, because my grandfather would have been too proud to accept the money. It was classic. He had the plastic on the furniture, the white furniture with the blue stitching. He died the first day of finals week and I had to drive to the funeral, there and back. It meant I couldn't study. I just drove. It was so depressing to be with these relatives, none of whom had called me, all of whom were jerks. My mother's dad acted horribly. Eventually we became close again, but when my mother was dying of cancer, he took us out to dinner and said to me, "You're killing your mother. You kids are killing your mother the way you act."*

We were in the Ponderosa eating dinner, and I took my salad, with blue cheese dressing, and I threw it in his lap. I left and started walking home, which was interesting because I was fifteen, and we lived a good two towns away from the restaurant.

Pop died with fifteen thousand dollars that he left for his three sons. Since my dad was dead we were supposed to get five thousand dollars. The next summer, Edie and I wanted to do something for Gary, and so we decided

to use the money to send him cross-country on a teen tour for six weeks—
Trails West. But my uncle Seymour never gave us our five thousand dol-
lars. At the unveiling of my grandfather, a year later, I told two of my
father's cousins about what Seymour had done. They said, "Hey, Sey-
mour, you got problems with money? We'll give the kids the money. You
pay us back." And he gave us the money the next day. Gary went on Trails
West. And to show you what kind of friend Gary was, at his funeral were
two guys he'd met on that tour.

TUESDAY, OCTOBER 9

"Here we go," Howard says, taking a seat next to Allison on the bed.

"A Story of Love and Loss," Larry King says, leaning over his desk in navy suspenders and a pale blue shirt. "Joining us tonight is Anne DeSollar. Her boyfriend was the late Gary Lutnick. She is the former CEO of the Duchess of York's foundation Chances for Children."

Anne wears a blue blazer over a light blue shirt, and a simple strand of pearls. She tells Larry about her first date with Gary and how it lasted a whole weekend. It's a rapid-fire love story that had just ended the week before.

"So you go to Hawaii to Tony Robbins's seminar. This is before the tragedy on Tuesday . . . " Larry says.

"Yes, on Tuesday I got a message on my voice mail from Gary at 8:56 in the morning, which was 2:56 Hawaii time. He was calling from the Trade Center."

She says friends phoned her about the attacks and then she checked her messages. We're all now bracing for what will come next. Howard and Allison look disgusted and distraught.

It's Gary's weakening voice apologizing for the difficulties he and Anne had been through lately, saying that he loved her, and that his life was probably going to end very soon. There are shouts in the background, people yelling instructions to close doors, cover vents. The moment just before Howard's brother's death, and a national television audience is listening.

*   *   *

The next day Howard will tell me he didn't sleep well after hearing his brother's voice on the tape. "It was all . . . too specific. I could see too much. It's not anything I wanted to picture."

A COUPLE OF WEEKS *after the attacks, Kyle's school called to tell us that when the children discussed September 11, they talked about jumpers—how people had jumped out of the windows and died. That night Kyle and I sat down and I asked him if he knew how Uncle Doug and Uncle Gary had died. "Yes," he said, "they jumped out of the building."*

I said, "No, no. They didn't jump out of the building, and while some people maybe did jump because of the fire, you would never want to jump because then you'd never be able to play again." I wanted him to understand that jumping from buildings was a terrible thing to do.

I explained to him that Uncle Doug and Uncle Gary had wanted to escape the building. But they couldn't get down the stairs, and when the buildings fell they died.

And then Kyle went to sleep. Around midnight he came into our bedroom. Allison and I were still awake. We asked him what was wrong. He told us, "I had a dream. I was a ghost and I flew into the Trade Center and I grabbed Uncle Doug and Uncle Gary and everyone else in there and I put them in my tummy and I flew them out so they would be safe." Allison put her arms around him and held him tight.

"Let's do a show of hands," CNBC reporter Maria Bartiromo suggests at the beginning of her report. She has two unidentified women and one unidentified man seated in a studio. "Howard Lutnick went on television, on this program, and said that he was going to take care of his employees' families. How many of you feel that he has done that?"

They sit expressionless.

"How many of you feel that he has *not* done that?"

Three hands go up.

"When you go on national television," the man says, "and say you're going to do all these things for these families . . . I don't see it. I don't see it in his deeds. I've heard the word. But I have not seen the deeds."

Maria Bartiromo's voice-over says, "There was *one* deed, though, these families say, but it wasn't one that made them *believe* in the CEO of Cantor Fitzgerald."

On the screen, rescue workers pull up rubble from the devastated Trade Center site.

"On September 15, just four days after the tragedy, Cantor Fitzgerald stopped paying the salaries of their seven hundred thirty-three missing employees."

Toward the end of the report, after more criticism has been leveled, the plan is finally explained—the ten years of health care, the hundred thousand dollars per family, and the 45 million in bonuses—and Howard states that as high a bar as the firm has set for itself, it will be the only company to jump over that bar.

"On September 13," Maria Bartiromo says then, "you went on national television and told these families, 'Don't worry, we'll take care of you.' On September 15, you *cut their salaries*. What kind of reassurance is that?"

He grimaces, then answers once again about what was needed to save the company and what they would do for the families in the coming years. It is distressingly clear that despite all he's done and all he will do, this issue is going to stick.

A THIRD PERSON in South Florida tests positive for anthrax exposure—all in Boca Raton. Examiners find traces of anthrax in the woman's nasal passage. She's taking antibiotics. Officials say there's no evidence the incidents are connected to September 11.

Firefighters at the Trade Center site are still searching for bodies. The number of confirmed dead rises, but the bodies aren't intact. At the victims' homes there's a knock on the door, a police officer outside with news they've found a loved one, found his arm or a leg, or, in one case, his chin. Families must determine when they have enough of a body to have a funeral. The identification visits begin a whole new process, because whatever a spouse or parent knows, it is different to *really* know. It just is.

Howard experienced the Connie Chung broadcast as a series of body blows. He was watching it late in the evening at the office. He had with him Josh Isay, who has joined his PR team, and Mike Weinstein, his economics professor from Haverford, who had come by to talk about what to do about all the bad press.

Barbara Walters looks out from her desk in the *20/20* studio.

"Two days after the Trade Center attacks," she says, "Connie Chung brought you one of the most moving interviews to come out of the tragedy: Howard Lutnick, the CEO of Cantor Fitzgerald, *sobbing* on national television after losing more than seven hundred of his employees, pledging his bond trading company would take care of the families.

"But what happened *after* the cameras went off turns into *another story*. As Connie discovered, actions sometimes speak louder than words—or tears."

"To many it was the interview that embodied the tragedy of September 11," Connie Chung's voice says. "Howard Lutnick, the CEO of the nation's largest bond trader, Cantor Fitzgerald, sobbed when he pledged to take care of the families of his seven hundred employees who were working on the top floors of the World Trade Center when the first plane hit. But today some of those families are furious at Howard Lutnick, accusing him of a cynical PR ploy to gain sympathy and, even worse, to attract business.

"Carol Herron, who has four children, says her concern over her missing husband turned to anger when she saw Lutnick on TV.

"Do you think Howard Lutnick was sincere?"

"No. Not at all."

"Why *would* he cry, *sob* on television if he didn't mean it?"

"Because of the image he wanted to portray to everyone."

"Are you suggesting that he just *turned on* the tears?"

"Oh, yeah."

They show Howard crying, but rather than showing the buildings coming down, or people running from the rubble, or pictures of Gary or Doug, they show these angry wives, and then Howard crying.

"But don't expect these women to cry for Lutnick," Connie Chung says. "Days after the tragedy, he did something they can neither forgive nor forget. He *cut off paychecks* at the same time their families were hoping they were alive."

The screen shows a covert shot of Howard and Edie after they've given their eulogies at Gary's service. The camera is pointed through a van window as though they are criminals.

We then see a woman crying as she holds a photograph of her dead husband. "He was almost thirty-five years old, a father of five, nicest person in the world," the woman says.

"When Howard Lutnick stopped your husband's paychecks, what did that mean to you?" Connie Chung asks.

"I was disgusted. Because I didn't accept that he was dead at that point. He was *missing*."

Connie Chung wears the same pained expression she wore when

she was calling Howard a remarkable man a month ago. Lost in all this bile is that the deaths were brought about by a terrorist attack. All the rage and anger is directed at Howard.

It goes on and on this way. Howard would say later that each time someone said something critical about him—that he faked his tears, that he never cared about the families, that he stole the firm from his dying mentor—he slipped lower and lower in his chair until he was practically under the desk.

And he knew too what this could mean for the company. Already *The O'Reilly Factor* had decimated the relief effort, hurt the equities business and eSpeed's stock. This wasn't going to help matters.

"It didn't have to be so brutal," says one spouse. "They could have given us at least two weeks to grieve without having to think that our husbands were gone."

"He calls everyone his family," says another widow, Susan Sliwak. "This is the first he's ever called them family. He's never treated anyone kindly in the firm."

"Howard Lutnick is not going to tell me that my husband is dead. That's not how I want to find out, on TV with the rest of the world."

The issue is potentially combustible. It's not the salaries so much as whether Howard has the right to declare the fate of their husbands. But Connie Chung seems uninterested in mining for insights. She says other firms are paying salaries and it would "hardly have bankrupted Cantor" to do the same.

She doesn't point out how hard it would have been for three hundred people to pay the salaries of seven hundred others. "Why would Howard Lutnick so publicly promise to support the families one minute and cut them off at the knees the next?" she asks. "Wall Street watchers say that's the Howard Lutnick they know."

The "Wall Street watcher" Connie Chung digs up is Tom Jaffe, a writer who went after Howard in a 1997 article for *Forbes* magazine.

"When I saw Lutnick cry, I thought to myself, *I've seen this man cry before*. I've heard from *others* how he's cried. How he could turn it on and off like a faucet," Jaffe says. "Howard Lutnick is regarded as aggressive, ambitious, ruthless, and willing to step on or over anyone to get what he wants."

The malevolence is stunning. At the end of the report, after an almost fifteen-minute litany of Howard's supposed broken promises, Connie Chung pulls a journalistic sleight of hand. She shows the television audience the plan, and then tells the people she's interviewing about it. The woman who said Howard had disgusted her now says the plan actually sounds terrific, and if it's true, she wants to apologize to Howard and to tell him he's a man of honor.

"Is that net or gross?" another of the wives asks of the money Howard has pledged.

Later, several wives, including Joan Kirwin, Jennifer Gardner, and Bonnie McEneaney, will call Howard to tell him they had been interviewed by Connie Chung and told her that they liked the plan. But their interviews never aired.

She never let the truth get in the way of her need to show teeth to those who accused her of melting in the face of Howard's tears.

The salary issue had everything to do with the emotions of the first weeks, the absence of a safety net, fears both real and overstated. What was needed from people like Connie Chung was a perspective piece that would bring to the matter a greater level of understanding.

The plan had ruined her exposé of Howard, but she ran it all anyhow. She repeated O'Reilly almost to the letter, including among her wives Lynda Fiori and digging up her own Lutnick authority from *Forbes* magazine. Howard Lutnick had staged his tears and betrayed the families of his dead friends and colleagues, she was saying, whether or not it was true.

LATE THE NEXT NIGHT I get Howard on the phone.
He says, "Did you see the bounce?"

I tell him I'm not sure I know what he's referring to.

"After they beat the crap out of me for fifteen minutes, she reads them the plan in the last two minutes and they like it. They actually apologized. And then it turned. And it turned even more today." He proceeds now to read several articles that say positive things about the plan and the firm, and then he tells me stories about two wives who

"The last good moment of my life."—Howard and Kyle on Kyle's first day of kindergarten at the Horace Mann School. The photograph was taken at 8:45 A.M. on September 11.

Howard with Connie Chung during their second interview after
September 11. "It was tabloid journalism. I've become a
Chicken McNugget of news," Lutnick later said.

The second Larry King interview, February 22: Howard thanked hi
team in the wake of Cantor Fitzgerald's impressive fourth-quarte
earnings report. On the September 19 show, Howard broke dow
when asked about his brother Gary's death

Three thousand people attended the Cantor memorial on October 1.
After several surviving spouses, Maura Coughlin *(top right)*,
Eileen Varacchi *(bottom right)*, Joan Kirwin and son *(below)*, and Sam Ellis
and Nancy Shea *(not pictured)* spoke
movingly of their late husbands and
wives, Howard Lutnick *(middle right)*
expressed his pride in being a member of
the Cantor family. New York mayor Rudy
Giuliani *(lower left, behind Lutnick)*
praised the company's "great
determination, unity, and courage in
the aftermath of the attacks."

Equities sales traders Chris Sorenson and John Law. So few of their friends survived. "I just think about all the people I knew. This one who got married, this one who just had a baby. This isn't anything anyone should have to go through."

The London office took over the jobs of their lost New York counterparts during the most difficult weeks and kept the business alive.

Prince Charles *(fourth from left)* met with Cantor's London office post–September 11.
Left to right: Shaun Lynn, Phil Norton, Lee Amaitis, Jim Johnson, and Clive Triance.
"The London office should be covered in medals," Howard said.

Relief Fund volunteers at a Cantor-sponsored children's holiday gathering in December. Pictured third from left, back row, is Howard's sister, Edie Lutnick, and in the bottom left is Edie's boyfriend, Lewis Ameri, who worked with her at the fund. The relief fund has raised and distributed over 23 million dollars.

After the attacks wiped out Cantor's human resources department, Karen Weinberg and Lynn Granat, Allison Lutnick's high school friends, ran a makeshift command center out of the Lutnicks' apartment.

At five in the morning of September 12, Allison Lutnick came up with the idea of the crisis center, a place for Cantor families to meet and share information. She has also organized support groups and hosted monthly meetings for pregnant widows and fiancées of Cantor victims.

Washing up before Men's Night Out. Since September 11, Howard has served as a second father to Michael and Julia Gardner, his best friend Doug's children. Every Thursday, Howard takes Michael *(middle)* and his sons, Brandon and Kyle, out on the town to a candy store or arcade.

Bernie Cantor and his protégé, Howard, on one
of their ritual Saturday-afternoon visits.

Howard's relationship with Iris Cantor started amicably but became
increasingly rancorous after Bernie's death in 1996, when they
battled publicly for control of the firm.

Gary Lutnick and David Kravette, a managing director and Howard's childhood friend. Kravette was the last person to make it out of the Cantor offices alive. He did so because he needed to clear a client through lobby security.

Howard, at twenty-nine, with Stuart Fraser on the day Howard was named president of Cantor Fitzgerald. The two started at the firm in the summer of 1979 in a training program set up by Bernie Cantor. For years they were resented by senior executives because of their close relationship with Cantor. "We had bull's-eyes on our backs," Fraser says.

Howard's parents, Solomon and Jane Lutnick, with Howard in Venice. Howard's mother died on February 19, 1978, when he was sixteen; his father died on September 12, 1979, during Howard's first week of college. Howard says that after that day he had a 21-year, 364-day string of good luck.

The Lutnick siblings, Gary, Howard, and Edie, circa 1971.

After their parents died, Edie *(right)* raised Gary *(center)* like a son.

Howard on a trip to Florida with the Haverford College tennis team. After the death of his parents, Haverford told Howard not to worry about tuition—a gesture of kindness Howard has repaid many times over by becoming one of the college's largest donors.

Howard's impressively appointed office on the 105th floor of Tower One. Above his desk is a portrait of the firm's founder, Bernie Cantor.

Bernie Cantor had the world's largest private collection of Rodin sculptures.
His office was often referred to as the "World's Highest Museum."
Pictured here is *The Three Shades*.

Howard at the Fresh Kills Landfill. The engine and landing gear of one of the planes are mixed in with the destroyed Rodins. The torso in the lower left is from *The Three Shades*. The head on the right is the remains of Rodin's *Pierre de Wiessant*.

Ground Zero, photographed by Allison Lutnick in October during the Lutnicks' tour of the Trade Center site. Looking at the building was "like looking at an unburied corpse."

"People would come by and the office would just disappear for them—they'd just stand there looking out the windows."

called and told him they hated the Connie Chung report and they appreciated all the work he was doing on their behalf.

He starts reading one of the stories aloud to me.

"'One Month Later: America Fights Back. Cantor to Aid Victims' Families.' They quote one of the wives, Nancy Moroney. Her husband, Dennis, was in charge of bonuses. She called me tonight. She says, 'When I heard you talking about bonuses, all of a sudden I realized, Oh my god—of course he's having trouble doing the bonuses, he doesn't have Dennis.'"

He reads on. The article goes through the plan in detail and doesn't make much of salaries being cut off. "Here's another one. The Associated Press, 'Cantor CEO Keeps His Promises.'

"The thing is, it's not any different from what I said I'd do on *Larry King*. I said I'd give twenty-five percent. But people just ignored it. Now if I'd actually figured this out and announced the details on *Larry King*, maybe I would never have been in this position in the first place.

"You know what's terrible is that Connie Chung set up the interview in a particular way. She tried to get me to sit in the office of the president of ABC, so I'd be sitting in front of this big, giant mahogany fancy desk. So I'd look like an ass. It was a total setup, so that when she's interviewing me I look like I'm still on top of the world, instead of nowhere, which is where I really am. It's tabloid journalism. I've become a Chicken McNugget of news."

*C*ALVIN'S CHURCH, *the Christian Cultural Center, invited me to an anniversary candlelight memorial service, and they wanted me to give a testimonial to the congregation. They called and offered three minutes. I said I'd like to be able to say what I want to say. So they gave me five.*

It was an African American congregation, with few exceptions. I had been there earlier for Calvin's service, and it felt nice to be invited back with all that's been going on in the last days, all the bad press.

The service I found out would be simulcast in eighty-one churches, then beamed by satellite across the Christian Television Network, and played over the radio. It's a big deal.

They'd been using my name to draw more attention to the evening. And then supposedly—because of O'Reilly and Connie Chung—there'd been some talk about asking me not to come, for fear of their being associated with me.

The Pastor A. R. Bernard told them, "This is a good guy. I saw him when he was at Calvin's service. This is the real thing."

They had pastors from all over the world speaking. One in Korean, the next in Chinese. Everyone talked about the Trade Center and those who died. They honored the fire department, the police department, and all the victims. The central message was that Christ was still on the throne, that bad things happened in biblical times just as they happen now. And then the Reverend Franklin Graham, Billy Graham's son, beamed in from his church in Fresno, California, and said turn to Christ and he will save you.

I'm Jewish, but not particularly religious, not a big attendee of any sort of services. But I have to say that being in that room was a very powerful experience. They put one of those ribbons on me, with an open Bible and a cross in the middle. I never would have worn one before. But I kept it on. I actually liked wearing it. I realized at all the services that every religion clearly comforts a tremendous amount of people in pain, and I think that's fantastic.

I would have had no understanding of something like this before, but there I was looking at five thousand people all tuned to the same message. LaChanze says she's getting through this because she's dedicated her life to Christ. I find that amazing.

I got up and talked about Calvin, then about what happened to us and what we were doing for the families. At Calvin's memorial, they had all embraced me and wanted to be near me. I was a small part of this service, but they kept me at the heart of it. They didn't drop me because of the bad press, and that says a lot about Pastor Bernard. He knew there was some heat on me, but he came up to me when I got to the church and said, "We're behind you. We know you're doing the right thing."

On either the first or second night, I did something I'd never ordinarily do. I went looking for the Bible we keep in the back of the bookshelves. I wanted to look at the Book of Job to see what had happened to him. I hadn't read the Bible in a long time. I didn't have much reason to. I realized when I read it that I had lost a lot, but unlike him, I had not lost my wife; I had not lost my children; I had not lost my sister. I did lose my brother, and he was a deep part of my life. Gary was my family's safety net if anything happened to me. And so I had lost family. But I hadn't lost all my family, and though I lost way, way too many friends, I was still surrounded by others. I had not lost them all.

So I read the Book of Job and realized that when people say it can't get worse, that indeed it could get worse. When I'd look at parents who lost a child, I saw a depth of pain that was overwhelming. I could not imagine losing mine, but we had twenty families who lost not one child, but two.

I think of the Abate family, who lost both Vinnie and Andrew. Or the Egans, losing two daughters, from our human resources department, Lisa and Samantha. Tim O'Brien's sister lost her brother and her husband. The Gilberts, from London, lost Andrew and Tim. Victor and Christina Colaio—wonderful people—lost two sons, Stephen and Mark. June Colaio, Mark's wife, lost her brother, Thomas Pedecini, as well. Frank and Kathleen Pezzuti lost their daughter, Kaleen, her boyfriend, and their other daughter's husband. Imagine that. It's unthinkable.

So it could always get worse. It wasn't that I felt lucky, because you can't go through what I went through and feel lucky ever again.

The Media

BILL RICE

"I don't know what Howard was thinking, or if he was thinking, but he balked at a very critical time. The PR was handled poorly, and the backlash was violent. I had customers who'd been with me through thick and thin. One guy who's one of my closest friends called me up and he was *really* pissed off, because of the perception that Bill O'Reilly created, which was of course not true.

"It was peculiar. These women were in a sense biting the hand that was trying to feed them. They were damaging the company. And it made all of us pretty mad, because we were all working literally twenty-four hours a day to keep the seams from splitting apart. The stress level was unbelievable. We work in a high-pressure business every day, but I've never seen it this intense for this long a period of time, with no letup. And to have to watch them tearing us down when we were working our asses off for them in large part . . . because if you were going after Howard you were going after us.

"It was very simple from our view—the media thrives on controversy. They want to see you writhe in pain. You know the story of the snake and the turtle—the snake wants to ride on the turtle's back across the water. The turtle says, 'You won't bite me,' and the snake says, 'Of course not,' and then when they're in the water the snake bites the turtle, and the turtle says, 'How could you do that? We're both going to die now.' And the snake says, 'I can't help it. I'm a snake.' And that was the media."

AMY NAUIOKAS

"I had advised Howard not to rush to go on television, and he didn't for a couple days. Then it got to the point where I thought I can't keep him off anymore, I mean he really wanted to go on and tell his story. It was important to him. It was important for people to know the company was still around, but it was also important for people to realize that they were gone, that people had died. My gut was telling me it was going to make it bigger than it already was. We were already handicapped enough. I was concerned about the extra pressure we'd be putting on ourselves now that people were going to be watching us.

"We were at the Pierre. He asked me, 'How did I do?' And I told him he couldn't have done any better. Because it was real. No one coached him. I think he was pleased he did it, and he was able to honor his friends and say publicly that he wanted to take care of the families.

"I told him before *Larry King*, 'This is a new scenario now. If I put you out there, and you announce the twenty-five percent, you've got to come through, because if you don't, you're done, we're done, I'm done, the whole organization is done. And I need you to commit to me. Look me in the eye and tell me that you mean what you say.'

"And he did, he looked me right in the eye, and he said, 'God as my witness, I will take care of these families. These people are going to be so proud to be associated with us.'

"So I did it; I said let's go ahead, against what everyone was saying—Merkel and all the others.

"What was frustrating was that we got back afterward, and everybody was on a high, but then they all went back to their jobs. We had a business to rebuild. And I started thinking after *Larry King*—We've got to give them more specifics about this twenty-five percent. It's important. We've got to get it out, we've got to get it out fast.

"Now I think back and I wonder, could I have shouted louder? Could I have said no one's leaving this room until you fucking lay out what the twenty-five percent will mean?"

TOM TRILLO

"Whatever we gave the families wasn't going to be enough. We simply had to stop the negative press, and the best way to do that I thought was to get off TV for a while, then go out there and tell people what it is you're going to do.

"Howard and Amy Nauiokas asked me to go on TV to tell our story, and I told Howard, 'Think about what I do every day.' Every day at three o'clock I get to talk to the GSCC and work out where we are with our positions on the Street and how much cash we have and why aren't we clearing trade to the levels we used to. And at four o'clock I get the pleasure of talking to the bank. And say, 'I need you to lend me another eighty million dollars unsecured overnight.' 'Okay, Tom,' they say. 'So what are you going to do for us tomorrow? How are your deliveries going?' And at five o'clock, I get to talk to the head of regulatory reporting at the SEC, right? And I get to tell him we're not going to file our reports on time as regulated by the SEC because we don't have our systems to where they need to be. And, yeah, could you cut me some slack? So that was my day, *every day*—every day, the level of stress I was under in talking to depositories, the banks, and the regulators to try and convince them that we're okay. It was salesman work. How were they going to like it when they read in the newspaper Tom Trillo at Cantor says they've done a fantastic job—'It's been a miracle. A Herculean effort.' Right? I said, 'Howard, are you outta your fucking mind?'"

T HE TEARS ARE important because they have become his signature, what he is known for, because so many people following the tragedy kept their emotions in check. Those at the center of it, those who saw what happened, like Mayor Giuliani, avoided putting into words the extent of the devastation. They used words like "unspeakable," or "unimaginable."

What was distinctive—among six thousand things that were distinctive about the September 11 massacre—was that while in some sense the country went through it together, in another, everyone went through this at his or her own speed and in his or her own manner. And many of the divisions occurred because of this.

The lack of a body stalled the grieving process for many. Acceptance took months for some. The resentment of Howard, it now seems, had less to do with money and more to do with the fact that he cried on too many shows, and they reran them too many times. And it was hard for many of the family members to watch him cry for them, to watch his tears speak for theirs at a time when fear of the future was looming as large as their sadness for those they lost. Here was a man with his family— at least his spouse and children—intact, who was well beyond economically secure, weeping on TV, and at the same time saying he couldn't pay their salaries.

That was the line that drowned out the others—the other ultimately significant part of his *Larry King* interview when he was explaining that he was going to share 25 percent of the company with them. If that was indeed good news, why did this man feel terrible enough about it that he was breaking down?

It would be months before he would even partially unravel the emotional chain of events that had led him to that particular moment.

His very real breakdown in front of millions of people was painful to watch. Some resented him for it; others wanted to come to New York and work for him.

But it would be hard to say that his tears were faked, because the truth was, in those days he cried an awful lot, both on and off camera, and you had to be living in a cave somewhere not to understand why.

In an interview on MSNBC, Tom Brokaw speaks of his assistant who was exposed days before to anthrax. His team is a family, he says, near tears. There is a particular sort of pain a boss feels, he says, when an employee ends up in harm's way. Authorities have quarantined the main NBC newsroom while a HazMat emergency response team conducts tests.

Bioterrorism is fast becoming the main topic of conversation.

The letter to Brokaw and another sent to Senator Tom Daschle were both signed in a slanted scrawl, the Daschle letter masquerading as a fan letter from a fourth-grade class in New Jersey.

With all the human loss, few ever mention the material loss—the spectacular offices, the seven million dollars' worth of art, paintings, and sculptures, Rodins primarily.

In Howard's office, along with a crystal ball, a wall of family photographs, and several expensive clocks given to him by friends, there was a statue of a cardinal by Giacomo Manzù, three Rodins, including Howard's prized sculpture of Balzac, and a portrait of Bernie Cantor that hung behind his desk. On the 105th floor—once called "The World's Highest Museum"—there had been close to two dozen Rodins. The mangled remains of a few will be discovered in February.

But what Howard and Stephen Merkel are concerned with now is the loss of their position on Telerate, the screen system on which for twenty-nine years they've been displaying their bond pricing data to the world's banks, brokerage firms, and money managers. By the start of the next week, Moneyline, the new owner of Telerate, will replace Cantor data with BrokerTec's.

So now when someone looks for Cantor on page 500 of Telerate's information network—referred to as Treasury 500—they get the competition.

If the market can't locate Cantor's data, the firm will become less relevant every day. What riles Howard most is that those customers expecting to find Cantor may not know about the switch. Everything Cantor's marketing staff and brokers have done to familiarize the customers with Treasury 500 will now benefit their competitor. He contacts Reuters and Bloomberg to ask them to display Cantor's data. Surely they need us, he says, and within a week a deal is signed.

For Howard, nothing seems certain, and it has begun to feel as though the floor beneath him might soon give way.

There is something depressing about working as intensely and as single-mindedly as he has been and to see it played out so negatively in the public eye. People still stop him on the way into a restaurant to tell him he's a hero. But lately he feels his voice has been muted, his ability to argue for the families has been weakened.

It's harder now for him to reach politicians on the phone, even those with whom he's had personal relationships. The week of negative television has put the business into a tailspin. Contributions to the relief fund, which had poured in after his first TV appearance, have all but dried up.

If Bill O'Reilly and Connie Chung had imagined that by lighting into the company they'd be helping the Cantor families, it appears they've done the opposite. Many who'd once felt compassion for Cantor Fitzgerald now seem turned off by the ordeal—by the vitriol and dysfunction—and are directing their charitable impulses and business elsewhere.

O N SATURDAY, as Howard and Allison ride down to Ground Zero, Allison's mother, Geri, calls to tell them to turn on the radio. A national talk show host, Mike Gallagher, has devoted his whole show to defending Howard and ripping into Connie Chung and Bill O'Reilly.

Gallagher says, "The guy lost his brother, and his best friend, and seven hundred employees. Give him a break." He then commends Howard for rebuilding the company and calls him a hero for the way in which he's taken care of the families of his friends.

It is the first of several shows Mike Gallagher will devote to the subject of Howard Lutnick, one of which will feature Howard as a call-in guest.

It picked up his mood and Monday's business. "Finally," he says, "someone in the media who understands."

When they reach Ground Zero a fire chief hands him and Allison hard hats and walks them through the World Financial Center, to the Trade Center site, where the mounds of steel and rubble still smolder.

"It was unbelievable," Howard says. "A piece from our tower must have flown across the street and sliced into the Merrill Lynch building. You see those steel beams sticking out of the ground like toothpicks in an apple. There's a billion tons of steel and concrete. The guy said it was so hot at the center that the cement was glowing.

"A group of families was leaving, and one guy says to me, 'My cousin and my brother-in-law worked at eSpeed.' Then he tells me they're having a double funeral on Sunday. Can I come?

"I said I don't know. I didn't just want to say right out that I couldn't go. But I couldn't, can't do doubles . . .

Double memorials have been an issue for Howard. He'd made the mistake of arriving at Joe and Danny Shea's unprepared, and it had wrecked him. He had opted not to attend the memorial for the Grazioso brothers because he'd needed his composure intact for his eSpeed conference call that afternoon.

"So the firefighter is telling us how it looked when he got there two minutes after the first plane hit, says West Street was like a battlefield, bodies and body parts everywhere. You had to step over them to get into the building. I can't help but think how lucky I was not to see any of that, that I came in on the other side.

"If I'd come in on the West Street side, I don't think I'd have been able to hold it together, to talk to all those people at the crisis center. And I'm not sure I would have been able to work. I would have been shell-shocked. Where I was, there was just a massive amount of smoke. But on the West Street side . . . It's hard to even think about it.

"You know what it was like? You look around gathering details, like you would at an archaeological dig. And then you look up and you realize *it's all gone*. All of it. You can't believe it. And then all the faces come back, and all the people come back, and the memories come back, and it just knocks you to the ground."

THURSDAY, OCTOBER 18

Howard, Amy Nauiokas, and I arrive at the Midtown offices of Howard's PR firm. Producers and their assistants are adjusting the lights and cameras. CNN anchor Willow Bay, smartly dressed in a lavender jacket, white blouse, and dark slacks, greets Howard warmly. Bay spent nearly a week with him preparing what was to be a lengthy, flattering biography for her talk show *Pinnacle*. He had, in fact, boasted just a little about it when I saw him last spring in San Francisco: Wasn't it amazing that someone wanted to do a whole television show about him?

The *Pinnacle* profile hadn't run by September 11, and now the Howard Lutnick story needs to be reconceived and reshot.

In the week of the negative news coverage, Willow Bay had called Howard to warn him that CNN was considering a critical story, but she wanted to know whether what she'd been hearing was true. He told her the criticisms of him were off base, and she took him at his word. As of now there's no guarantee how this interview will play, and so he's prepared for tough questions. Glancing at the lights, Howard asks if he looks all right. Bay goes into the next room, then returns with powder and a puff, and proceeds to pat Howard's face and forehead, perhaps a promising—albeit strange—indication of amity, though nothing is for certain these days.

They sit in metal folding chairs and talk in the tones of friends catching up.

His responses to her questions—primarily explanations of his actions—are fine, but he's nervous. He can't blame those who've lost loved ones in the attacks for the way they feel. His position and his decision to take ultimate responsibility has made him a lightning rod, and he understands and accepts that. The company, he says, is doing the right thing, and they'll continue to do so. He explains the details of his plan.

At the end of the interview, after they shake hands, he tells her how disappointed he was in Connie Chung and her reporting—that she knew his plan and seemed to keep it from her interview subjects. The subtext of the story: *Please don't screw me over.*

In the elevator he says it bothered him that Willow Bay had used the word "vilified"—as in "you were vilified by the media." He repeats the word over and over to himself—"vilified." *You were vilified.*

5:52 P.M.

Park Avenue is teeming with packs of resettled Wall Street workers leaving their offices, heading home or to a nearby bar. Along with Cantor, Lehman Brothers has taken up temporary residence in Howard's building. There is a wedding up the block at the Waldorf Astoria; two bridesmaids in blue satin dresses giggle next to a suntanned man in a tuxedo. A vendor on the corner hawks souvenirs and baubles of September 11—the ubiquitous NYPD and FDNY hats, T-shirts emblazoned with GOD BLESS AMERICA or that show Osama bin Laden's face on a poster reading, "Most Wanted."

The first person I see inside Cantor's makeshift office is David Kravette. Reporters, most recently from *Time* magazine, have wanted to talk to him about how he survived the fireball in the lobby.

"They took a lot of pictures," he says. He's wearing a denim eSpeed jacket over his shirt and tie. Stock reports scroll across half a dozen televisions suspended around the room. Virtually everyone in this office is new. Phil Marber, the head of Cantor's equities division, has been bringing people in at a rate of twelve a week. The new employees are mostly in their twenties, some in their early thirties.

Kravette points out the four or five people who were with the company before the 11th. They survived because they'd been on business trips or shooting a round of golf. Howard was at a celebrity golf event during the Trade Center bombing in 1993, something he regrets greatly, and one of the reasons he felt so compelled to reach the building and his people after the first plane hit.

Kravette says he's going to a fund-raiser for the relief fund tonight, organized by people connected with the Ford modeling agency.

"I'll be the short bald guy looking up at all the models," he says.

He is doing better these days, having fewer nightmares. But he gets sad when he goes to the hospital and sees Lauren and Greg Manning.

On Tuesday the *New York Times* ran a front-page story about Lauren Manning. Like Kravette, she had been in the lobby when the plane hit and a fireball of jet fuel raged down from the 93rd floor. Whereas Kravette came within fifty feet of the fire, Lauren was engulfed by those same flames and was burned severely on 80 percent of her body. In such cases, doctors generally believe the survival rate to be indirectly proportional to the percentage of the body burned. Lauren has a one-in-five chance of living.

Kravette and Howard have been visiting regularly.

"I get sad," says Kravette. "I didn't think I wanted to see a counselor, but now . . . maybe I will. Just once or twice, I mean. Nothing more than that."

These are people who pride themselves on their ability to make split-second decisions at work, but here in their personal lives, they are less sure about what to do and what to feel.

As Howard finishes a closed-door meeting, people assemble outside to have a word with him. It is like watching a senator and his staff. There literally is not a minute in which he can daydream.

Cantor's senior managing director Harry Fry and traders Craig Cummings and Ted Smith will join Howard for the drive to Clifton, New Jersey, where he will meet with family members of Cantor employees who died on September 11.

Fry, fortyish, with blond hair and a ruddy complexion, was on a flight from Chicago to Houston the day of the hijackings.

"The pilot learned of the attacks while we were in the air. When we landed they led us all out onto the tarmac, where they tell us that two planes have hit the Twin Towers. I couldn't believe it. I got on the phone right away, but of course I couldn't reach anyone." The elevator opens and we all step in. Harry shakes his head. "We had one hundred twenty-four people in my division. A hundred and twenty of them died."

We drive through heavy crosstown traffic to the Lincoln Tunnel, passing along the way a poster for a real estate company, with a picture of the Twin Towers rising into the nighttime skyline. A couple is hugging and teasing each other in front of it, the man draped in gold chains. The poster is rare. Already commercial and film producers have started removing the images of the towers from their work. Seeing the buildings outside our window is a bit startling. It's as though someone out there still doesn't know what happened.

When Howard rides with colleagues, the seating is arranged according to how essential the person's conversation will be. Tonight Harry has the prime seat. Craig, Ted, and Diny Ajamian sit in the back. Howard and Harry discuss which businesses to keep, which to lose—where to expand or contract. In the weeks following the attacks, Howard closed Cantor's Frankfurt and Paris offices and greatly reduced staff at his Tokyo branch. Several other divisions—anything that wasn't currently profitable—were slashed.

Howard says his old goals of waiting for investments to yield results is over. The goal now is to make money fast, because he needs cash to help the families. Harry's ideas are compelling but long-term; the two men are attempting to find compromises.

Howard's cell phone rings and he breaks away from Fry to complain at length about how Telerate and Dow Jones treated Cantor in the wake of the tragedy, then he mentions Giuliani and how he's focused almost exclusively lately on the firefighters and the police. "I wish he'd talk more about ordinary citizens. My guys were heroes too."

He picks up again with Harry. The sign for the country club appears out of nowhere. We drive past the entrance and use the exit ramp instead, going against traffic—which is how Howard has been traveling these days.

*   *   *

The beige-carpeted meeting room is filled with three dozen circular tables, six or seven chairs around each. At the side of the room is a long table, holding trays of fruit and cheese, cookies, and pots of coffee. Down an adjoining hallway in another conference room a chorus group is practicing for the club's centennial celebration.

"*I want to be a part of it. New York, New York!*" they're singing, far too cheerfully, within earshot of a few bereft parents who file by to get to the meeting. Craig winces and says, "Who the hell is singing?"

A widow walks over and gives Ted a hug. "Hi, Teddy. How're you doing?"

"Not great," he says.

They stand looking at each other. She tells him about her days and how she's coping.

Ted has been having a rough time of it. For weeks after the attacks he stayed away from the office. Now he's back at work, but without the rest of his team. He hasn't yet figured out a new role for himself.

There are fewer than twenty people in the room now, seated at tables, talking in soft voices, or staring off, drinking coffee, and I wonder if it will be a small turnout. Soon more people trickle in—a few older couples, parents, and then a large group of young wives, stylish and attractive, primarily in their twenties and early thirties. My eyes drop to their wedding bands. On the jacket lapel of a young, green-eyed woman is a button photograph of her curly-haired, square-jawed husband. More people file in and quietly take seats. There are several pregnant women in attendance. A baby wails somewhere behind us. The room is long—half the size of a football field.

Howard enters and begins his rounds, pausing at each table, shaking hands and introducing himself with a "Hi, I'm Howard Lutnick" to those he hasn't met before.

They, in turn, tell him briefly about their husband, or son, or wife. And then on to the next table he goes. A heavyset older man grips Howard's hand and stares intensely into his eyes. Other exchanges are lighter.

"I'm very sorry about your brother," one man says.

Soon there's someone at every seat and every table. I had expected the wives, and there are dozens and dozens of them. What I wasn't prepared for were the parents.

Diny Ajamian hands out copies of the plan. Eleven pages long, it includes sections on life insurance, bonuses, health insurance, stock options, 401(k)s, and the Cantor Fitzgerald Relief Fund.

"The end of last night's family meeting was really harsh," she says. "People were yelling at him. One man shouted, 'Where's my urn?' And then asks, 'What are you doing to track down the body parts?' I'm not kidding. As though that's part of our job."

After completing his circuit of the room, Howard moves to the front, holding in his hand a large cordless microphone that a best man might use to make a wedding toast. There is no media here, only those connected to Cantor are allowed. The people at my table, two wives and an older couple, are sweet to me, and I understand that they think I'm here for the same reason they are.

"I'm going to answer every single question anyone has about each topic before going on," Howard says. "We're not going anywhere. I just want to make sure all of you understand how fundamentally committed our company is to each of you, and irrespective of what has been said, you're going to hear tonight, and understand tonight, that the people who are alive at Cantor Fitzgerald loved your loved ones, cared about them so much that they are willing to do whatever it takes to help you out. That is not normal. It's certainly not required. It certainly has nothing to do with anything other than the love of the people alive for the people they miss and who they lost, and so I'm just going to start at the top and go one by one." He talks first about company-provided life insurance. He explains how discretionary bonuses work and when the firm will pay them. A woman complains that when she called the house the man who answered the phone was rude to her. Someone named Tom. For a moment I wonder if I was rude to anyone. I think I answered the phone three or four times, but I took and delivered messages.

He moves closer to the woman. "I have a problem, which is that I'm a human being. I have two arms. I have two ears, one mouth, and I can't do it all. It's just not possible. Seven hundred families. And if you think seven hundred is the number why don't you look around you.

Two thousand parents, and brothers, and sisters, and sisters-in-law. I spend every minute of my life, when I'm not working, on the phone. And when I call you, I'm not just going to say hello and hang up quickly. That's not right. I call people back until one in the morning. I am doing everything I can. But I am just me, and I apologize—"

"I don't have a problem with you," the woman says, chastened. "It's this Tom person."

"No, no," Howard says, "I apologize because what I did starting Wednesday is I brought in every one of my friends to help answer phones in my house." He speaks about how difficult it was to get in touch with people, and to answer sufficiently every call that came in, then he returns to the plan, and his decision to pay ten years of health insurance for every family.

Someone stands and asks about the salaries being cut off. He knew this was coming; it's asked at every meeting, and by every reporter lately. He pauses, looks at the ground, then lifts his head and starts in. He explains how the company paid the last paycheck on September 15, but couldn't pay checks on September 30. He said Cantor Fitzgerald processes about 200 billion dollars of securities a day, buying and selling them. Monday, he says, went off without a hitch, meaning 200 billion in and out.

"Tuesday was a disaster. We lost all our people and presumably we may well have lost our business."

He details how the banks lost their offices, which meant they weren't clearing securities, how Cantor's stocks and bonds had piled up. People are taking notes, or just listening intently, and here is another oddity—how few here really knew precisely what it was their husbands or wives or daughters or sons did at work, how they moved and ultimately made so much money. Or that it took an incredible amount of money to make money.

"Thursday I go on TV, and they ask me emotional questions and I cry because I lost all my friends, I lost my brother, for those of you who don't know, I lost my *best* friend, his name is Doug Gardner, he has a five-year-old and a three-year-old. And I cried. Personally, that was a good thing for me to do, okay? When the banks came to see me Friday morning that was not the best thing to do. They were looking me up and down and saying, 'This guy owes seventy *billion* dollars. And his company's got three hundred fifty *million* in capital. I want to explain what they've been cutting out of my interviews, for those of you who think these programs actually tell the truth."

He allows a ten-second silence.

"Well, our capital is not some shareholder's money. This is not Merrill Lynch. It's Ian Schneider's money, it's Steve Roach's money, and it's my money, and it's your money." He steps forward two paces.

"When your loved one passed away we took that money and we set it aside for that purpose because it's *your* money. So when someone says, 'Well you have three hundred and fifty million in capital, why don't you give half of that away?' Cantor Fitzgerald has zero dollars of its own money. It's called a partnership. It's the collective money of the partners who work here. The partners who died are owed just under one hundred million dollars of it. Okay? So that's their money.

"The bank is looking at me because I cried on TV last night. And they're wondering, Is this guy together or not? On Friday if I don't answer every question like the most aggressive, in-control businessman, the bank takes the company from me by Saturday. I told them, 'Look, you talk to me about the people I lost I'm going to start crying, but if you talk about business, I am no dumber than I ever was before. And I convinced them to stay with me and lend my firm *seventy billion dollars* when every single person in the company died." He grips the microphone tightly; the muscles in his neck tighten. He's slept so little and it occurs to me he could be having a breakdown here, that he could be snapping.

"And that was a miracle. And it hurts me—you're damn right it *hurts* me—when people say, 'You cut us off.' The *hell* I cut you off," he's yelling now. "I was trying to make sure I could stand here today. That's why I made those decisions."

It's uncomfortable now, in the way a dinner table gets when a family member has lost his cool.

"It's *easy* now. I have a company. The bank gave me back my accounts. On Monday they held all of our money. They controlled Cantor Fitzgerald, everything except the Cantor Relief Fund. 'Why'd you only give a million dollars to the fund?' people asked me. 'You're loaded.' But every dollar I had in the world, except for three million, was in Cantor Fitzgerald, and the bank owned it. So I took one and sent it to the relief fund." The woman next to me takes a sip from her water. She's staring down at the table smoothing the top with her finger.

"At the crisis center I said that's all I've got and I'm sorry if that's not good enough. I understand it's difficult for some of you to grasp that it's not just about one or ten or fifty. It's *seven hundred*. And three hundred living employees cannot pay the salaries of seven hundred people, and we lost virtually all of the ones who made us money." His voice softens abruptly.

"If that's not obvious, then I'm sorry," he says. "What we can do is commit to giving you twenty-five percent of the profits of our company for the next five years, and we're going to pay ten years' of your health insurance." He's back to the plan again, confidently and unemotionally. He's shamed them, and now he's letting them off the hook.

At the end of the meeting he talks like a coach about what they can all accomplish together, that they are one and the same. They applaud for several minutes. The mood afterward is relatively buoyant. People linger, exchange phone numbers and addresses. Hug one another. A woman stops to talk to Diny and tells her that Saturday was supposed to be her wedding day.

"Oh my," Diny says. She reaches her arms around the woman and hugs her.

After everyone's left, Howard looks, improbably, more energized than at the start of the evening. Another burden has been lifted. What he's been wearing in his body language and on his face lately has been the weight of disapproval, doubt, and dislike. He has longed to make his case, and he's had a chance tonight. The meetings were supposed to be for the families, and they are, but of course they're also for Howard. The rest of us are exhausted. Everyone wants to go home.

"It was so much better than last night," Diny says.

"How?"

"Last night there were hecklers."

"There weren't hecklers," Howard says.

"Yes, there were," Diny says.

*   *   *

In the car on the drive back, Jimmy is telling Howard about the trip he took to the cemetery where his mom, who died in 1992, is buried.

"The week before the attacks, my mother's coming to me every night in my dreams, talking to me even though I can't hear what she's saying. So Sunday morning when I wake up, my wife says, 'You gonna play golf?' because that's what I do on Sunday, and I say, 'No, I'm gonna go to the cemetery. So I sat on my mother's grave and I cried for about an hour and a half, thanking God for what He's done for me, and how much I love my mom, how much I miss her. I cried about the grandchildren she's seen and the ones she hasn't. And I never did this before, you know? I was like a friggin' basket case. She was trying to tell me something, but I didn't know what the hell it was. I told that story recently to one my friends, and he said your mother pulled strings for you."

Howard puts his hand on Jimmy's headrest.

"She sure did. If you go down to Ground Zero, Jim, you will see, just like I did, that where we were standing is untouched, everywhere else, where you ran, fucking rubble. What's the odds of those two towers coming down and not touching where you ran, or the corner around it. You run another ten yards—"

"I was dead, I was dead," Jimmy says, soberly.

"Destroyed. Defuckingstroyed like you have never seen."

"I actually fell as I got to that corner."

"'Cause you're out of shape," Howard says, and laughs.

"I'm not," Jimmy says, offended. "I'm in better shape than I look."

The mood is easy, postadventure. It's not a sad conversation. They're not touching on everything that was lost here, only that they were in something together, that the only person who knows what they went through is the other.

"I was saying the only way I'm gonna survive this is if I get behind something big. You know I didn't think there was a chance of me or you living."

"Me too. I said to myself, 'Son of a bitch. I'm dead.'"

"And then when it got light, I said, I'm gonna live. Did I tell you some cop tried to make a gun collar? Tried to book me for having a gun?"

"I love it. He's gonna take you downtown. You're a looter!" Howard says.

"You did the right thing, Jim. I'm glad you went to the cemetery."

We drive past Nutley and Secaucus, New Jersey, heading for the tunnel. He talks about an employee who lost everyone in his division, then stayed away—AWOL—for four weeks. Howard is only partly sympathetic. "He determined that the right thing to do for the business was to go to funerals."

"But some people have been through trauma . . . ," I venture.

"Their psyches might be hurt, but they're no more hurt than anyone else's. I mean, Jimmy's psyche is hurt but he can still come to work, right, Jim?"

"Right, Mr. Lutnick."

WHEN THE BUILDING *came down there was a roaring in my ears like a jet engine. We just started running. Jimmy ran along the building, underneath the overhang. I thought, Why the hell are we running here? This is the last place I want to be when stuff starts falling. I peeled off to the right and looked over my shoulder to check on Jimmy, but I didn't see him. What I see is a wave of smoke coming toward me. It's like a horror movie. So I'm running from this tornado and I'm in the* lead. *Behind the Millennium Hotel there's a church graveyard, with an iron fence. And I can see another tornado coming across the graveyard. I remember yelling "Oh shit!" And then it overtakes me. I dive to my left, under an SUV. Shit starts to hit me, particles about an inch and a half thick. I move my head near the tire so as not to get crushed in case something falls on the car. My eyes are closed and my glasses are bent. Stuff is just crashing down around me. It was like I was being pounded with hail.*

All of a sudden everything's just black . . . *and quiet, dead. It was eerie. I'm thinking, I'm gonna die. My lips were dry, cracked. I'd take a breath of smoke and it coated my mouth and my teeth, then my throat. I was having trouble breathing at all. I didn't get mad at anybody, wasn't angry or afraid. I just thought, I'm going to die. That's what my brother said, "My life's going to end." Or what Fred said, "I can't see. There's a lot of smoke. We're trying to break the windows. I don't think I'm gonna make it." There's no anger, no violence. No one to fight, no one to run away from. There's nowhere to go, nothing you can do. You just have to breathe. But breathing is the instrument of your death.*

And then I see a light. I crawl out and there's a flashlight near me. The beam only reaches a short distance, but it's right there. I yell out, "Hey!" But there's no response. So I get up, and there's this guy there. With a flashlight. I grab him by the collar and yell, "Let's get the hell out of here!" And the guy takes three or four steps and just sits down. Like a zombie. I'm standing. clearly alive. So I start walking, and I'm using my hands to feel my way along the cars.

I'm in the street, feeling for cars. It's still black out. Absolutely still. Perfect silence. And there's particles everywhere, and with each breath I'm taking more of it in. Gradually the world changes from black to a very dark gray, and I can see my hands.

That's when I thought, I'm gonna live. I still had no idea what had really happened. The ground was covered with soot, three or four inches deep. You could taste it. It had a nasty bite, like acid. Or scorched metal.

Then I see a coffee shop. A Starbucks or Coffee Republic sort of place. All the glass is blown out. But I need water. So I go in. And there's two women inside. I go behind the counter to the sink and I turn on the faucet. Out comes clear water. I rinse out my mouth, and then I just hacked up this stuff—this black solid shit from my insides. It was like a rock. I try to take another sip but hack up more of the stuff. I couldn't get the water down my throat. I just spat it out. The water came back out black.

Then one of the women says, "Hey, I found some water." I took a bottle.

I asked her, "Where's the bathrooms?" She pointed me around the corner. I went in, grabbed a roll of toilet paper, and I walked back out onto the street.

I don't take hot showers. But that night I kept turning up the heat, way past what I'd normally be able to handle, and it still wasn't hot enough. Finally it was like burning water coming out, and I was still shivering. I was trying to scour out the particles that had baked into my head, the smoke from my skin. I started rubbing like crazy, as hard as I could to scrape the stuff off me. Ash and concrete dust, chunks of it stuck so deep . . . I let this burning water pound on my head until it started running cold.

F RANK WALCZAK grew up in Boston, Massachusetts, and Westchester County, New York. He graduated from Denver University
and now lives on the Jersey shore. He's been a surfer for sixteen years,
and looks the part—broad shoulders, thick, light brown hair, with sun-
induced crow's-feet around his eyes. People that live by the water are
generally a lot happier than people who don't, he says.

Quite a few of the Cantor Fitzgerald brokers and traders were
surfers. They'd meet in the cafeteria line and talk about how the waves
had been the previous weekend, or the latest buoy readings on the In-
ternet.

Walczak, who goes by the nickname "Zack," worked on the foreign
exchange (FX) forwards desk on the 105th floor. We speak after work
on the steps of the building across the street from Cantor's interim offices.

"We had eight guys. We were a good desk, well functioning. We'd
slimmed down a lot from the years before because when the Euro
came to fruition, they took twelve currencies and made it one, basically. The profit margins were slowing down. But we had great guys.

"I was the only one of us who lived because on Monday afternoon,
Hurricane Erin was coming up the coast, and I'd heard from some
friends that Tuesday would be the biggest day. I went around and asked
the guys, 'Anybody mind if I take tomorrow off?' And they all said no,
go ahead.

"The next morning I was down at Sandy Hook, at the top of the Jersey shore. I remember how clear it was because you could see Manhattan. It's only eighteen miles as the crow flies, and I could see the whole skyline from the water. The water was about seventy degrees. I'd told my wife the night before I might take a vacation day, to go surfing. And then she looked at me like, *You're forty years old. Are you ever going to grow up?*

"In the morning, I threw my board in the car and left the house around the time I usually leave for work. I was out in the water from around six fifteen right until it happened. Then I looked at the skyline and thought, *Oh my god, there's* smoke *coming out of the Trade Center.* I rode the next wave in, ran to my car, and got on my phone. From the other cars I could hear radios saying that a plane had hit the World Trade Center.

"I tried calling the desk, then I called Chris Panatier and left a message on his cell."

Panatier had two children, a six-year-old daughter and a four-year-old son. He was thirty-six when he died. His wife, Carolyn, had been his high school sweetheart.

"Then I called Chris Gray, Robert Spencer. I went down the list. I was standing on the beach leaving another message when I saw that fireball engulf the second tower. Then the phones went down and I couldn't call at all, not even my house. I live ten minutes from where I was surfing, and I couldn't reach my wife to tell her where I was.

"She'd run to a neighbor's house, a guy I usually surf with, and he'd told her he hadn't seen or heard from me. So she'd thought I'd gone in. She was crying when I saw her. The phone rang nonstop with friends and family calling to see if I'd been in the building.

"I didn't know what to feel. I was scared and nervous. But I felt I should be doing something. That night I started calling up people on my desk, the wives. All these people—we used to ride in on the boat together. We became close with one another. They kept saying, 'I can't believe it. I can't believe it. Do you think they got out?'

"And I was telling them, 'Yes, I'm sure some people got out.'

"But how could I really know? I hadn't heard anything positive.

"That night, I awoke to the sound of the siren from our volunteer fire department. When I heard the wail, I ran to check on the kids because I was sure it was an air raid. Something had happened. I was terrified. And then I just broke down. I sat downstairs in my living room by myself and cried.

"The next couple of days, nobody knew what to do. I went into the crisis center. I went to a couple of hospitals for some of the wives. We scoured those in Lower Manhattan. We didn't find anything.

"Everybody was holding out so much hope, but I knew in my heart that none of those guys got out. I was just hoping that it was quick for them. I have a recurring nightmare where I'm with those guys and the building's crashing in. And we're all just together. There's the big scream. It's a cold-sweat nightmare. I still have that one."

PASSAGES

After taking the kids to a play, Howard tells me on the way home, "I watched the tapes last night. And it made me even angrier." He leans forward. "There was nothing I promised that I didn't do. I said we had to put the company back together so we could take care of the families. In that order. I didn't say anything about paying salaries.

"I mean, look, I had just committed to paying for ten years of health care for the families, paying one hundred thousand dollars a family, and paying forty-five million dollars' worth of bonuses, that is one hundred seventy-five million dollars from a company that three weeks before had everyone killed. And here's Connie Chung on national television brutalizing me as if I'm a villain.

"It's so misplaced, so completely misplaced. I'm not a villain. My brother was killed, my best friend was killed, and all my friends were killed, all the people that I worked with, and my company, and everything that I have lived for before had been killed, and I'm a villain?"

For his sake I wish Howard could let it rest. But there are reasons he can't let it go. For all the firm has done, there are still stray comments in the paper, family members who doubt his word and voice these doubts publicly. His goal now is to reach every member of every family, either by phone or in person. He's traveled to hotel ballrooms and churches and a baseball stadium club room. And he's spent at least half of every workday calling families. He listens patiently, explains what the firm is doing, takes their calls even if they call back twice in the next hour. He is trying to win over this group one by one if he has to, and the method is already paying dividends. The meetings go from hostile to communal—each time he fields animosity by explaining what the company's been through and what they're planning to do—never one without the other.

M ARYANN hands him a stapled list of family members who have said negative things about the company or about him. Listed are phone numbers and the names of the deceased.

Every five minutes or so she reaches someone and signals for Howard to pick up the phone. "Hi," he says. "This is Howard Lutnick from Cantor Fitzgerald calling," as though there are other Howard Lutnicks who might be calling. "How are you doing?"

His other major tasks with regard to the families—the families are his biggest job these days—is writing condolence letters, and responding to the people who have written him. The list of households receiving condolence letters contains thirteen hundred names, including spouses, parents, and siblings. Howard ended up handwriting notes to all of them, a job that took countless hours and became a personal mission. On weekends he brings home his e-mails, printed out by Maryann. The stack lately has been knee-high. Weekend afternoons he meets with his new PR staff. Howard has fared much better since the terrible stretch of news coverage in the fall, and some credit is due to the group he's assembled. On the day the bonuses went out, hundreds of news organizations were contacted and dozens ran stories. The idea was to reach them before any families called to say that their checks hadn't arrived yet, or were too small, or that they doubted Cantor would fulfill its promises.

He tells them where things went wrong for him before, how Connie Chung let him down, then takes them through the Iris Cantor story, detail by detail.

Before September 11, people didn't know much about Howard, but if they did, it more often than not had to do with his struggle with Iris Cantor, over control of the company in 1996. The *New York Times* ran a feature on the front page of the Sunday "Business" section in which

Iris claimed Howard had stolen the firm from his dying mentor.

He speaks to them about the partnership agreement Bernie Cantor set up that specified Howard would run the company, and that Iris Cantor had signed the document in 1993, 1994, and 1995. He talks about the *Pinnacle* piece on CNN that would have settled the matter once and for all. He wants these people to like him, to understand that he's been maligned.

A N ACCOUNTANT named Paul Pion, Diny, and Howard are going over numbers as they apply to bonuses for employees who worked less than a year. After Howard leaves, and we've introduced ourselves, I ask Paul where he was on the day of the attacks.

"I was working across the street," he says. His company, Deloitte & Touche, had offices in Two World Financial Center. "I was looking out the window when the first plane hit," he says. "I just thought it was a small commuter plane. An accident. We evacuated the building when the second one hit. I saw terrible things."

Pion's tone is flat, but he's clearly shaken by his words, like a kid talking of something awful he's seen but doesn't yet understand.

"I saw bodies dropping—twenty or thirty of them. They were people I knew, friends. I used to work on the floors below Cantor. Right where the plane hit. It seemed unreal, like something from a Schwarzeneggar movie. The bodies bounced."

This is the worst detail I have heard.

"The bodies were mangled. The heads were destroyed. I'm too young to have ever been in a war, but this was worse than anything from any war I could imagine. We started walking up the West Side Highway. There were bodies on the street. The buildings were melting."

"I still can't think of that as real. If I did I couldn't live through this." Everyone I've spoken to has reported experiences like this, and making sense of them will likely take years. Processing the deaths of friends is one thing, but facing the inferno and all the falling bodies is another. And now he's faced with the task of helping calculate annual bonuses for these same people. The issues they're dealing with here—financial, legal, and personal—are all profound and heartbreaking.

*   *   *

A T THE END of the day Maryann has been handing Howard a
stack of letters and forcing him to read them. The great majority
of the more than two thousand that have come into Cantor Fitzgerald
since September 11 are positive, most emphatically so, but lately Howard
has had a tendency to focus on the worst.

Tonight, before he leaves for another town meeting—this one in
Staten Island—she gives him six or seven.

A woman from Arkansas writes:

> I can only say that Cantor Fitzgerald families do not have much to be
> grateful for right now, but where would they be if you had not been
> delayed that morning?

Another from Petaluma, California, says:

> Please allow me to carry some of your pain. It is too much for one
> man. My hope is that we will begin to lighten the weight you have cho-
> sen to carry. It is not yours alone. It belongs to all of us who have cho-
> sen to live in a free society.

One sentiment expressed repeatedly in slightly different form in
four of the letters is:

> We wanted to reach through the TV and give you a hug.

A letter addressed to *Good Morning America* reads:

> It is humanly impossible for this man [Howard] to be everything to
> everyone when hundreds of his support team are dead and his com-
> pany threatens to crumble before his eyes. It matters not one iota what
> he makes in personal salary, or for that matter, what the surviving
> spouses' issues are with what kind of an employer he is or was. Noth-
> ing could be less relevant to the people of New York. It is useless gossip
> and has no place right now.

Most of the letters are from women, from all over the country. One from West Dundee, Illinois, refers to the critical *20/20* report:

> If I lost my husband, even under natural circumstances, there is absolutely no way I would be able to appear on a television show before even the first month anniversary, there would be just too much grief. These people spoke as if YOU flew these planes into the buildings, as if you are responsible for this. What on earth do they want you to do? I'm certain you did not have people come to their homes every morning, handcuff their spouses and force them to work at these buildings in the skies. I'm certain these spouses enjoyed a wonderful life due to the positions you gave their family members . . . This was not grief speaking. I'm not sure exactly what it was besides down right mean. How on earth are YOU supposed to keep a company afloat making money when your entire work force of 700+ employees is gone???? YOU are one person, how on earth are you supposed to pull yourself together after your own personal loss in such a short time. How are YOU supposed to do all this, in less than a month????

He folds them neatly into their envelopes again and places them carefully in his briefcase, so that they can be read again tonight with Allison.

T HE MEETING TONIGHT will take place in Richmond County Park, home of the AA Staten Island Yankees. Howard will address the families in a club suite at the stadium.

In the sport utility, Diny and Ted sit in the back, and Howard in front, talking on his cellphone.

Three blocks from the Trade Center site, we pass floodlights and cranes. Ted points out where the buildings are, or, rather, were.

"They found Michael LaForte's body," Ted says. "His upper body, anyway. And Steve Roach's too. There were no burns."

In all, the remains of ten Cantor Fitzgerald employees were found that day. The talk turns to how the building fell. Diny says, "I heard the top of the North Tower came off in one piece. That's why some of the bodies are intact."

"*Okay*," Howard says, staring out the window. "New conversation, please."

O N THESE LAST FEW trips we've been talking about Bernie. These days have been fairly miserable for Howard. Weeks of sleep deprivation have worn him down, and the negative media has added to his exhaustion. I ask Howard about Bernie again, in part because his mood lifts when he speaks of him.

He talks of the time he spent with him in California, working on the equities desk, and how on weekends he'd often have Bernie all to himself.

"He'd say, 'Let's go see Beverly Hills,' and off we'd go in his staff's Peugeot station wagon. And he very rarely drove. I remember Iris telling us to be careful because 'it's more dangerous than you think.' We just drove around Beverly Hills with Bernie pointing out Lucille Ball's house, and places other celebrities lived. It was great.

"Then we'd go to his house and as soon as we'd sit down he'd offer me a beer. I'd decline, and he'd say, 'Come on, it's Saturday, Howard. You can have a beer.'

"So I'd have a beer—really two beers, it turns out. His cook, Max, would pour two beers in one giant mug. I once asked Bernie why the mugs were so big, and he said, 'So you don't have to get up. We can sit and talk and you don't have to get up and get a refill.' That's how he was in those days.

"Sometimes friends would come by and take him out, just to get his legs moving and have him walk around. But usually it was just Bernie and me, walking down the street, stopping for a cappuccino, just the two of us together talking."

He smiles now in a way I haven't seen for a while.

"In California I'd have these *whole days* with Bernie. There, if the senior executives were having a meeting, they'd invite me in, give me lunch. In New York the senior executives wouldn't give me the time of day. They'd make me stand there answering questions, and once I finished they'd make me leave.

"One thing Bernie really liked was that I wasn't afraid to tell him what other people wouldn't. I'd give it to him straight. Always with tremendous respect, but never holding anything back, either."

Later, in the kitchen, Howard tells me about the day he first interviewed at Cantor Fitzgerald, dressed in a suit that he and his grandfather Morris had purchased over the weekend.

"The place was just incredible," he says. "A sculpture gallery on top of the world. You would get off the elevator, make a right, and there's a room with a domed ceiling and Rodin's six-foot *The Thinker* sitting right there. It was just staggering. If you had a ten o'clock appointment with Bernie, he'd write ten fifteen in his book. The first thing you'd do was walk right by *The Thinker*. And then a young woman fresh from the Yale Graduate School for Fine Arts would give you a tour while you were waiting. And she'd know everything about all eighty sculptures— *The Three Shades*, the one that sits atop the *Gates of Hell*. When you were done she'd drop you off at Bernie's office. *Power*. That's the word you thought of. I'd see the most puffed-up, arrogant blowhards knocked down to size simply by visiting Bernie in his office.

"The place I worked before joining Cantor was chrome this and chrome that, to create the appearance of money. Cantor had *marble*. I didn't know enough to truly appreciate it, didn't have much to compare it to. I just thought, *This must be how a big guy on Wall Street does things.*

"But with Bernie it wasn't just power. He had style. Back then I didn't really know how to dress. I had one jacket. I wore that and a tie. At the interview Rod Fisher sat me down with Jim Avena, the company's number two guy.

"Avena hands me this prospectus from some random company, which I start reading, and he leaves me there for maybe . . . half an hour. When he comes back, he gives me maybe five minutes, that's it, and he tells me to call him.

"When I do call, I speak to his secretary and she's the one who offers me the job. Later Avena tells me I'll be starting the same time as Bernie's nephew, Stuart Fraser. Stuart takes off for some wilderness camp, so everyone thinks I'm Bernie's nephew. When I tell them I'm not, they don't believe me. Ten years later there were guys who still thought I was his nephew. Back then they thought I was a spy, so of course they gave me bullshit work. My boss in municipal bonds had me copy down classified ads from the paper."

Stuart too has told me about this period, and how it set the tone for their respective careers. Howard, whose first long-term job was managing Cantor's accounts, was always seen as Bernie's boy. His rapid rise coupled with the fact that he was also the boss's confidant, briefing him on events within the firm, both good and bad, only created more animosity and resentment within the executive suite.

I THINK BERNIE *appreciated how I took his concepts and ran with them. He taught me arbitrage, trading one bond against another. He was proud of his ideas, and that this kid whom he'd picked out was turning them into profits for the company.*

Senior year of college I applied to business school and was accepted at Northwestern. Harvard and Stanford asked me to get some work experience and reapply. I had worked at Cantor Fitzgerald for a year and a half when I decided to start filling out applications. I asked Bernie if he would write me a letter of recommendation.

"Why in the world would you want to go to business school?" he asked.

I told him it'd always been one of my goals to go to business school and get an MBA.

"Let me tell you about MBAs," he said. "The best way to get an MBA is to hire one." Then he tells me a story about how after he left the army as a private, first-class, he set up his own company, B. G. Cantor and Company, and the first thing he did was to hire a brigadier general.

I laughed. "Come on, Bernie, can't you just write the letter?"

He said, "Imagine you're at business school. You're reading a course catalog and it says, 'An industrialist, famous on Wall Street, the developer of the bond markets of the world, who's done everything from bought and sold Channel 13 to owning the Dallas Municipal Bus Company.' If that course was offered, would you take it?"

"Sure."

He said, "That course is right here. I'm offering you private lessons."

I thought about the offer overnight. It wasn't a hard choice. I had a relative who worked at Goldman Sachs. And he thought it was nice to work at Cantor Fitzgerald, but that it was fundamental to go to Harvard Business School because if you didn't go to Harvard Business School, you couldn't become a partner at Goldman Sachs. And to him, being successful on Wall Street meant working at Goldman Sachs. I didn't know any better to disagree with him, and being a partner at Goldman would certainly be a wonderful thing.

But when I told him I was going to stay at Cantor rather than go to business school, I think he lost respect for me. He never really spoke to me after that.

Shortly thereafter I formed a division called the Investment Strategies Group, and what I did was manage money for Bernie and his friends. We would buy and sell bonds for insurance companies and pension funds. Before long we were managing almost a billion dollars.

I was still a kid and to me the numbers were mind boggling. But it was great fun, and I was good at it. And Bernie noticed. Over time we grew very close, because we liked each other, and I was making a lot of money for him and his friends. Bernie came to trust and rely on my judgment of what to buy and what to sell. We kept adding new strategies. When I'd come up with a new idea I'd go to his office and we'd talk about it. Ten, twelve times a day, we'd talk.

Then, in 1986, there was a series of events that changed our friendship, and my place in the company. I'd purchased a discount Swissair ski package. It included a flight to St. Moritz, lodging at the Palace Hotel, and lift tickets, all for the price of a Club Med vacation. My girlfriend and I were really looking forward to it.

I knew that when I told Bernie I was going on vacation he'd be angry. In the three years I'd worked at Cantor, he'd never taken a vacation. Two weeks before the departure date I was still sweating it out. Finally, when I told him, he made it clear that I was letting him down. "Why are you taking off?" he said. "You should be working."

A week before I left, he called me up and asked if I was still going to St. Moritz. When I told him I was, he said, "Fine, I'm going too. My first vacation in five years." He asked me where I was staying. I told him the Palace Hotel. He said, "Great, I'm staying there too."

His friend Branco Weiss, who lived in Switzerland, would spend the week with us in St. Moritz. In the afternoons, when I was done skiing, Bernie and I would get together and talk. Later Branco and Bernie and I would go out to dinner, or sit around and drink wine or hot chocolate.

Later that week Branco and Bernie were commenting about how youth is wasted on the young. Then they pointed at me and said, "Except for him." I just loved that.

At the end of the trip, Bernie asked me if, instead of flying back to New York, I'd go to Paris with him. I asked him, "Don't I have to get back to work?"

"No," he said, "just come with me. I'll pay for the ticket."

So we went to Paris and he checked us in to the Bristol Hotel; I think it was a thousand a night. Bernie had flown in Stuart and Elise as well. It was all like some great dream: I'm in Paris with one of my best friends and Bernie, who was becoming like a father to me.

Bernie had a limousine and driver who took us to all the best restaurants. One night when we arrived back at the hotel, Bernie handed me five hundred francs. I asked him, "What's this for?"

"It's spending money."

He gave Stuart some too and told the limousine driver to take us out and show us a good time. I think Bernie enjoyed that as much as we did.

Bernie told me that week that he was considering selling the company and he wanted me and Stuart to help him start a new firm. We'd be deal makers, and all the investment banks would come to us. Bernie would introduce me around. I would be his eyes and ears. The deal fell through, but it was clear that at twenty-five I had earned Bernie's confidence, and that my life had just undergone a major change.

Bernie wasn't just teaching me the business. He was teaching me how to live, how to wear fine suits and how to pick them out. He taught me about wine, and how to use multiple sets of china and cutlery at dinner; where to go on vacation; taught me about art, and the protocol at an auction house. He spent long hours teaching me about Rodin. We spoke fifteen times a day.

When I walked by Bernie in the early days, he'd reach over and touch my suit. He'd say, "What is this crap you wear?"

At the time I was wearing Norman Hilton, which I'd buy at Barneys whenever they had a trunk sale. So Bernie starts taking me to his tailor in California, who shows me something called Super 100s and Super 120s. Bernie explains to me how it's woven per square inch, and he talks to me about the different types of wool, and who makes the finest fabrics.

I used to say Bernie lived in the "material world"—he was a man of touch. You would give him your business card—he would hold it and say, "This is eighty-pound paper." His particular knowledge was so extraordinary. He would teach me about fabrics. And then he would buy me two new suits.

It was clear to me what he was doing. He was inviting me into his world. He was saying, You don't know? Come on, I'll teach you.

I would have suits made only by his tailor and sometimes he'd buy them for me. We would spend the day together in California and then he would take me to a barbershop in Beverly Hills for a manicure and a shave.

When we were done he'd grab my face and say, "Now that's a shave."

Fast forward to 1994. The men's fashion designer Ermenegildo Zegna comes out with Zegna Trophy winner, a Super 150. Completely ridiculously expensive. I buy two of them. Can't be more expensive, but it's just for one particular reason. I walk by Bernie, I grab his suit, and I say, "What's this crap you're wearing? Feel this."

He says, "What?"

I say, "Super 150."

He says, "You've got to be kidding me."

I say, "I'm not." And then I send his tailor the fabric for three suits.

For a long time I didn't spend much of my paycheck. My needs were simple and I really didn't know what to buy. My one extravagance was my 1987 Porsche, which I had until 1990. I'm a player in the firm at this point, but I'm not in the executive suite. I'm making Bernie a lot of money trading and I'm also making a ton for myself. I'm twenty-eight. It's unbelievable. Then one day Bernie calls me up and says to me, "What kind of car you got?" I say a Porsche. He says, "That piece of shit? Get yourself a real car."

Now legend had it in the late '70s Bernie went to Italy and bought four

Ferraris. He kept one for himself and gave the other three to his senior ex- ecutives as gifts. Bernie's was a 400i that Stuart used to drive everywhere in Los Angeles trying to pick up chicks. The problem was the license plates read MRS BCG. And it was an automatic.

Bernie's insistent—I should have a Ferrari. I tell Gary about it that night. Gary agrees—"Definitely. You should have a Ferrari." And you know why? Because he wanted my Porsche. He knew I'd give it to him. He says, "Don't worry about a thing." A few days later he comes back and says, "I got the car you want—black on black, the 348ts, the roof comes off—it's perfect. So we go see it. He's already negotiated. Contract's done. "Here you go!" he says. So I buy the Ferrari, toss him the keys to the Porsche, and we both drive home in our new cars.

With Bernie there was always a balance. He expected me to work around the clock, but he also wanted me to live the kind of life he was living too. It took a while for me to get there. I wasn't going to take a single thing for granted.

When Bernie made me president, it's not as though I stepped back and thought, My God, I've made it. I knew I was doing well, but I was twenty-nine, and in those days Bernie owned me. If even one day I came in late, Bernie would nail me. If I left early he'd nail me. If I didn't know every single topic he'd nail me. My responsibility was to tell him everything that was going on. That was the deal. I'd spend every other week in California. I never made decisions without him, and he never made them without me. It was a tremendous gift. In New York, we'd spend Saturdays together at his house. I'd get there early in the morning and stay until evening. We'd talk business, watch football, college basketball. More often than not it was business, but in time it became much more than that. We filled a role in the other's life. Every night before I'd go to bed, I'd call Bernie to see if there was something important he was thinking, or something I might have forgotten to tell him. We relished this. It was work but it was personal too, and I miss him.

HARRY WAIZER

"I was in the elevator when the plane struck," Harry Waizer tells me. "I still can't remember whether I was between 0 and 78 or between 78 and 104. They told me that with the way the elevators functioned I was likely between 78 and 104."

While his colleagues fought for the company's survival and weathered an increasingly hostile media storm, Harry spent the last weeks of September and most of October in a coma. His voice when I call him is faint; his words the result of some effort.

Harry was inside an elevator when the first plane hit. He remembers the explosion. "I recall the physical shock. The shaking. Part of the elevator burst into flames. I grabbed something—I don't know what—and tried to beat back the fire. Then a second fireball hit us and caught me flush in the face. It happened quick, and then it was over.

"I burnt my hands fighting the flame, my fingertips up to my elbows. My legs burned above the knees, six inches or eight inches up. And my face was burnt. I remember the elevator plummeting, the screech of metal on metal. There were sparks shooting all over from the car braking or hitting the shaft, and then all of a sudden it caught itself and glided to the 78th floor.

"There was one other woman with me. The odd thing was, I had my briefcase, an over-the-shoulder bag, with my Palm Pilot, calculator, papers, and things in it, and I was debating whether or not to carry it down. I must have been in some kind of adrenaline shock.

"I knew that I was hurt. But I was so focused on getting down, finding an ambulance. All I could think about was *Get downstairs. Find an ambulance.* It was a very calm, focused feeling. So I found the fire exit and I started downstairs. I was shouting at people, asking them to step to the side because I needed an ambulance. People mostly were very kind. We were all in the same boat. Some people reacted a little annoyed, but then they'd look at me and their jaw would drop and they'd move over to give me room. I must have looked pretty bad. I didn't think about it. Floor after floor I walked. At some point I run into an EMS person coming up, and he just turns around and goes down with me. He did my shouting for me, which was a real relief, because as it turned out, I had taken a lot of flame and hydrocarbons into my lungs. Also, I ended up with calcium deposits in both my elbows and in my knees, from all the trauma.

"When we finally made it down, we walked through the lobby and out to the street. All the ambulances we saw were already filled. Finally, on Church Street, we found one that could take me, and they drove me straight to the burn center. When we got there, someone told me that to help me breathe better they were going to have to intubate me.

"I said go ahead, do what you have to do. That's the last thing I remember for a very long time. I didn't wake up until sometime right before Halloween. I was in my own little world. Neither my wife, Karen, nor the doctors and nurses would tell me what had happened. All she said was, 'There was a fire in the building. You were burned; you're going to be okay.' One day, maybe a week later, she came in and I said to her, 'Tell me what happened on September 11.'

"'A plane hit the building,' she said.

"I asked was it a terrorist attack. She said yes. I asked how many people had died, and she said around five thousand. I started naming names.

"The astonishing thing is Karen told me there were moments I was conscious before that, and I had no memory of them. She told me the things I said were, 'Pray for Howard,' and 'We have to warn them,'" and 'How did I not suffocate,' which tells how I must have been feeling.

"Howard visited me shortly after I was admitted to the hospital. He said, 'Harry, if you recognize my voice, raise your hand,' and I put my hand right up. Later, when I spoke to Karen, she told me I was still on Cantor's payroll. I can't say enough about how much that meant to me."

"It took a whole month before I could even call the families of my friends. I'd pick up the phone, then couldn't think of what to say. I worried that when we talked they'd think *Why you? Why were you and Karen the lucky ones?* I realize how lucky I was. A few seconds earlier and I would have been above the fire line and unable to escape. And even though I knew they'd never ask me those questions, it was impossible to ignore the thought process. Finally I did start calling and I'm glad I did. I feel better about calling them. Even now I still feel a terrible sense of loss. We had an exceptional legal department, top-notch minds and good people. I would get up in the morning and look forward to going to work. At Cantor I worked with people I could rely on, and it made all the difference. And that's not something everyone can say."

*I*T WAS THE LAST WEEK *of February. 1993. I was president of the company, but the people weren't mine. They were people brought in when Jim Avena was president. Same CFO, same general counsel. I didn't change them. At the end of a vacation with Allison, I went to Florida to play in a celebrity pro-am golf tournament, at the Don Shula resort. Dan Marino was in our foursome. Allison had her picture taken with O.J.*

We were rained out on the seventeenth hole and I went inside and tried to call the office. I couldn't get through. And then someone said there's been an explosion at the Trade Center. The TV was on in the clubhouse and you could see people covered in soot. And they were all our guys. Cantor people were being interviewed, talking about fighting their way downstairs through the smoke. We flew back home.

The difference in '93 was that none of our people died. It wasn't a human disaster so much as it was a business crisis. The way people responded, or in many cases didn't respond, was very significant—and changed the way I viewed work and the company from there on in.

We had to find a place where we could work and do it immediately. Wall Street certainly wasn't going to wait for us to get up and running again. This was a major undertaking. That Sunday, I went to the Trade Center. Our floors were smoky, smelly, dirty, and we'd have to replace some of the computers. Structurally everything seemed fine, but we couldn't get back in the building for a month.

We had to rebuild from scratch. I made a pact with one of the executives. I said, "I'm going to push as hard as I can to get front-office trading

*open, you worry about the back-office settlements. But if either one isn't
ready we won't open."*

*We built our government securities business over that weekend. Dow
Jones, which owned Telerate then, gave us a room at their offices, and we
had another floor at Salomon Brothers. Our back office worked out of
Chemical Bank. I slept on the computer room floor at Dow Jones. I was
talking to the phone company around the clock, trying to figure out how
to integrate everything.*

*There are compassionate people on Wall Street. We've certainly seen
that recently, but if there's an opportunity to grab market share, our competitors will do it. I knew this, which is why I wanted to open right away.*

*When I met with the executives, to decide when to open, it immedi-
ately became clear how at odds we were. I'd been president for two years,
but to these guys I was still an outsider. They worked for themselves, and
maybe they thought they worked for Bernie, but they didn't work for me.*

*Monday, U.S. Treasury trading volume was down eighty percent be-
cause we were closed. Tuesday it was down only sixty-five percent. That
meant the world's banks were figuring out ways to trade without using us.
I knew right then we had to open or we'd never get their business back.*

*Tuesday there's a coup attempt. Three of our top executives—Joe Mal-
vasio, Harry Needleman, and Bob Graustein—make a play to oust me.
Malvasio and Needleman are Avena's men. Graustein had recently joined
as chief administrative officer.*

*The three of them called Bernie and told him, "Howard's out of con-
trol. He's trying to force the company to open before it's ready." They said,
"Bernie, the company can't open. Howard's crazy. It's too risky. The regulators will shut us down. We're not in capital compliance. Howard's demanding that we open and we think you should suspend him."*

*Bernie called me and told me what they said. The first thing I did was
to lose my cool, which wasn't a smart move on my part, since they were
saying I was out of control.*

*Bernie brought us together that afternoon, to talk about what had
happened. He'd decided that Malvasio and Rod Fisher, who ran our data
company in Westchester, and I would run the company jointly until
Bernie could figure out a plan for the long haul.*

I talked with Rod Fisher, who had been my friend and was influential

in my decision to join the company. I was sure he'd back me; he would un-
derstand that I had acted in the best interests of the company. There was
no reason why I shouldn't continue running the company as I had been
doing. Instead, he suggested that perhaps he and I should run the com-
pany together.

I remember telling Allison it was the worst business day of my life.
Someone I'd known since I was a kid, who'd helped me get the job in the
first place, used this as an opportunity to promote himself. He wasn't
throwing me out, he was saying—You and me, we'll be co-equals.

I told him if that was the case, I wouldn't be sticking around. I felt he
should have supported me, rather than just think of himself.

Fisher called me the next morning and said, "I spoke to Bernie last
night and he's picked you." He pledged his allegiance. Bernie called me
and asked me what I thought.

I said if we don't open by Friday, I think we're done. If we're closed an-
other week, no one's going to remember us when we reopen. We're the
bond storefront on Wall Street. If they see the storefront is closed, they're
going to find another store. They'll work around us.

He asked me, "What about the capital compliance issues?"

I said, "Bernie, the Trade Center was hit, not our bank vault." At the
time we had 125 million in capital, and after the attack we still had the
same 125 million. Our books and records were fine.

I just defeated their arguments with simple logic. They were specious
arguments. He said, "Okay it's your show. We'll open."

We opened that Thursday, six days after the terrorist bombing, and for
the most part there were no snags. It was the right move, and Bernie and
everyone else knew it.

FRIDAY, OCTOBER 26

In the evening we head down to see LaChanze Gooding and her new baby at Saint Vincent's Hospital. There's a copy of the *New York Post* next to me with an article on how Cantor plans to pay out more than 45 million dollars in bonuses, along with quarterly distributions from the firm's profits. At the end of the article the reporter writes:

> Unlike other devastated firms, Lutnick stopped paychecks for deceased employees on Sept. 15—leaving grieving families high and dry.
>
> Moreover, Lutnick's tear-stained promises made in the wake of the tragedy sparked scrutiny as complaints arose that the chief executive— who lost his brother in the attacks—was reneging on his promises to take care of "the Cantor family."

"What does *'tear-stained'* mean?" Howard asks.

He begins calling wives to see if they understand the plan.

"Hi, Claudia. How ya doin? . . . Yeah . . . A little day by day."

After talking about the bonuses and health care, he answers a question she has about Bill O'Reilly:

"O'Reilly said, 'Looks like Lutnick finally did the right thing. We roughed him up enough.' How ridiculous is that. Haven't I been roughed up enough?" He tells her about Gary. "Smoke inhalation. You know why I think that? Because I was standing outside and the smoke almost killed me." After a pause, he says, "You're not ready yet. It's too raw, but you'll get there. Give it time." He tells her how Edie took care of Gary, how they all took care of one another. He's still talking as we get out of the car and walk into Saint Vincent's.

When we pass through the revolving door Howard's cell signal fades. "Can't end a conversation like that," he says. He goes outside and calls her back.

LaChanze's hospital room is softly lit. Inside are heart-shaped helium balloons announcing IT'S A GIRL! and CONGRATULATIONS. "Howard!" LaChanze says.

"Hi, Sweetie," he says. "You look fantastic."

Zaya, the baby, is named for Calvin's great-grandfather Jozaia. "It's biblical," LaChanze said. "It's a real name too. It's Nigerian." Zaya sleeps in LaChanze's mother's arms. LaChanze's father, Walter, sits on the other side of the room, along with two friends. Howard leans against the air vents by the window. Here he is no longer the boss, the man everyone's been reading about and has seen interviewed on television. LaChanze tells him about the birth, her second C-section. "It wasn't bad at all," she says.

We talk about Calvin some, then about the wives.

LaChanze's father tells me, "When I saw the plane hit I thought, *Calvin works in the World Trade Center.* But they'd been in Martha's Vineyard, so I kept hoping they were still there. I called LaChanze but couldn't get through. Later I found out he was at work."

Across the room they are talking about Lynda Fiore and her desire to have her moment on television.

"That's it. That's it exactly," LaChanze says. "I want to go on those shows. I'd tell 'em, 'First off, Howard didn't *fly the plane.* Because that's how they're acting. Secondly, he lost seven hundred people who worked for him.'"

Howard smiles, punches the air like a boxer. "We gotta get you out there."

He tells her about a dinner he and Allison had recently and how the people at a neighboring table stopped their conversations so they could eavesdrop on them.

"I see people out at dinner walking around having a good time, and it's like they're back to their lives now," Howard says.

"I think of that *every* day. Every time I see a father put his child in a stroller. Whenever people ask me where Calvin worked and I tell them Cantor, they just have this look. They know right away what happened."

On the drive back uptown, Howard makes more phone calls. It's become an obsession with him, and it's taking a toll on him. He holds his stomach. He's got terrible heartburn. His appetite is down.

"Hi," he says to the woman on the line. "This is Howard Lutnick from Cantor Fitzgerald calling. How's the baby? . . . Thank you, you're very kind."

SATURDAY, NOVEMBER 10

Each of the towers of the World Trade Center was like a midsized town. They had their own zip codes. There was a security force, shops, restaurants, medical facilities. Fifty thousand people worked there, decorated their cubicles or offices with pictures of their friends and family. A book I'm reading about skyscrapers has a small section of statistics that gives an idea of the mass of these things: 43,000 windows; 600,000 square feet of glass; 200,000 tons of structural steel; 6 acres of marble; 40,000 doorknobs; 200 elevators; 1,200 restrooms; 10 million square feet of office space. Each floor was an entire acre.

Howard and I walk down Lexington Avenue and stop at a bookstore. He wants to buy a book on old French châteaus for Allison.

On the front table, staring up at him, is Bill O'Reilly's face. Howard smiles and picks up a copy. He's considering buying it. He's curious about how they've packaged O'Reilly and what he might have to say. But at the counter he can't bring himself to plunk down the cash.

"I don't like him," he tells the clerk. "He's not a *nice* person. He hasn't been nice to me."

The clerk is puzzled. Howard is just one of a hundred customers.

"Hasn't been nice to you personally?"

"Right." Howard's testing his notoriety. He doesn't explain. He puts the book back and we walk out. It's odd to see him this way, not in the office, not in his car or in his house. Out in the world where he still fits in, somewhat.

An hour later, Stephen Merkel and I are in the park near his house on Jane Street. The day is oddly warm, in the seventies. People are out in shirtsleeves and bright colors in November. The weather has been all wrong this fall—sunny, muggy even, and it makes one feel as though time has stood still since September 11, that the climate makers too have been knocked off course.

The playground is packed, as are the sidewalks of Greenwich Village, with children and couples arm in arm. The mood has lightened some, but of course you have only to walk a block and look downtown to become somber all over again.

Earlier in the week, Merkel went down to the site and found it far worse, far more raw, than he'd expected.

The fires, two months later, are still burning. Workers in man-baskets sift through millions of tons of debris. Construction teams wearing masks and goggles move carefully and swiftly through the wreckage, forty-ton steel columns splayed about like the ruins they are.

"It was like looking at an unburied corpse," he says.

It has been a difficult week, even by the standards of late. On Thursday there were two bomb scares at the Cantor offices at the UBS Warburg building. Rumors had it the bomb threat was issued in response to Warburg's freezing of al-Qaeda funds the day before. Or it may have been triggered by Salman Rushdie's recent op-ed piece in the *New York Times* titled "Yes, This Is About Islam." Random House, Rushdie's publisher, has offices in the building.

Friday brought two more bomb threats. The calls will continue for the next month and a half. "It's a terrible way to have to work," Merkel says.

Later we stop for food at a diner around the corner from the playground. Merkel's son, Gabriel, sits in his high chair, eating what his father feeds him. When Gabriel nods off for a while, Merkel talks about the first weeks.

"We were a crisis within a crisis within a crisis. Because we were in a city that was in a crisis, that was in a country that was stunned. We were several layers into it. When you walked around the city, you saw the crisis and it was remarkable. The fact that the country had been attacked, the fact that the city was frozen—these were endless logistics to work out. What other people found difficult to absorb we had to accommodate instantly. There were decisions to make. You either deal with it or you shut down. I didn't sleep well for a while. The first time I cried was when I woke up on Wednesday. On Tuesday I had to speak with the families and so I tried to stay calm. But the next morning, and for several mornings after, it would all just overwhelm me.

"When Howard and I spoke with Joe Noviello and Tom Trillo, I think there was a feeling we might not be able to put it back together. It was baffling that the bond market was rushing to open again.

"The Bank of New York had terrible problems with their clearing operations. BrokerTec was openly trying to steal our business after so many of our people died—that was opportunistic and cold-blooded."

He talks more about the business, but even more about the people he misses. His eyes look tired. "What haunts me was how close I was to being one of them. I can't shake it. All those people, I spent so much time with them, and I was so close to them, and I was just . . . *not there*, and they *were* there. That's what I can't get over.

"There were flames and there was glass and I ran and I thought I was going to die, but that isn't what bothers me. If it hadn't been a nice day, if I hadn't decided to walk, if I hadn't taken that particular route, or stopped to give someone directions, or if I'd taken a different elevator bank. I easily could have been in their circumstances."

THE ONE POSITIVE by-product of the battles with Iris Cantor was the bond the senior executives forged with one another, Jennifer Gardner tells me.

"That's when they really became family," she says.

Jennifer met Iris and Bernie in October of 1993, the same night she met Howard and Allison, at a lavish affair the firm threw at the Metropolitan Museum. Cantor had a reputation for extravagant client parties, she said.

"I met Doug there after work. We walked up the big steps and through the Egyptian gallery. I was introduced to Howard and Allison. It was the sort of over-the-top party you read about in the society pages. Howard was immediately warm. He teased me and paid attention when I spoke, which I liked. And when we left they had a car service take us home—I'll admit, it was nice. Iris was this incredibly glamorous woman with jewels as big as Christmas ornaments. Bernie couldn't have been more of a gentleman. Sweet, like your grandfather or a great uncle. And I know that's not who he was, that he'd been something of a curmudgeon, and a tyrant at times, but you couldn't tell to meet him in that context."

The battle for control of the firm is something she remembers vividly. "I always had the feeling with Iris that for all her charm and all her great stories, she was just moving chess pieces around. And then when Bernie died, she took an untenable position that she couldn't let go of. She painted herself into a corner. I think it had more to do with control than money. She watched how everyone ran around for Bernie, tended to him, and she wanted that to continue. She wanted 'yes people' around her."

The court battles, she says, were every bit as venomous as the newspapers reported them to be. A residual effect of the constant trips to Delaware, the late nights preparing their arguments, was that it brought her husband, Doug, Stephen Merkel, Stuart Fraser, and Howard closer together.

"It was a turning point for those guys. In a sense they were just kids before that, all of them under forty, and they'd just been through the fight of their lives. Bernie was gone now. Iris was gone. Howard could run the company the way he wanted."

But the battle left scars, and damaged their reputations, even with the court victory. It was there that the us-against-the-world philosophy was born. Howard was labeled litigious, and power hungry, but in the end he'd won, and a new chapter in his life could begin.

*I*T WAS BERNIE'S COMPANY. *He built it. His name was on the door. And I loved and respected him. He was the real thing. But sooner or later he was going to need a successor, and he knew it. Together Bernie and I had more than doubled the company's profits. Before then our earnings had been flat. I had a track record. So, there was me and there was Iris, his wife. Ultimately he decided that I would run the firm, and Iris would have two votes.*

I couldn't put debt on the company of more than twenty-five percent of the partners' capital, and number two, I couldn't sell the firm without her consent.

The first sign of problems was a night when I went over to Bernie's apartment. Iris and her lawyer were there, and they had a letter of resignation for me. I said, "What is this?"

Iris's lawyer said that while I now had the authority to run the partnership if something were to happen to Bernie, Iris wanted a standing letter of resignation from me so that she could take back control of the firm if she didn't like the way I was running it.

I looked at Bernie. "Is this what you want me to do? What's the point of the whole partnership agreement, then, if she can just throw me out? There's no reason for me to sign this."

Bernie told me, "I don't want you to sign it."

"Why are you doing this, then?"

"It's for Iris's protection."

I said, "It's not my job to protect Iris. If this is what you want, I'll do it. But I'm not going to do what anybody else wants."

And Bernie said, "I don't want you to do it." So I left without signing her letter.

Soon after that we ironed out the details of what would happen if Bernie died or became incapacitated, how it would work between Iris and me. Iris signed the agreement; we all signed, and signed it again each year until Bernie died.

When Bernie went on dialysis three days a week, he had an apartment in the Helmsley Building in New York Hospital. He had a big tube coming out of one arm and going into another. Basically all of his blood would come out, go through a filter, and go back in. On one of my visits, I brought Bernie a thirty-five-inch TV so he could see it better. Bernie's eyesight had deteriorated so severely during the second half of 1995—in part from retinal bleeding that occurred from his dialysis—that it had become hard for him even to read. His ability to comprehend business circumstances began to diminish as well.

It became clear to me when his secretary had sued him for sexual harassment and wrongful dismissal.

It made little sense to anyone who'd spent time with Bernie and who knew him. Bernie was an incredible gentleman and the last person who'd make inappropriate comments to anyone, especially a woman. But when it came time for his deposition, he was non compos mentis. He would admit to anything, from eating a chocolate cake at breakfast to the Lindbergh kidnapping.

He could not defend himself, and so Stephen Merkel came in and talked with me about whether Bernie should be determined incapacitated with regard to running the partnership.

I told him there was no reason to do anything now, to make any changes. Bernie was aware enough to know he wasn't well.

I still spent all my Saturdays with him. But it was different. Now it was simply the two of us spending time together. It was the beginning of his decline, and it was worsening quickly.

Allison and I went to his apartment on his birthday, December 17th, 1995, and while he looked good—Bernie had style in spades—he was having difficulty speaking, and often he just kept his head down during dinner. He could say hello. He knew who you were and could chat with you, but when you asked him questions, he'd get defensive and say, "I'm

*not going to tell you," or, "Don't be asking me questions like that. You
know the answer." And the question would be something no more trou-
bling than was it Tuesday or Thursday.*

*Just before Christmas he fell very ill—physically this time. Soon after
he was rushed back to the hospital. He lost consciousness when he got
there, and the doctors asked Iris whether she would want him to go on
life-support. He'd had a "Do Not Resuscitate" order in his living will, but
Iris decided he should go on life-support. I was there when she made the
decision, and I believe it came from her heart.*

*Still, it was a terrible thing to witness. The following morning, while
he was hooked up to a respirator, Iris told me that she wanted power of attorney over his affairs.*

*It's important to talk about this, because I want to make it clear what
the discussions were like then, what happened and why, because a lot has
been said about me—before and after September 11th—how I stole the
firm from my dying mentor, and I want people to understand that this al-
legation couldn't be further from the truth.*

*Iris asked me to get the necessary documents together so that she could
have Bernie declared incapacitated. The options were to make the decla-
ration temporary or permanent. She chose permanent and asked me to
get two doctors to do the proper tests and to sign the documents. I didn't
question her motivations. I called Bernie's lawyers in California, and I received two copies of the necessary certificates.*

*I gave them to Bernie's doctor, a kidney specialist at the Rogesin Insti-
tute, and his associate. They signed the document.*

*I then sent to Iris notification about the partnership agreement and
how it would work when Bernie could no longer run the company.*

*We had procedures in place in case anything ever happened to him.
The partnership agreement had a shield stipulating that if Bernie were
incapacitated, the control of the firm would pass over to me, and Iris
would have only her two votes. Otherwise, the company was not hers to
take over and operate.*

*Remember, the partners had put their life savings in the firm, and they
hardly wanted anyone's spouse to run the business, no matter how capable she may be.*

So Fraser, Fisher, and Phil Ginsberg signed a document that had one sentence in the middle of the page—"I hereby determine that B. Gerald Cantor is incapacitated."

It was a simple document—just one sentence.

I brought the doctors' signed certificates to Iris and I gave her a copy of the partnership incapacity language. I asked her to sign it. She wouldn't. She said she wasn't ready to turn the firm over to me. I asked her how was it that she had declared him permanently incapacitated with regard to his personal affairs but not for the company. This began the process that ended up bringing so much acrimony and negative publicity. Iris Cantor against the partners of Cantor Fitzgerald.

The relationship with Iris finally fell apart on leap year, February 29, 1996. Rod Fisher called and told me he'd changed his mind. He was changing his stance on the issue of whether Bernie Cantor was incapacitated. Essentially, he'd jumped sides. He was egging her on now, and everything was getting nasty.

Rather than fighting with her, we filed something called a declaratory judgment. We went down to the Delaware courts and said please resolve for us in a very quick fashion who runs the company—is it Iris Cantor or is it me?

What it came down to was this: If Bernie was incapacitated, then the agreement we'd made stood. If he wasn't incapacitated, then he ran the company and there was nothing to fight over.

April 7th, all the partners at Cantor Fitzgerald and I received a FedEx-ed letter from Iris and Bernie, stating that they were firing me and taking back the company.

I knew it was bogus for a couple of reasons. First of all, if Bernie was back to himself, he would never say "Iris and I are taking back the company." It was his firm, and he'd never use "Iris and I" with regard to company business. Secondly, Bernie had a very particular signature. It was like a declining mountain range. The first letter was a big peak and then it got smaller and smaller. When he was going blind, he would sign more vertically than horizontally, and couldn't get his name on the line because he could barely see. Here was a letter and his name is signed right on the line.

Whenever Bernie received a gift, a calendar, or a souvenir, and his secretary wrote the thank-you note, she'd sign for him. She would sign a big "B," and then the declining mountain range. That way Bernie knew whether he had signed a particular letter or if his secretary had sent it out without showing it to him. I realized immediately this wasn't the signature of the Bernie Cantor I knew.

Until then, I'd thought our problems, while large, were our own, that the world wouldn't care about the affairs of a private company. My wife and I were expecting our first child, my son Kyle, and so I was preoccupied with that as well. He was born at eight A.M., April 10th, and he was beautiful. About an hour later I told my wife, "I hate to do this to you but I have to go into the office."

I told her I had to because Iris tried to fire me over the weekend, and if I didn't go in, people might think I actually got fired. I said, "I'll walk around shaking everybody's hand." I wore a hat that said KYLE'S DAD. I could answer a lot of questions with my hat. I explained how ridiculous this move by Iris was. Then I went back up to see my baby boy.

That Friday I got a call from Diana Henriques from the New York Times. She said she'd been speaking with Iris and Iris's PR people for a week, and the story was going to be rough on me. I was going to be on the cover of the Times "Business" section on Sunday. I could speak to her or not—the story would run, anyway.

If I wanted to speak with her, I had until seven P.M. that Friday. So I figured I had nothing to lose. Iris and her PR team would have certainly gotten their digs in.

The piece on us in the New York Times Sunday edition of April 16th could not have been larger—my picture was two inches square, Iris's picture was two inches square, and Bernie's picture was six or seven inches. The article was on the cover and two whole pages inside.

Both of us could not have looked worse. We were all jerks, the article was saying. And maybe that was progress, because before the interview I was the only jerk in the writer's mind.

We resolved the trial quickly because I made Iris basically the same settlement offer I'd made before the lawsuit. At ten o'clock a videotape would have been played showing his medical exam, done by the head of cognitive neurology at Johns Hopkins. Bloomberg news had sued to have the videotape played in open court, in the interests of journalism. We had offered to show the judge the tape in private—"in camera" it was called—because we knew it would put to rest the notion that Bernie was able to run a company or make important decisions.

Iris signed the settlement agreement at 9:59.

That was the end of the case, but not of our feuding. Iris and I spoke a few times after that, and then she said we wouldn't be talking anymore. Bernie died July 3rd.

The night before his burial, Stuart called me at around midnight. Someone from Iris's camp had called from Los Angeles to say Bernie had died and was being buried the next day. Stuart said, "Why didn't you tell me earlier?" They had waited until the last commercial flight had left New York to tell him. They hadn't wanted him or me at the funeral.

He was very depressed about it. He was saying there was nothing we could do, and I said, "We have to go."

He asked me, "How?"

"Well, it's earlier there," I said. "We'll figure out a way to get there."

It was the middle of the night. I called around and found a plane we could charter. We stopped first in New Hampshire and picked up Phil Ginsberg, then in White Plains for Stuart and Elise. We picked up Stuart's mother, Enid, and father, Tom, in St. Louis and landed in the morning in L.A.

We knew where his mausoleum was. It was in the cemetery where Marilyn Monroe was buried. I was familiar with it because I'd gone with him the day he began building what he called "the little house." Bernie's mausoleum was next to Armand Hammer's.

We booked hotel rooms in Westwood. Stuart called Iris and told her we were there and we wanted to come. He was furious with her. He told her Bernie was his friend and she had no right to keep him from the funeral. He got so angry that he broke the phone. I called back and tried to negotiate a truce. The result was that Phil and I would not attend if she would let Stuart's family come—Stuart, Elise, Enid (Iris's sister), and Tom.

She agreed. She said, "If you don't come, I'll agree to let them attend." So Phil and I drove to the cemetery. They went in, and I stood at the gate.

The reason I stood there was so she couldn't make the point that I hadn't cared enough about Bernie to attend. I watched the procession going in. I didn't see many of his closest friends. They had not been informed.

After the cars had left, I went into the mausoleum and said good-bye. I loved Bernie and I had to be there for myself and for him.

For their daughter Casey's first-birthday party, Howard and Allison have hired a singer, a face-painter, and a man who makes balloon animals. When I arrive, the thirty or so guests are all singing childrens' tunes like "If You're Happy and You Know It." The kids have been made up to resemble vampires, lions, and fairy princesses. The mood is cheerful, relaxed; the parents are in faded blue jeans and thick sweaters, clothes they might wear to a football game at their alma mater. They begin shaking a huge multicolored parachute, sending dozens of blue, yellow, and red plastic balls into the air. Much thought and care has been put into the party by Allison. There's a need to do this right, especially now, when it would be so easy to spend a Sunday thinking too much, or reading another article in the Sunday newspaper about why the buildings collapsed.

The kids act like kids, and the parents find their mood raised. It's a difficult time to be a parent, because the kids know what happened on some levels and don't know on others. It's not only the children who lost parents who will be affected. Parents have described morbid cartoons their children have created about buildings falling down, or people jumping, or fires overtaking their homes.

A New York Board of Education study in the spring will find thousands of schoolchildren experiencing severe anxiety, chronic nightmares, and fear of public places months after the Trade Center attacks. And these are children outside the communities that were devastated.

And it hasn't only been the Trade Center collapsing; there have been the anthrax attacks, and the plane crashing in Rockaway, Queens. New York children have been acutely aware of death. Some problems have been harder to see—diminished attention spans, trouble sleeping, talking too much about the attacks, or not talking about them at all.

Howard is enjoying the fact that a day like this is still possible, that there's still a community left. I stand next to Charlotte Gardner as she watches her grandchildren. Two-year-old Julia Gardner is holding maracas at her side without knowing what to do with them. Charlotte makes shaking motions with her hands. Julia moves her own hands ever so slightly.

"Come on. Come on, Julia," Charlotte says. She points out her grandson Michael. "Can you see him? Can you see Douglas in that face?"

Charlotte wears a dark blue sweater and dark blue wool slacks. Her long white hair is tied back. She is a striking woman in her sixties. "This party is a good thing," she says. She keeps thinking she's getting better, and then something will set her back. She was reading the Sunday *Times* that morning and found herself scanning the article about how the buildings fell.

"I got a paragraph or two into it, and then I thought, *Whoa. I can't do this.* I had to set it down. I don't know what I was thinking. I can't read something like that."

When the singing stops, the balloon artist takes over. Howard drifts from conversation to conversation, putting his hand on friends' shoulders.

Someone says they heard about the Willow Bay *Pinnacle* piece, and he says, "It's coming on soon."

By now it would be hard to find a person associated with Cantor who hasn't been featured on television or in a magazine or newspaper. On the news one night is a child being born to a Cantor widow, and in the paper the next day is a feature on four brokers who loved to play basketball. The men are shown shirtless on an asphalt court. Then there are the more general stories about how everyone's grieving, or talking to their kids, or seeing psychiatrists, or taking antidepressants.

For Howard, the media has become a daily report card, which he allows too often to affect his spirits. Today, with the *Pinnacle* piece scheduled for six, he is as buoyant as he's been in a long while. It's his daughter's first birthday, he's surrounded by family and friends, and in two hours a television show will present his side of the story—without rounding up another critic from *Forbes* or another three angry family members.

"It's not bad," he tells me when I ask for the preview. "She lets me speak in full paragraphs."

Some of the parents and kids have left, but about twenty-five friends and family members remain. People settle onto the couches and onto chairs and the floor, as though we're watching the Academy Awards. An unusual way to spend an afternoon, really—throw a party for your daughter, and then watch a show about yourself on TV.

Downstairs, in Howard and Allison's bedroom, the TV is on.

"Before September 11 business was fun," Howard says on television.

The next image we see is of Tower One, in a huge cloud of black smoke, collapsing.

"No American company has ever seen such destruction," Willow Bay says. "And no CEO has ever had to live up to such a promise."

We see Howard crying on *Larry King*. Then we watch the plane, no more than a small speck, flying into the North Tower, footage shot by a French documentary filmmaker that many in the room haven't seen before. Howard winces. Edie and Stuart can't watch.

The *Pinnacle* music pipes in. "Howard Lutnick, CEO of Cantor Fitzgerald, was one of Wall Street's brightest young stars, a forty-year-old running a fifty-trillion-dollar-a-year trading empire."

There's footage of him on the trading floor in the World Trade Center in June, and then Tower One engulfed in smoke. Another shot shows the building crumbling, then dust-covered people running through the streets.

"In the days that followed [September 11], Howard Lutnick and his firm became symbols of the grotesque devastation of the worst terrorist attacks in U.S. history. Lutnick grieved publicly and watching his ordeal unfold on national television, a nation grieved with him."

The interviews of Howard done in June look as though they were shot ten years ago. There are no circles beneath his eyes. He is tanned and rested, confident. The Trade Center offices are shown in all their splendor.

"Fantastic," someone says, during the commercial break.

"He looks great, doesn't he?" his mother-in-law says.

When the *Pinnacle* piece resumes, Howard reflects on his decision to discontinue salaries. "I made decisions that were fundamental to the survival of the company, and I don't expect people to understand what it means to lose *every single person* who made revenues for you, who supports you, and helps you, but you know what—I made the decisions that allow me to sit here today, and say, *We're going to make money. We're going to deliver an unbelievable amount of support to these people.*"

He talks of the firm's reconfiguration, dropping some departments and keeping others, principally the equities and bond businesses. He says the choice was to "climb back up or to strap on skis and ski on down."

She asks the question he's been waiting for. "Will there be profits this year?"

"I say this to the families, that while it's a miracle—and I do believe it's a miracle—I expect Cantor Fitzgerald to be profitable in the fourth quarter of two thousand and *one*. That is, *this* quarter, and it's because the people who work for me are just incredible and our customers—insurance companies, pension funds, hedge funds, banks—they've been so supportive of us and helpful to us, that we will make a profit this quarter, and we will start making distributions to the families in January."

When the report is finished, the room reacts as though he just won a five-set tennis match. The phone is ringing with well-wishers, and his friends gather about him as they leave, telling him he was terrific.

"She did a good job," he says. "Thank God."

A few days after the party, we sit in the kitchen of Jennifer Gardner's house, eating bagels and drinking coffee. The children both know what happened, and they talk about it often, especially Michael. On the first day, she had told him there'd been an explosion at his father's office, and they couldn't find Daddy.

"Michael first thought that maybe he couldn't cross the street because the light wasn't changing. And then the second day he said, 'I think Daddy died.' And I said, 'I think you're right.' In the morning, I'd take him on his bicycle and he'd ride around Tavern on the Green parking lot. He'd ride a little and then stop and talk, ride some more and then stop and talk. He understood immediately that his father was gone. But he was very clear that he'd tried to get out. He asked a lot of questions, like, 'Was he running?' Or, 'If he was stronger, could he have gotten out?'"

She's smiling. "Michael said, 'I'm strong. I could have gotten out.' I said, 'You know your daddy's the strongest person we know. You know that all he wanted to do was come home. He tried really hard and we're proud of him.' And now Michael says stuff like that. 'He tried really hard, we're proud of him,' and 'He didn't have enough time.' And then he'll say airplanes can't hit this building, and we're on the second floor, anyway. He needs *facts*. He's a very smart kid. 'There was a bad man on the plane,' he says. 'He did it on purpose. It wasn't an accident,' he told his class. 'Bad guys died too.' We read the 'Nation Challenged' section of the *Times* together. He knows all the companies that lost people— AON, Marsh and McLennan. I think it helps. It makes him feel like he's managing it. At school the other day they had the 'Nation Challenged' section out. It showed a billboard hanging over the turnpike with all the names. Michael pointed to Doug's name and said, 'There's my daddy,' and proceeded to tell the class what happened. One kid said, 'Your daddy didn't die.' Michael said, 'Yes he did. There was a big fire at the building. It was a very tall building. Two planes hit it. They didn't have enough time to get out. They tried really hard. I'm very proud of my daddy.'

IT IS AROUND Maryann Burns's desk where all the best dirt gets slung. People gather, peer at a newspaper, dissect their weekends. All this happens on their way into Howard's office.

Maryann grew up in Bayside, Queens, the daughter of an accountant and a nurse. She is a person who develops close personal relationships, banters with the guys like a sister. She is focused, efficient at her job, but there have been days since the 11th when it's all she can do to rise from bed in the morning. She thinks often of her friends Jody Nicholo and Debbie Bellows, who sat next to her. She's had dreams of finding Debbie's remains in the Trade Center rubble. And then she thinks of Gregg.

After years of unsatisfying dates, of being single, Maryann had finally met someone—a young trader named Gregg Reidy. And they had been falling in love, or at least Maryann had hoped they were.

They'd become friends in the late spring of 2001—and then Maryann had to leave for the Cantor office in London, where Howard works in the summers. She'd e-mailed Gregg and they spoke on the phone regularly. By midsummer they were on the phone first thing in the morning and right before she went to bed.

She collected items from shops and hotels as gifts to bring him. He sent her a compass engraved with the words "SO YOU CAN FIND YOUR WAY HOME. LOVE, GREGG." She is uncomfortable telling these stories—in part because love stories all sound the same and rarely do their participants justice, and also because it was only starting. It's as though she still doesn't want to jinx it—to place too much on it too soon.

What gets her most is that they never got to test it—to see if they could fight and work it out, negotiate a bathroom, vacation together.

Just before the attacks, Gregg Reidy and Maryann spent their first weekend together. The phone calls were a prelude to something more significant.

They spoke late on the night of the 10th, talked in soft voices as though the weekend hadn't ended and they were still in the same room. And when she closed her eyes, Maryann felt happy and excited about her future.

At his funeral she wasn't sure if his family knew who she was. They hadn't made it to the meeting-the-parents stage yet. But his father said he knew all about her. He'd seen Gregg up at daybreak on the family vacation. He'd just had his wake-up call from Maryann in England.

Howard is starting to get into a rhythm with the town meetings, and I suspect that he needs them more than he knows. The issues of the second round are bonuses and the Victim Compensation Fund.

As the crowd gathers, Diny tells me that her cell phone bills are in the thousands. Many of the family members call just to talk. Off to the side of the room is the same setup of grapes and cheeses, crackers, cookies.

"Some people haven't picked up their bonus checks yet," Howard says. "If you haven't got your bonus, it is ready and waiting for you. We really want you to have it. So, please call and get it. If you need help with the documents and the paperwork, we have lawyers to help you."

There are other issues. "I have had at least ten families tell me that their loved ones were supposed to receive compensation of a million dollars. Ten, okay? And those ten, their loved ones had never earned a million dollars before. One of them had worked in the firm—I looked this up before—for seven years and had never made more than two hundred fifty thousand dollars and never made less than two hundred twenty-five thousand dollars. And this year the division he was in had a gross revenue of only seven hundred fifty thousand dollars. Does it seem that he should be making a million?"

He stops for a moment and lets those words stand. "It was a small division, a couple of guys. So, I understand people have a need now to talk it over with me, and we'll make it work correctly. The company doesn't have a million dollars to give to everybody. But we absolutely want to get it right. For every single family."

He tells them about the Victim Compensation Fund, and explains that it works as a bailout for the airlines—that if a family agrees to never sue anybody in the U.S. for the wrongful death of their loved ones, the government is supposed to pay them an amount commensurate with what their loved one would have made over the rest of his or her working life.

"This is very, very, very serious stuff. We have twenty-five-year-olds, thirty-five-year-olds, forty- and forty-five-year-olds. These people had a lot of work time left."

He describes how the firm proposes to argue the Cantor families' case with the Department of Justice. "You may think the reason why your loved ones worked at Cantor Fitzgerald is because they liked being part of a team that was *winning*, that was *growing*, and you'd be right. It was a great place for people to work, a great place to make money, a great place to build a career. Now the government is saying it's going to set aside a fund for your families. You can bet I'll be all over that fund to make sure the money gets to each of you. If we're together on this our voice will be so loud, it will be thunder.

"But if we split up, and I'm just looking out for me and you're just looking out for you, they will have divided and conquered. This is what's happened so often in the past, which is why the Red Cross has never given out money before. The first time the Red Cross gave money directly to victims' families was during the first two weeks after the attacks, and that's because we at Cantor Fitzgerald spoke to them, and when we did our voice was thunderous. Then, as a lot of you know, some families started making *comments*, and people started thinking we weren't together on this, and so my ability to get money from the United Way was limited. I am most effective when I am *working for you*. Let me work for you, and I'll make this *fund* work for you. I'll go to the Justice Department, the United Way, the Red Cross, and make them do what is right."

A woman stands up. "What does 'together' mean?"

"It means, as one—not apart."

"How can six hundred fifty-eight families all different from one another, different needs, problems, all be as one?"

"Right now, to the people watching us, it seems as if Cantor Fitzgerald is fragmented into twelve or thirteen or fourteen separate sections. So when I talk to them, they're wondering, *What section do you represent? How many people do you really have behind you?* What we need them to know is that we're united in our purpose and that we share similar concerns and common goals. We're together on this."

He tells them Cantor will be preparing a legal brief on their behalf and that while they each need to hire a lawyer, they shouldn't sign anything yet. "For now, keep your pens in your pockets." After the meeting is over, a group of twenty or so linger, exchanging telephone numbers and e-mail addresses. They have formed a community, and for many these last weeks represent a time of greater involvement with the firm than they'd ever had before.

In the second week of December, the first 9/11 widow commits suicide, the cause of death is a self-inflicted gunshot wound at her home in East Stroudsburg, Pennsylvania. Her husband had been a broker at Euro Brokers Inc. in Tower Two. While it isn't another Cantor victim, the story hits hard within the community of Cantor survivors and family members.

The days are getting shorter and the cold weather is kicking in. A newspaper article details deficiencies in the fireproofing of the buildings. A Gambino crime family member ran the company that applied the fireproofing, the article said. The man, Louis DiBono, was gunned down in 1990 by John Gotti.

No one wants to examine, or even hear, the ways this might have been prevented. What haunts Howard these days is that in 1993 someone tried to kill everyone in the World Trade Center. They killed six.

If he hadn't been on vacation in 1993, if he'd had to walk down those stairs holding a shirt over his face, breathing smoke like everyone else, he might have pushed Bernie to move Cantor's offices to a different part of the city.

In the last month there have been bomb threats each day, twice a day. And though the Cantor staff has stopped reacting to them, they are a reminder of how unsafe their world still is. It is not a peaceful, contemplative time, and while things to some extent have slowed down, they haven't really gotten easier. The outlook for the firm is improving. Cantor will make a profit for the fourth quarter and will soon be able to begin payments to the families. Howard will be able to follow through on all the promises he made in September and October, and it's hard for him not to want to shove that fact in the face of his detractors.

But he doesn't have the energy for that. Days after Thanksgiving, he finished his condolence letters, having worked every night. He'd first decided on a letter written by someone else, but one he'd edited and approved. Then he'd written his own that was to be sent to the families. In both instances, he'd balked at mailing them because they just "looked wrong." So he started handwriting each of more than a thousand messages. At the height of the letter-writing period, he traveled to Chicago with Edie to take Gary's place at the wedding of his brother's best friend, Patrick Troy. He wrote letters on the plane out and between the wedding itself and the reception. On the plane back he wrote more. It became a source of pride for him, and a weight that by his own care and labor he removed from his shoulders.

A ROUND THIS TIME, a missive is sent around to the Cantor equities personnel from Bill Rice in the L.A. office.

> I was in New York and Boston last week where I had a chance to spend time talking with many people at the firm, veterans and new additions. Each of those people are very different in their viewpoints and backgrounds, yet all of them, I notice, linked by a common commitment: To honor our lost loved ones and friends by pulling together to rebuild Cantor Fitzgerald to a level beyond its stature previous to September 11th. We must do so to ensure ample care and support for their surviving families. The spirits and memories of the 658 members of our family must live on each day through our words, thoughts, and deeds. Every single one of you reading this missive carries a burden by being here—a responsibility no longer only to your family at home, but also

to literally thousands of others who depend on your efforts. It is a noble effort. It is a far, far better reason to do what we do. It is, quite simply, the right thing.

Each of you is about to embark upon a difficult journey, but one of which I am certain you will be proud.

It is incumbent on each of us to practice and teach the faith of Cantor Fitzgerald in its purest form to the new people. This is a religion of sorts. The effort we make now will magnify the benefit exponentially just one or two years from now. If we choose to ignore our responsibility, we will find ourselves with a menacing disease that would be very difficult to remedy.

There are two main components to this mantra:

1. Embrace the speaker system, for it is our lifeblood. Use it to negotiate, place orders and indications, and provide information on anything over 10K shares. Being religious about this eliminates errors, politics, and favoritism.

2. Share information. Each individual must contribute something to the system every day. If you only take from the well but do not give something back you do not belong in this family. Imagine if no one contributed but intended to only take from the system. The business would die and so would all of us. Ask yourself each day if you have thrown some fertilizer back upon the fields.

The new people at CF&CO must come to understand and participate in this creed, but can only learn to do so by the penchant of the firm's veterans to lead them by example. We are counting upon all of you to make a difference, and by doing so we are sure you will improve your own business and enrich how you feel about working here. Great things are about to happen at this firm—believe me when I say that. Godspeed, and do good work.

F OR A WHILE," Frank Walczak says, "I just wandered around in a cloud. The emotions came from so many places I didn't know how to handle them."

This is how nearly everyone will describe the fall of 2001.

"There's no playbook for this kind of thing. Sometimes I'd find myself getting short with my children and with my wife over nothing. My wife and I would argue and then we'd think, *What are we doing?* I think it's that I never worked through this that's doing this to me.

"I was just trying to keep moving—keep busy—and try to see what I could do to help the other families in our area. My wife was calling other wives, helping with their kids. There's so much you need to do, but you just can't get started. You take a step and get halted, as though you're paralyzed. At nighttime, we were bringing baskets of food to different people, to different houses. It made us feel like we were helping. And that's what I needed. I needed to do that. There was such a loss there, and I really didn't recognize it at first. I had blinders on. And after a while, when it all quiets down, it really starts to sink in. Your emotions start to well and then flare up. You start to reevaluate your life—what's important, what's not. I used to think always about *making the money, making the money, making the money.* Now it's, *Hey, you need money to pay the bills, but that's not what it's about.*

"Workwise, my group was gone, and I just wanted to help where I could. I wanted to work, to *do something.* I started driving three hours in the morning and three hours at night, commuting up to the Connecticut office, when they reopened the following Monday. Whoever was alive from New York equities was there, and they already had an existing office. So I just sat down at a desk and said: 'What do you want me to do?' And they gave me a list of phone numbers and orders to call in, told me who to talk to and what to say. Maybe the third day, Phil comes over and says, 'Who are you?' And I tell him I used to work on 105 doing FX forwards. 'I didn't know where to go. I wasn't in that day,' I say.

"And Phil says, 'Okay, I'll talk to you when I get a minute. Right now, just keep doing whatever you're doing.'

"Over the next days there was so much business coming in we couldn't keep up. I thought we were going to have to turn some of it away. It was too much. But so many customers knew what had happened to us and they wanted to help. Everybody was working long hours, and lots of us had crazy commutes."

Frank stayed with Marber's equity team. FX forwards, like the majority of Cantor's voice brokerage businesses, was shut down for good after the attacks.

"It would have been very hard in lots of ways to rebuild," Frank says. "A change is as good as rest sometimes. I think the guys when they look down at me and see where I'm working, they're happy about it. But yeah, I miss them. We spent more time together than we did with our families. I have friends in other parts of the company so I mourn the company as a whole, but our desk . . . I think of them first."

RECOVERY

MONDAY, DECEMBER 17, 11:00 A.M.

Howard sits alone at a table in a conference room at the company's interim offices at 299 Park Avenue. His image is projected onto the top right corner of the screen in front of him. An assistant works the controls and members of the Cantor Fitzgerald London office appear on the television monitor. (In 1995 Cantor opened offices at One America Square near the Tower of London. Howard has spent his last seven summers working there.) People sit in rows facing us. Their movements are choppy and slightly liquid, like the nightly news reports broadcast from Afghanistan.

"I would have thought we'd have a bigger crowd," Howard says. "Is that Lee who just came in the back?"

His voice then echoes back to us from the London conference room.

"Yes, it is," Lee says.

Howard begins with the partnership distribution numbers, and reports that Cantor will make a substantial fourth-quarter profit. This method of communication takes some getting used to. Howard says something slightly funny, there's a ten-second delay before the laughter bounces back. He takes them through the plan, reassuring them along the way that the company remains strong—their share of Cantor's profits will not radically change. This is the other side of the story— whatever is paid out to the families from Cantor's bottom line will come from the paychecks of the surviving partners. The faces all stare ahead. One man leaves the room briefly and then returns.

Howard says he's proud of them, that they've done an extraordinary job seeing the company through one of the worst business tragedies in history. "The London office has covered itself in glory," he says. "All of you have done an incredible job of keeping us going . . . You're first-class people and I just want you to know that we in America love you for it." He talks then about the divisions they've closed, emphasizing at the same time that the two powerhouse businesses, equities and U.S. governments, are still going strong. He tells them that eSpeed's stock has risen to levels above September 10 and that the partnership is secure.

He pauses, wipes his glasses, and puts them back on. "It's not that we're going to survive. Survival was from Tuesday, September 11, to Tuesday, September 18. We're not about surviving anymore—we're about succeeding." He talks about BrokerTec and Icap, and how they tried to force Cantor out of business.

"Some of our competitors are not good people."

Then, referring to the negative media coverage, he says, "You shouldn't let someone else who doesn't wish us well influence your view of what the company is about. We're taking care of these families." It's hard to tell if the people in the London office are taking all this in. There's silence on the other end.

"I'm very, very proud to be a part of Cantor Fitzgerald and eSpeed, and I think each and every one of you should wear it as a badge of honor."

He ends by saying, "We're going to do the right thing. But more than that, it's going to be the *Cantor Fitzgerald* thing, and it will be legend—the most a company's done for those they lost, and loved."

The London personnel applaud at the end. Then they're blipped off the screen and Howard is alone in the room.

T HAT EVENING, Howard and I along with Stephen Merkel, Kent Karosen, and Stuart Fraser ride up to the New York partnership meeting at the Hudson Hotel. In previous years the meetings were held on the 107th floor of the Trade Center. They were social events, as well as opportunities for people to talk about the firm and where it was headed.

There were cocktails and jumbo shrimp. Howard would end meetings by asking people to stay, have a drink, talk to someone you don't know. He'd introduce colleagues to one another, encourage camaraderie.

On 58th Street, he realizes he's late, and he and Stuart step outside ahead of the rest of us and start running toward the hotel. It's not something I've seen Howard do—run to get anywhere—but he wants the meeting to go well, to be able to set the tone, and so he doesn't want to be late.

It's drizzling out as we make our way into the darkly lit, stylized hotel and take the elevator to the meeting room on the third floor. When we get there, we see Howard and Stuart are alone. It's now that it hits Howard—170 of his partners, the majority of them friends of his—are dead.

It's not that he didn't know it, and it's not that he doesn't think about these things every hour of every day—it's just that for some reason he was expecting a packed room. They'd even ordered liquor and hors d'oeuvres for fifty. Soon seven or eight people trickle in, but no more than fifteen eventually show up.

He begins talking to the partners in the room and others listening on the phone. He does his best but he's clearly shaken up.

7:30 P.M.

After the partnership meeting we head down to the Marriott Hotel in Times Square, where Howard will talk with Kenneth Feinberg, Special Master of the Victim Compensation Fund, the government program Howard's been telling the families about.

On the way into the meeting, Feinberg tells us about his day with Hillary Clinton, Rudy Giuliani, and a group of family members of the firefighters. "That was a real mess, really rough," he said. The firefighter's wives, sixty of them or so, were complaining about the likeli-

hood that pensions and life insurance would be taken out of their possible settlements.

Feinberg, a fifty-six-year-old former aide to Ted Kennedy, speaks
with the senator's strong Massachusetts accent. Before becoming the
Special Master (one of the family members will refer mistakenly to
him as the Grand Master) he mediated disputes over agent orange, and
the Dalkon Shield birth control device. "Have you run any numbers as
to the average income of Cantor employees?" he asks.

Howard says, "Two-thirds made less than two hundred and fifty
thousand dollars, but it was a young company. Young with rapidly in-
creasing earning potential."

"But it's clear from what you say it's not a place where most people
were making millions. Because you know that Cantor Fitzgerald gets
sited regularly as being a place which skews way high—across the
board multimillionaires," Feinberg says.

Once the briefing is done, Feinberg will address a group of family
members, somewhere in the neighborhood of three hundred, he expects.

When we step into the ballroom, there are easily fourteen hundred
people there. It's the most staggering sight I've seen in these months,
and to contrast it with the empty partners meeting is to understand a
great deal about what's happened.

Here is where the life is, in the remaining family members. It's at
times like this that I comprehend within Howard both his sadness and
tremendous resilience. He views the chance to speak to these groups as
a gift he's been granted, an opportunity to fill some of the empty
spaces in his world.

Feinberg has arrived from a series of meetings of no more than one
hundred family members. He'd expected this one to be somewhat
larger, but it is clear from his expression that he hadn't anticipated this.
"Holy shit," he says.

After Feinberg's opening remarks, a young blond woman stands up.
"Excuse me, Mr. Feinberg. I have a very general question, and then a
more specific question. I would like specifically for myself to know
how you're going to determine my husband's retirement age. We've all

heard things, that traders and people in the financial industry retire at earlier ages than people in other industries. Since when did that become a statistic in this case? My husband did not have the option to retire. That was taken away from him. And believe me, I think most of the people in this room think that our government failed us.

"Okay, so let's assume then that my husband would retire at sixty-two. He makes three hundred thousand dollars a year from age thirty-three, and let's say one hundred thousand dollars in life insurance, what might my economic recovery be? Is there a cap?"

"How many kids?"

"Three." The woman says.

"I want this to be clear: There is no cap. *No cap.* Your award would be in the multimillions. I don't know what the exact amount would be. We haven't decided that, but that sounds like a very high award. And *certainly* one hundred thousand dollars in life insurance would be a rather minor offset to any multimillion award."

"I lost my wife and she was seven months pregnant. How would you handle someone who is pregnant, or a case like this?" a man among the group asks.

Feinberg looks stricken, chastened.

"I don't know. I mean, you're saying do you have more than one claim, because of the pregnancy?"

"Would you consider that a child—"

"The question is, you lost your wife who is pregnant, so do you really have two claims? One for the wife and one for the fetus. I should be thinking about something like that. That's a good question. I don't have an answer for you yet."

The conversation is both theoretical and practical, because Feinberg holds sway over the federal purse strings, but the issues are so abstract: the idea of different dollar amounts for varying degrees of pain, and the notion that the families will be bringing themselves before a judge essentially to argue the economic worth of their daughter or husband. They are not as excited by Feinberg's plan as he anticipated, but instead are angry at all the bureaucracy and the lack of a clear-cut formula. He has already gone on record saying that those who opt out

of the plan will have trouble resolving the cases to their satisfaction. As
the meetings progress, he'll be more blunt with his feelings, saying of
the plan, *"It's the only game in town."*

"Why are we on trial here?" one woman will ask, and the crowd will
erupt into applause.

A white-haired man in a dark blue sweater stands up. "Mr. Feinberg? Uh . . . I lost my son in this tragedy. And I want to know, and I
don't want to beat a dead horse, but my son was married, and his wife
is entitled to make a claim. Does it mean that I'm precluded from making a claim on my own? And if I wanted, expected, any recompense
from this, I would have to take it from my daughter-in-law?"

"Yes, you're precluded," Ken Feinberg says.

"Mr. Feinberg, my three children can't sleep at night," a tall woman
in her midthirties says. "My son in school is unable to participate in the
sports he loves. My three-year-old is afraid of who's going to disappear
next. My daughter has recurring nightmares." Her voice is stern, strong.
"I want to know how you're going to value their pain and suffering—a
dollar amount that you're going to assign for their pain and suffering
and mine."

"There is no dollar amount I could ever put on that."

The mood in the room is becoming volatile. It isn't only a discussion of the plan, but also of the nature of the loss, the value of it, the
extent of it. Money is a proxy for the loss. It is the only option available.

"We are anxious and nervous," the woman with the three children
says. "This has put us in a stressful position, so we're asking you to give
us an idea. I don't care if it's the same dollar amount for every child."

"We've considered all sorts of amounts. I don't know if it'll be one
hundred thousand dollars, two hundred thousand dollars, five hundred thousand dollars, seven hundred and fifty thousand dollars, a
million—I can't tell you yet what that will be. But you'll know in the
next three or four days."

Feinberg points to a woman in the twentieth row or so. "Last question, this woman here."

A woman with short dark hair and a dark jacket says, "Mr. Feinberg, everybody in this room has been through enormous pain and
suffering. What I understand is happening, is that there will be one

claimant per victim, which I think is a mistake that could become extremely troublesome. Keep in mind that the people who died were, on average, in their twenties and thirties. There are a lot of parents here. There were a lot of single men who died. I think that cutting out relatives of the victims who are not entitled under state statutory law to make that primary claim for economic loss is a mistake, because this wasn't a traditional death. This was unprecedented in the history of the United States. There should be awards given to people who don't have the primary claims for economic loss, but who have *extraordinarily* strong claims for pain and suffering. Fourteen members of my family will never be the same.

"We don't really want money, quite honestly. But I also don't want to have to go to my brother's wife and tell her to give something to my mother. Under the circumstances, you should allow room for changes to the regulations."

The audience breaks into applause.

Feinberg, distressed, raises his hands in a placating gesture. "What would you have me do when you clap and say please take into account these other individuals who suffered? What can I do? It's not the time or the calculation I'm concerned about. That's objective. It's deciding *like Solomon,* and I'm not Solomon—let's give thirty-eight percent to the wife, and notwithstanding state law, let's give sixty-two percent or whatever it is to the parents."

The woman suggests that additional funds be set aside.

"Let me just say before I adjourn, I'm trying to run a program that hopefully will bring a thimble of relief to what you're suffering. And I want you to know on behalf of the program, I'm going to do my best. And I want to thank everybody. I've learned a lot here tonight . . . And a particular thanks to Howard for setting this up."

The room erupts into the loudest ovation of the night.

Afterward, Howard stands on the stage and a group of around thirty crowd around him. It is an image that will fix itself in my mind for a while. I see the backs of heads, and Howard, like an evangelical preacher, or a politician, leaning over to shake hands, or just to talk. People are pushing each other aside to speak with him. This is where he's most comfortable. He isn't waiting for this period to be over. He's growing into the part. There are still a thousand people in the meeting, and more and more of them are moving toward him. When he leaves the stage he goes to a corner where there's another twenty or so people waiting to ask him questions. There is now a hopeful feeling to the proceedings. There is the sense that something can be done. And there's a new sort of anxiety revolving around that fact.

On the afternoon of the Cantor Fitzgerald holiday party, David Kravette and I are seated at the oval table in Howard's office while Howard talks bonuses with the mother of one of his deceased traders. This has been ongoing for more than a month. Where usually the trader would come in and talk about his bonus, now many of the traders' wives, or mothers, or fathers, are coming in or calling on the phone and disputing the numbers.

The mother tells him she'll "keep her lips sealed" if he raises her son's bonus. Several family members have threatened to go to the media if their requests aren't met. In 90 percent of the cases, Howard has worked it out, and in a some instances paid more than what was due. He'll live with that, he says.

"Your son was tremendously successful," he's saying now, "which we liked, incidentally. Not that we didn't like all our employees, but we *really* liked the successful ones. And your son was a real star."

The conversation continues, with Howard being warm and supportive, but reminding the woman that, in fact, "that desk wasn't doing so well. A lot of the divisions were stagnant in the last year."

Kravette's attention moves to the windowsill that looks out on the Empire State and the Met Life Buildings. He's looking on Howard's shelf at a photograph of Doug and Fred, Joe and Gary and Calvin.

"I've got to tell you," Kravette says, "I am so glad I'm not in one of those pictures. It's been rough. I've been having trouble sleeping. I keep thinking how close I was, just how close."

The loss is hitting everyone harder these days, partially because the first intense push at work is over, and then also because it's the holidays, and nothing is like it was last year.

The partnership meeting on Monday was only the start. Tonight's party will be another test.

Howard winds down his conversation, explaining that the division was having a down year, and that while the young man in question was still doing great work, no one on Wall Street had a particularly good 2001.

"It sucks to be him sometimes," Kravette says.

O N THE WAY over to the party I think about the bonus negotiations. Every night at around ten, Paul Pion—a partner at Deloitte who is acting as interim CFO—has made the trip uptown to Howard's apartment and goes over bonus numbers for fifteen or twenty more deceased employees.

There were plenty of threats people made, and honest mistakes. A few of the wives of those in the agencies division brought in documents from other companies claiming their husband did multimillion-dollar transactions on a particular piece of business when in truth three people worked on it, not one.

There is some desperation in these negotiations, a feeling that this is the last bonus the spouse will ever get. And of course the award deserves to be high—he died on the job, after all. That's what they believe, and it's a thankless task to negotiate against that thinking even when the numbers support you.

T HIS YEAR'S GATHERING is at a midtown restaurant and bar called Town, which will be mentioned in an episode of *Sex in the City*. Karen Weinberg, Allison's high school friend, has set up the event, and Dave Kravette and I are among the first to arrive.

Waiters and waitresses pass stylish appetizers that resemble tiny sculptures more than they resemble food.

Phil Marber, wearing a black golf shirt under a black-and-white plaid jacket, is talking to two new lawyers at the firm about a fundraiser he attended where he sat at a table with Phoebe Cates and Kevin Kline. "Phoebe Cates is off somewhere and it's just the two of us. He asks me, 'How are you doing?' So I say, 'Well . . . I'm going through a miserable divorce, I'm working seventy hours a week, and all my friends are dead.'" Marber smiles sadly.

Last year's holiday party was up on the 106th floor, at Windows on the World. People danced, joked, and drank the occasional shot of tequila or Jagermeister, Maryann Burns tells me. What she remembers most vividly is the easy camaraderie between the executives and the level below them, and the level below that.

Everyone was cutting loose. Howard drifted around, introducing employees from different departments. "Matchmaking" he called it. In another hour, after his ritual "Men's Night Out" with Doug's son, Michael Gardner, and his own two boys, he will join the party and dutifully fulfill that role again. There are lots of introductions these days. This room is packed with the fresh, untroubled faces of the new hires. They're easy to pick out. A few of the old guard are standing in the corner talking. Harry Fry, a Southern Californian, possessed of a relatively sunny disposition, is at the bar, reflecting on all the friends he'd hired in the last months.

"There were at least five people. One guy, Carl Valvo, I knew since we were kids."

They'd gone to high school together in La Canada, California, outside Los Angeles. Harry is godfather to Valvo's daughter. "He had these funky dark-framed glasses. Interesting guy."

The pain is visible in his face.

"Eric Stahlman, he was in my wedding party. I've known him for sixteen years. It's hard for me to even think about it. Talk about survivor's guilt. These guys were there because I brought them in. They had nice lives. I kept telling them there was no way they'd be able to turn me down, and they didn't."

We turn to other topics then, the baby he and his wife are expecting, his role in the company, the "eight weeks of hell" he had interviewing survivors whose division had been closed, reassigning them, placing some on disability or releasing them from their contracts.

"A lot of people moved on. The first person was a woman named Gloria Fox from the interest rates options desk. She was devastated by what happened. She came in and asked me what she should do, and I said, 'Gloria, we're not doing interest rate options here anymore. Maybe out of Chicago or London,' but she didn't want to move. I know the CEOs of a few companies, and she ended up taking a job with Euro Brokers." He sips his drink, then says, "Now that that period's over I'm not entirely sure what my role is. But Howard will let me know." He smiles. "He always does."

More people pile in, mostly the new reinforcements, who are enjoying the locale, the jazz music, the food, and the trendy drinks. Marber is standing next to a barrel-chested man in a tight, black V-neck shirt and a dark blazer, Barry McTiernan, an equities salesman in the Darien, Connecticut, office. Marber motions me over. He's been telling Barry about the book Howard and I are putting together.

"Let me tell you something about that guy I'm sure you know. He's self-made, right? An orphan. He's maybe the richest thirty-nine-year-old, self-made guy in the world. That's why people are jealous of him. He's doing more for the families than any other company. Twenty-five percent of the company's profits? That's *huge*. Ten years' health care? Other companies aren't doing that. When that bad press happened, I told the wives, 'Just wait and see what he's doing.'"

Barry leans in close—he's had a lot to drink—and tells me virtually the same thing Harry Fry has just told me. "It's fucking sad," he says. "I lost four people I hired personally. You feel responsible." He shakes his head. "That first day we had five hundred calls. More the next day. The phones lit up like Christmas trees. Wives calling in wanting to know about their husbands. We had to tell them their husbands were dead. I talked to them myself. It was brutal."

The firm was designed so that traders and salespeople and brokers would have each other's back, many have told me. A broker with a pile of good accounts whose phones are ringing off the hook will need an assistant broker, or someone in a slow patch to help him or her through, and that person will be rewarded financially, and in words, or favors in kind. For ten to twelve hours a day, they sat little more than two feet from one another, literally shoulder to shoulder, took bites from each other's sandwiches, shared their Cokes.

"You look out at the trading floor, and it looks and sounds like a family," Stuart Fraser told me once, "people screaming and yelling and ready to kill each other during the day. Then at the day's end buying one another beers and saying, 'Man, you really know how to yell.'"

Barry McTiernan talks about being in the Connecticut office on the day of the attacks, of how he barked directions to his colleagues after the plane hit. As he speaks he grows animated and then a little angry at those friends who couldn't get out of the building. For a moment he looks embarrassed because everyone around us seems to be having fun, and he's getting emotional.

Several survivors, most recently Matt Claus and Gary Lambert, have told me how exhausting social events become, how they wind up repeating painful stories to those with no knowledge of the friends they're referring to. Sometimes they don't disclose where they work so that they won't have to begin.

"It's all still with me. You know?"

FRIDAY, DECEMBER 21

I meet Marber at seven A.M. and he's been in the office for nearly an hour. He talks about bonuses and how few people on Wall Street will be getting them this year. "They're throwing Enron at them," Marber says, "and the Argentine crisis, anything to bring their expectations down." He points out that Cantor will be paying full bonuses to all employees, living and dead.

Marber leans back in his chair and looks through his glass office wall at the trading floor and team he's thrown together.

"For me this has never been work. It's kind of like being a baseball player, who goes to work, but he's still, you know, playing baseball. It's not like I move garbage cans. *That's* work. What better place could you be than to work with a good group of guys, have something interesting to do, talk to your friends on the phone, your customers? What has happened is that I feel a greater responsibility now. September 10th we were a well-oiled machine. Everything was perfect; when something broke, you called someone and it was fixed in five minutes. Now when it's broke you don't know who to call anymore. Part of me feels when I get it back to where it was, then I'm done. That's my endgame. The goal before was just to make money. Now the goal is rebuilding the business. The first couple of months we all had the same goal. I didn't have to worry about someone saying, 'I'm out of here, I'm gonna work somewhere down the street.' Now the reality is setting in that we're not quite the same firm. We've lost a lot of quality guys. And there are pressures. Our customers were loading us up in the first week, but they can't do that forever. Other businesses on the Street are down, and I have to face the possibility of some defections in the near term. No one's left yet, but I'm talking to everyone more, calling the other offices and the salespeople and customers. Just to tell them I appreciate what they're doing."

He takes a phone call, then one of the brokers comes in to ask a few questions. The equities guys—and everyone except one are men in the room—love Marber, look up to him. The personal aspect of the business is still crucial in equities. In bonds Cantor had already begun the process of going electronic—but equities was different—it was still all about relationships, phone conversations, dinners out with the client.

"It was like a black hole the first weeks—too much death. We were trying to process all the business. And at the same time you have all the wives of your dead partners calling you, clients calling you, reporters calling you, and it all was so fractured, and you couldn't concentrate on the business really."

T HAT AFTERNOON I talk with John Law, one of the few from Marber's equities New York team who survived. "I never went to college," he says. "Wall Street, Cantor, fills in those gaps." Law is tall with short dark hair and a confident, warm manner. His accent is thick and his voice deep. And he seems at once relaxed and charged up. Clearly he likes his work. He cannot count the people he knew who died in the terror attacks. He writes about them each night on his computer—sketches, details—so he won't forget them.

Law was out of the office, in Los Angeles for a wedding, when the plane struck. He had recently proposed to his fiancée, and the trip to California was among the best times he can remember. He says he stopped in the Los Angeles office for a day and made a million-share trade. It was that kind of a week.

He was staying at a nice hotel with the woman he would marry, playing a little golf, going out for dinners, and drinking California wine. Tuesday morning he was scheduled to play golf at Pebble Beach. "I was just so *psyched up* about everything."

The division Law had left behind for a week was filled with close friends he could grab a drink with at the end of the day, or scarf down lunch with at his desk. "Whatever you did with your time, these were the people you did it with. They were friends with your friends and you with theirs. It was like a big puzzle. I mean, we kidded each other sometimes about, you know, 'How much you make this month?' But the idea was that we all made money, and we did it together. They told me before I came here, 'If you can make it at Cantor you can make it anywhere.' Everyone made a good living, but everyone had a different approach—whether this one's an entertainer, this one's just on top of his game and all his customers love him. There was ball-busting. Even when the market was crapping out we were all doing big money."

At six in the morning on September 11, when John Law was sleeping in his hotel room, he received a phone call from his brother. "Where are you?" his brother asked. John told him. "Do you see what's going on?" his brother asked.

"I turned the TV on moments after the second plane hit. I was thinking first of '93 when everyone made it down. But then you saw the building melting . . . you knew it wasn't going to be the same. I knew my friend Chris Sorenson was in Bora Bora with his girlfriend. I found out about Bart Loehner—his wife made him stay home because he had bronchitis. But the rest of them . . . There were too many angles to it, you didn't know where to turn first. I write about them now so I can, you know, stay close to the situation. I wanted to feel this. Normally I shield myself from painful situations. It's a condition from growing up. But I didn't want to this time. When you look around now, as sad as it is, people are sort of forgetting. I think it's just human nature; you want to put bad things out of your mind. I had a drink with Freddy Gabler a week before he died. What do you say?

"I went to about six funerals, and then I called as many people as I could. But there are just so many." He closes his eyes, then looks away. "We lost a hundred people out of a hundred fourteen. Forty salesmen, fifteen traders each with a wingman, foreign stocks, stock options, a couple of secretaries, some support staff—I just think about all the people I knew. This one who just got married, this one who just had a baby. We were a real team. We looked out for each other. This isn't anything anyone should have to go through."

I'd asked him earlier about guilt, whether he had complicated feelings about surviving. "The therapists are trained to ask you about that, do you feel guilty about living. I don't. I'd planned that trip a long time ago. I guess it just wasn't my time."

*   *   *

W E'D ACTUALLY GOTTEN to the point where we'd rotate," Chris Sorenson is telling me. "We'd send one person out and another would stay and work, or we'd send people to separate funerals, one in Long Island and the other in Connecticut, so no one among the surviving spouses or parents would feel left out. This went on for a long time. We were on autopilot," he says. Not workwise, but emotionally.

"Our equities desk is like a private society. We spent time together constantly. Dinners, weekends. My parents knew all the people I worked with."

Sorenson's friend Martha had an apartment in his neighborhood, and the two of them would get dinner or drinks three nights a week. She'd scrutinize his choice of girlfriends, look after him in a variety of ways. She was his big sister, he says. She was thirty-nine years old when she died.

"That was a fairly senior age for the desk. There were areas of the trading floor where the average age was twenty-six. Plenty of kids twenty-three, twenty-four were running around, barking into phones, making good money. A few were straight out of college."

Sorenson wears his hair combed back away from his forehead. He's thirty-one, but the stress and strain of the last months shows on his face. His desk is the center of activity; the new kids stop by to ask him questions. He's been looking lately at pictures of all their parties, he says. He had his thirtieth birthday party a year ago, a big bash at a nightclub in the city. "You'd see a picture, five guys—four gone. Three guys—two gone. Four guys—all gone." His eyes redden as he speaks.

Eddie Mazzella was planning on retiring the day Chris Sorenson returned from vacation. "That was especially hard," Sorenson said. "Because he was waiting for me, and he would have been gone if I was there."

T HERE ARE MOMENTS of opportunity for a stock," Bill Rice, head of Cantor Equities Los Angeles office says, "where all the moons are lined up, and a block of stock can trade."

We're seated in an empty back office in Cantor's San Francisco location. Rice is fit and relaxed-looking. His speech is slow and deliberate. He is articulate and decidedly Californian. He wears a gray linen shirt, khaki pants, and the sort of metal bracelet favored more by graduate art students than equities brokers.

"They are quantifiable things but they are also emotional things, with the buyer and seller. The bond business is much more commoditized. It's not so with the stocks we sell. The stocks themselves are like people." He stops for a moment to make sure I'm following him here.

"Each one has different pants and inseams and shirt sleeves. We're not trading General Motors and IBM. We trade secondary and tertiary stocks you haven't heard of. And all of them have different personalities. It takes some *sensitivity* to sell them. Enormous sensitivity to trade large volumes without destroying the market."

It's the art of trading stock that begins to get into your blood he says, but it's also the specific philosophies he and others have stuck by. He talks of the speaker system, the squawk boxes, and how after a few months you can pick out the voices, hundreds of them from the other offices. There are several hundred people on the speaker system doing business at the same time, the conversations are succinct—no grand ideas are imparted. People talk over one another, though they try not to. On a given day, Rice says, he might be on the hoot a hundred times. On a slow day only ten or fifteen times.

"The hard part with all the new hires is that so many of the voices are unfamiliar, and so we sometimes don't know where they're coming from, which office. It's essential you learn the voices. We rely on each other. If I'm on a couple of phones and it's my stock that's trading, and someone from Boston is querying me about it, we have a buddy system. My buddies next to me are helping me out, they'll respond for me over the hoot."

On the morning of the 11th, Rice says he got in at four A.M., as everyone does in the L.A. office. He says after sixteen years he's still not used to waking up that early. He just does. "I was on the phone before the markets opened with one of my clients, and at the same time I was talking with Val Silver, one of my very good friends. She constantly played practical jokes. We had that in common. Me, Val, and Randy Fowler—we very early on figured out we were afraid of one another, and so we made a pact: that we'd never fuck with one another. Val never violated that pact. And that morning, Val and I were cooking up a rat fuck when the plane hit.

"It had to do with one of the guys in my office who wants to be an actor in the worst way. He's got the headshot, he's got the cameo appearance on *Friends*. He'd just sent out an e-mail to everyone in the firm about this new movie he's in, and I couldn't believe the self-promotion. So we had to do something. We were going to say something about a TV show he'd been given a part in or an agent calling him with a new script. I was talking to Val via an instant message when the plane hit.

"I remember Jeff LeVeen saying over the system, 'I think the building's been hit by a plane and we're going to evacuate. We're getting out of here.' A customer called so I was a little preoccupied. I thought it was kind of ridiculous. Some little Cessna had flown into the building by mistake. We didn't think about a commercial airliner hitting the building. I remember when I realized it was a commercial plane. I was watching on TV. And I see from my peripheral vision a guy named Steve Larrabee, and he's walking behind my desk and he's *sobbing*. And I'm thinking, *Why is Steve so incredibly upset?* I mean, nothing definitive has been declared, and I went up to him and he said, 'He's such a good kid, he's such a good kid,' and I realized what he meant was, I had hired his son three months earlier and sent him to New York to work there and train for a period of time, and then he'd come back after a few months to L.A. And I'd forgotten that his kid was there. I hugged him, but Steve knew.

"His son had called him when it happened. He told him, 'Dad, I'm scared, I'm scared. I don't know what to do.' And his dad just told him, 'Get the hell out of there.' When he hung up the phone he knew how desperate it all was. Steve had given me his son's résumé. He'd always done that—he'd come to me and say, 'This young person is looking for a job. Can you look this over and see if it can be improved?' This time it was for his son Chris, and I said, 'Why don't we hire him?' And he said, 'I don't know if I want my kid working here with me . . . I think it would be too difficult.' I told him, 'I think it's a great idea.'

"And he came up to me a day or two later. He said, 'Were you serious about wanting Chris to work for you?' I said, 'Yeah. I happen to need someone right now.' So I hired him. And he was great. Very positive. Very well liked. He looked like his father. Same square jaw. His father was a football player. I haven't done any grieving yet. I think there are a couple of reasons.

"At the six-month point, I was asked to speak at a vigil about September 11 and about Cantor Fitzgerald. It was to be at a Catholic church in our area. They asked people of all denominations—a rabbi, someone of Islamic beliefs, priests and ministers. I forced myself to think carefully about everything. And I realized that myself . . . and everyone I work with, we're all in some kind of denial. Very clearly. Some have defense mechanisms that have kicked in. Not a day goes by when we don't think about it, or talk about it. But we don't really face it. It's hard enough to think about one of your friends dying. But when, literally, hundreds of people you knew are gone, you just don't know where to start.

"There is a bizarre juxtaposition where we come to work, because it's something that we know and know well, and feel good about. It's a place where we can be together and comfort each other. And yet it's a place where there are so many ghosts. You can't avoid any of that. I sort of liken this group—those who were there in all the offices that day—to people in a quarantined hospital ward. We have this thing in common where we are physically together every day in an area others stay away from. We can't describe or explain what happened to us. No one wants to. And certainly no one can understand.

"I was in the room the other day. And there was a woman who'd worked for us. She said, 'You know, I can't look at my wedding pictures because my whole wedding party is dead.' So it's peculiar. Those of us here. We have this deep wound. Most things in life are reparable; most roads in life, if there's a mistake, you can back up and go a different way. This is a road where there's no reverse.

"Anyway, I seem to remember about fifteen minutes of silence. Then all of a sudden I hear in the speaker, 'Hello! Hello!' And it was Timmy. Timmy Grazioso. We yelled, 'Get the hell out of there! Get out of there!' He says, 'We can't; we're trapped.'

"Another guy, Mark Zeplin, is describing into the speaker how they're trapped. 'Get to the roof!' Frank Harrison from Chicago is yelling. 'Get to the roof of the building.' Everyone's yelling, all these voices at once. We're trying to get them to the roof, thinking if we got them there maybe a helicopter could pick them up. But they tried to do that, and that must have been what that fifteen minutes of silence was. They must have all tried to get out. They must have tried every possible way to get out of that building and couldn't, and at that point then came back to the trading room.

"Mark is yelling, 'You guys got to call somebody. You got to call someone and get help.'

"It was so pathetic. I got on my cell phone and called 911. It just exemplified how helpless we were. The only thing I could do was call 911 in Los Angeles. There was just nothing you could do, but listen to your . . . *friends.*"

He's looking away from me, and it's as though he's hearing all the voices. No attribution, he just speaks in the voices:

"'The smoke is really bad.'

"'Use your shirt as a mask!'

"'Stay down! Stay down!'

"Timmy said, 'Call for help! Tell them we're under the desk!' Then the last thing he said was, 'You guys have no idea how *desperate* this is.'"

"'*No idea how desperate this is,*'" he repeats. His face is wet with tears now.

"And you hear voices in the background. Then nothing . . . Those voices will never go away. Not one of us will ever forget them.

"Somebody from New York dialed up, dialed our listed trading desk in L.A. One of the guys answered, and said, 'What's going on, what's going on out there?'

"'We're fucking dying here. That's what's fucking going on.'

"It was Alvin. Alvin Bergsohn. He just picked up the phone, maybe hoping it was someone who was going to help, who was going to tell him what to do."

Lee Amaitis wears a crisp blue shirt over dark blue slacks. His thinning hair is slicked back like Howard's. When he talks he rubs his hands together furiously, moves them back and forth on his legs. It is hard for him to sit still, not because he lacks concentration, but because he has so much energy and intensity. He speaks with a Brooklyn accent, which clearly delineates him from the bulk of his British colleagues.

He sits in a well-appointed CEO's office lined with pictures of racehorses and boxing, two of his passions. Amaitis's impressive rise to the head of Cantor's international businesses was one accomplished without a college education and with a few notable missteps.

Amaitis's father, Stanley, immigrated from Lithuania. He spent a decade in the coal mines of western Pennsylvania before moving to Brooklyn, where Lee grew up. His father was employed there as a construction foreman and moonlighted as a building superintendent. Lee worked alongside him from the age of nine. After high school he got a job training horses.

"I liked the whole idea of being at the racetrack. I went from being a hot walker to a groom, taking care of horses. I taught myself how to ride. And then I became an outrider, which is someone who takes the horses to the post in the afternoon. Eventually I became a pretty good trainer." He says he never cracked the top tier, because "I didn't bleed blue."

Amaitis eventually moved on to an owner who found him a position on Wall Street working in the back office for a Cantor competitor called Fundamental Brokers. For a short while his income actually went down, but within a year he became a broker on the company's mort-gage-backed securities desk.

"I was one of their best producers. I mean, I made them a lot of money. And then I got caught up with the excesses of the eighties; I fell off the rails."

One day when Amaitis was arriving at work he heard his name mentioned by some men who'd been talking with the receptionist.

"I said, '*I'm* Lee Amaitis.' One of the guys spun me around, threw me up against the wall. They were cops. I was handcuffed and taken to the courthouse where they have these holding tanks. Couple of *strange* people in there. Humiliating thing. They kept asking me to give 'em names. And I said, 'I don't know what you guys are talking about. I buy drugs, I use drugs, and that's the end of it.' My lawyer bailed me out—it was a misdemeanor—and we left. It was rough. I lost my job, I went into rehab in Summit, New Jersey, for twenty-eight days. Toughest thing I've ever done in my life."

Since Amaitis's arrest in 1986, he says he's remained clean and sober. But his firm renounced him, and his friends and colleagues deserted him as well.

"Basically, everybody was like, 'Don't touch Lee.'"

Eventually he got a job with another brokerage company, worked his way up, and then joined Cantor in the mid-nineties. In the weeks following September 11, Amaitis was nearly as present in the British press as Howard was back in the States. Almost every day following the attacks there was another feature. Prince Charles, among others, came to visit the offices.

"The media people were all over. I was interviewed every other minute of the day to the point at which I didn't know what to say any-more. A BBC reporter came in doing a feature on who we were, what we'd done, because most people didn't know us at all. When they started to learn more, and know what had happened, they were amazed. Ultimately I thought it was good to talk about it. I'm so proud of how we held up. We wanted people to know we were still here, and that we'd held together. And the press seemed genuinely interested in our story. They spent time with us—not the normal quick news bite. And unlike the States, we really didn't get any negative press here in Europe.

"It was just pure adrenaline in those first weeks. Guys were sleeping on the floor. We wouldn't stop for a minute. I'd just take a breath, go home, shower, and come right back. Clive Triance and I were clearing transactions until the middle of the night. Figuring out if we had positions, errors, and risks. The behind-the-scenes stuff was intense.

"People were asking, 'Are these guys going to make it?'

"But my men and women managed the task. I had kids here, midtier employees, who never went home. You talk about loyalty. I had to chase them out of the building. I'd say, 'Go to the hotel across the street and get some sleep,' please. But they wouldn't leave.

"Nothing surprises me in this place, nothing. Because we had such a will to survive. And I know if it had happened to us here in London, New York would have done the same for us. Part of it is instinct. Your adrenaline kicks in and says, This is what I do for a living, I have to do this."

I ask him how life is these days, whether things are beginning to get back to normal.

"I don't sleep well. And I probably work too hard. But that's self-imposed. There's a lot to do and never enough time to do it in. For a while we were doing the work of two companies here in London, but after the first four weeks or so that all went back to the U.S. Now we can focus on our own issues."

In a couple of months those issues will include a high-stakes fight in a London court with Icap, the British brokerage company accused of trying to destroy Cantor Fitzgerald in the wake of 9/11 by poaching key staff.

The case will be dragged out, and there will be mention of both the workplace pressures and the after-work excesses of the traders and brokers. The rivalries will be revealed as far more than a professional competition. It's a street brawl.

Howard has said to me that the firm was always made up of Hawks and Doves: the Doves being the diplomats, the "relationship" people whom the clients and even their competition tended to love. The Doves were Doug Gardner, Joe Shea, Shaun Lynn, Dan LaVecchia, and Tim Coughlin. Stephen Merkel (a tested veteran of the Iris Cantor feuds) and Amaitis are the Hawks, he says. (Howard counts himself as a Hawk.) Fred Varacchi and Phil Marber could be either, depending on what the situation called for. The fight with Spencer, who tried shortly after September 11 to buy the firm, Howard says, will be both public and at times almost comically acrimonious.

Spencer's "Put one up their bottom" and "This is the time I've been waiting for" e-mails will be splashed across the front pages of tabloid newspapers on both continents. At stake is not only the issue of corporate ethics but also potentially billions of dollars of trades. Each broker Icap poached brought with him millions upon millions in client activity, and when the broker leaves he tends to take his customers. Now Amaitis is talking about Howard, whose London office is on the other side of the wall from us, and has a huge painting of Bernie Cantor hanging behind his desk.

"When that first building came down, I'm sitting over here, he's over *there*, right in the middle of it. I don't know if the people are gone. But he knew. And he made some tough decisions. I think it could have been handled better from a PR standpoint. He could have said clearly why he was doing whatever he was doing and what they'd all get. But really no one's ever going to win in that situation. Everybody's going to point the finger and say, 'You stayed alive. You have millions of dollars. That makes you a bad guy.' My feeling is bosses make tough decisions. You don't want the job, don't take it. He wanted the job.

"The first time when I went back to work from rehab, I got interviewed to be a boss. I got asked, 'How many people have you fired?' And I said I haven't been in that situation. And the guy who interviewed me said, 'Well, you will here.' And I knew I had to do things that I might not want to do.

"It's control." He points toward Howard's office. "Now he's a control freak. You say that to him and he'll say thank you. A lot of people are afraid of him. When they have problems with him I encourage them to talk to him. Because what's he gonna do, bite you? There are things you have to do as a boss that won't always make you popular and you have to do them anyway, or move out of the way and let someone else do it."

T HE EIGHTIES WERE a wild time in our business," Stuart Fraser is telling me. "Lot of craziness and excesses; entertainment was out of control."

We're in an empty storage room where Stuart goes to smoke cigarettes.

"It was more than dinners. They'd ask for ten tickets to the hottest play or a sold-out Knicks or Rangers game, and they'd take all their buddies. I remember taking people to the Palm Restaurant, and they'd order a five-pound lobster to take home for the wife. The budget was unlimited." He gives me a moment to imagine what that might entail. "We'd fly them to the Masters, or the NCAAs, or the Super Bowl. Hey, let's go see the fucking World Cup in Italy. Let's go to Oktoberfest in Munich. Let's golf in Ireland. The parties, the dinners, the nights out on the town. It was the nature of the business. That's how brokers cemented their relationships."

What fueled Cantor's success in the eighties was Reaganomics, plain and simple. Governments needed to finance the record deficits and more often than not they did so by issuing bonds. There was more *product* out there, as dealers say, more auctions, more liquidity, than ever, and that meant massive volume for Cantor. Cantor made their money on the small commissions it charged when a bond was bought or sold, but as the trades multiplied, these small amounts added up.

During this time Howard moved his way up the hierarchy, eventually carving out a name in the industry nearly as large as his mentor's.

Everything that Bernie did for the world of bond brokerage in the 1970s, Howard did again in the late 1990s with eSpeed. But this time it was a tougher sell. He had to get customers to stop using the phone, or a Cantor broker altogether, and he was essentially replacing voice brokers with an unglamorous black box.

The technology itself created a similarly wide range of reactions—from outright enthusiasm to dread. People either saw Howard as a prescient genius for introducing eSpeed or as a profit-driven boss whose move to technology would render obsolete hundreds of voice-brokering jobs.

"The black box," as they call it, made them feel a bit lonelier, a little lost. David Kravette said he'd been unhappy working for eSpeed right before the attacks, that he'd missed the dinners, the human contact. Others said the same thing.

But in terms of setting the standard for the business, it was an enormous success. And Howard, like his predecessor, was seen as a maverick. The difference was that while Bernie had expanded the industry to create more jobs, Howard had in a sense contracted it—and many brokers blamed him for that. Even some of those who remained with the company had difficulties with the move to eSpeed.

The View

CHRIS SORENSON

"You'd look out in the morning," equities broker Chris Sorenson says, "and you'd see the top of the Empire State Building, and the two shadows of the World Trade Center stretching across the clouds. It was an impressive sight. We'd seen plenty of planes go by below us. After the Rangers won the Stanley Cup, a blimp came by. The wind forced it off course and pulled it almost right up against the building.

"I liked working at the Trade Center. It was beautiful being way up in the sky like that. On a clear morning in the spring or the fall, it seemed like the view went on forever. What amazed me was looking north, how green New York was. After a few years, you took it for granted, but there were some mornings when you just couldn't. The view was so spectacular, you just *had* to look."

HOWARD LUTNICK

"Straight up, you see the arch of Washington Square; to the left, the George Washington Bridge. On a clear day you can see planes landing at LaGuardia. Sometimes in the early morning I'd see clouds below me and I'd have these 'Jack in the Beanstalk' moments. It looked as though you could step outside and walk on those clouds all the way over to the radio tower on top of the Empire State Building. In the summer, when the city was still and the smog clung to the buildings, you'd see blue sky above, and foggy brown below. It was like a layer cake. Nights, though, were my favorite—you'd see the lights and you couldn't stop staring. It was amazing. People would come by and the office would just disappear for them—they'd just stand there looking out the windows."

JOHN LAW
"On a clear day you could see the hair under the arm of the Statue of Liberty."

E ILEEN AND FRED VARACCHI met in high school biology class when she was in tenth grade and he was in eleventh. Fred was a year behind in science. He told Eileen jokes, and they were funny enough to get the two of them kicked out of class together. They started dating after that and never dated anyone else again.

Fred's story— son of a plumber, working-class Long Island kid, who becomes president of the largest electronic bond exchange in the world—would seem more remarkable if it didn't seem to those who knew him over the years to be so inevitable.

"He was always very driven," Eileen says of her husband, "but in his own way. He always wanted to make money. He'd do any kind of job— wash windows, be a gas attendant—anything. And I figured, this guy is gonna go far, because he didn't care what it was he did. He'd always have the same positive attitude."

On a sunny day in February, we're at the Varacchis' house in Greenwich, Connecticut. There's a pool and a tennis court out back, and wherever you look is another contraption for the kids to play with, or on. We're sitting in the den, and there are pictures of Fred everywhere. In one he's snowboarding, in another he's dressed as one of the Blues Brothers. He was tall, and thick-haired, and he was one of the brightest young superstars on Wall Street.

Greenwich is a world of fourth- and fifth-generation millionaires. Prep schools kids and Ivy League grads. The Varacchis both commuted to college and lived with their parents for two years after graduation.

Howard likes to tell about following Fred after a morning meeting: Howard was in a cab and Fred had gone ahead on his motorcycle. Traffic stalled in a tunnel, and Howard was told that there'd been a motorcycle accident up the road, and it had been serious. Howard got out of the cab and started running through traffic. As it turned out, it wasn't Fred. When Howard found Fred he grabbed him and kissed him, and told him how happy he was that he was okay. Howard had envisioned the worst. He told that story at Fred's memorial, to say that he felt fortunate that he'd been able to tell Fred while he was alive how much he meant to him.

"Fred and I are *so* different," Eileen says. "He's outgoing and loud; I'm quiet, reserved. He's very athletic, very coordinated, very musical; I'm not." She stops, realizing, like so many others I've talked to, that she's been speaking in the present tense. "He was the fun one, and I was the serious one."

She thinks for a moment, then smiles. "He loved to have cookies and milk before dinner. It drove me *crazy*, absolutely crazy. And it's a great thing for the kids too, you know. I'd look at him and say, 'Don't you see I'm cooking here. '" She nearly laughs. "He loved to sing, but he'd always ask me, 'Does that sound good?' He wanted to sound like the people on the radio—oh, who was it just recently? . . . Creed. So he'd blast that song. And he'd say, 'I sound just like him, huh?' He was always proud when he blew the speakers out."

Corrine, her six-year-old, is seated in a chair outside the room, listening in. I point my eyes to show Eileen. She nods to indicate she knows. "He always had stomach problems. I don't know if it was because of nerves or how he ate. He eats too fast, too rich. He loved sunglasses. *Loved* them. He'd always lose 'em. He thought he could play golf better than he did." She shakes her head. "He tried so hard. I think that was his biggest challenge—to learn how to play golf better, because he enjoyed it so much, but he never entirely got it. But whoever played with him was always patient because they just wanted to be around him."

The fear many of the wives have isn't simply financial, and it isn't only that they'll have to raise the kids alone, it's that so many of these marriages—the best ones—are blends of personalities. And it is the hope of a mother that their children will have a little of both parents.

She talks for a while about Howard, how he and Allison have called often, and taken her out to dinner several times, how he advises her financially. She says the negative press made her angry and that she wishes they'd understand what the company was up against. I ask her how she thinks Fred would have reacted as a survivor. "He would have thrown himself into saving the company, and he would have taken on so much with the families. If he felt somebody needed something or was hurting, he'd do anything to help them. That's how he was."

"Can I tell something?" her daughter, Corrine, in a pink Powerpuff Girls T-shirt, says. She's made her way into the room and now seats herself on the couch near her mother. "On Amelia Island he helped somebody because she fell off the bike and hit her head."

"Right, right," Eileen says.

"And was bleeding."

"Right," says Eileen. "Daddy stopped and helped the woman who fell off the bike."

"She was bleeding on her head. 'Cause she fell down." Corrine says proudly. "She had to get a paper towel; he was 'Hurry, hurry, get a towel!'"

"I actually had put something on the back of his memorial program to have people write letters to the kids, telling them experiences or stories of their father. I've gotten so many and it tears me up reading them, but I know that it's something they'll cherish."

"Mommy, can I watch the tape of Daddy tonight?"

"Umhmm."

Corrine then sprints upstairs.

"He made a tape of his TV appearances—CNN and other channels—and then we had the video of his ZZ Top and Blues Brothers imitations . . ."

Corrine returns wearing slippers of her father's, in the shape of gorillas. "Look at my feet! These are Daddy's," she says.

"Yeah, Daddy's feet always got cold," Eileen says.

"Daddy's shoes," their two-year-old son, Tyler, says.

Eileen talks more about all the letters that have come in from friends and people who'd read about what has happened to them. We hear clomping then. It's Corrine and now she's wearing her father's dark leather cowboy boots. "I haven't taken anything out of the drawers or the closet," Eileen says. "I just can't get myself to do it yet."

"Daddy lets us watch Austin Powers," Corrine says, then imitates the movie spy. "Oh, be*have*." She names two other movies her father lets her watch. They're both R rated. What is most remarkable is how present Fred is. It is literally as though he's out late to dinner. He isn't a memory. His word still stands.

It strikes me, partly because she told me this and also because I sensed it, that Eileen Varacchi hasn't spent much time talking about what has happened to her family. She hasn't seen a counselor. She's been in support groups, but it feels as though she's just begun this process.

I'm thinking of those boots and those gorilla shoes as I wait on the lamp-lit platform for the train. And I imagine that little girl forty years from now remembering a gesture of kindness her father made on a vacation when she was five, the sort of thing that by the next day he'd probably already forgotten.

O N THAT FRIDAY morning I meet with Maura Coughlin, wife of executive managing director Tim Coughlin, at her apartment on the Upper East Side. She has short blond hair and a suntan. She's fit and pretty, and quick-witted.

"Timmy was all about work and he was really all about the people. As a result, he probably had a harder time adjusting when they went to eSpeed because he loved the relationships he had. He was always pushing the brokers to entertain the traders and the customers at night. Timmy had a zillion friends, a zillion. He knew everybody in the business."

Cantor was Coughlin's third stop in his career. He'd started at RMJ, a brokerage firm that closed in the early '90s, then he went to Garban, where he developed a reputation as one of the top ten-year brokers on the Street. Howard convinced him to join Cantor in April of 1995.

Coughlin ran Cantor's U.S. Treasury ten-year desk until 1999, then all U.S. government bonds. He'd been urging Howard to move him from management to a position where he could produce again, back into the action—on the phones, making trades. He thrived on all the yelling, on having fifty or sixty guys at a desk shouting at each other. "It made his day," Maura says. "When he was in an office by himself he went stir crazy."

She describes her husband's relationship with Howard as being of the love-hate variety. She laughs when she says this, but adds that some of Tim's old friends were surprised that they got along as well as they did.

"Howard hated that he couldn't keep Tim on a leash. But to his credit, Howard gave him the freedom he needed. Timmy respected Howard, but they didn't entirely *get* each other. Howard always seemed more studious, more comfortable in an office. Timmy was not one to sit behind a desk and do people's payroll and stuff like that. Timmy was the type to bring beers to the desk on a Friday afternoon. I can't see Howard walking in with a six-pack. You need both types in a company, I suppose, that's what makes it work so well. The part of Howard Timmy liked best was Allison. Timmy really loved Allison. Whenever he could get her away from Howard on trips, he loved drinking beers with her."

Both Coughlins grew up on Long Island. They met at a bar called Suspenders in 1991. He was thirty-four, she was twenty-five.

"He had long hair and he was just so much fun. That's the best way to describe him. He worked hard and played hard. That was his motto. He was always positive. Even when he called me on September 11th right after the plane hit. I don't think he had any idea how bad it was, but he told me to turn on the TV. He didn't want me to be scared, he said. He was going to leave the building. That was it. There was no 'I love you, take care,' because I don't think for one second he thought that he wasn't going to make it out. There was really no panic or anything like it in his voice.

"When Timmy called me, my children hadn't gone to school yet, so they were on the couch with me. My kids went to work with him five, six times a year, so they knew it was his building on fire when they saw it on TV. I turned it off."

About a week after the attacks, two police officers came to the Coughlins' door to tell them they'd found Tim's body. Maura said she was both relieved and in shock. She had already had his wake.

Coughlin's body was found intact. "I have every dollar bill from his pocket, everything. All the credit cards, his wedding ring. I was very happy, because we were able to bury him, because it gave me some closure."

I asked her what she'd told her children. "I explained it to my daughter, who just turned five, that a plane hit Daddy's building and he died and everybody he worked with died. So she gets it. I didn't tell her people did it deliberately because I think she'd be scared then that someone would fly a plane into this building. She's too young for that, I mean, she was four and a half when he died. I said it was an accident. My three-year-old has begun to talk more about heaven and Daddy dying. The baby of course knows nothing, and that's refreshing in some ways."

I ask her what the effect was of the communal aspect of all the mourning. "It's been comforting, not because I want people to wallow in my sadness with me. It was such a national tragedy, and I really feel like there's so many people who are going through the same thing I am. If Tim had died of a heart attack, it would have been just as horrible. And as it is, we've gotten so much support from friends, from Howard and Cantor. The negative aspect is that it's always on TV and it's always going to be part of my kids' life. The war and patriotism and all the coverage. For the first two months I wanted nothing to do with the flag, nothing. I didn't want to see the bumper stickers or the pins. And now I feel differently. I don't want to say Timmy died for his country. He didn't. But Timmy's a part of history now, and I have to embrace that for my children. They're learning in school about how their dad died. But they're so young that I just . . . it's painful."

"I met with Mr. Feinberg on January 8th," Howard informs a hotel conference room full of family members. "I thought I'd tell you what our conversation was. You can determine what you think of it. I walked into the office and he asked me, 'Howard, why don't your families trust me?' I said, 'Why do *you* think, Ken? Maybe it has to do with you're telling them there was no cap.'

"He says, 'I told them there's no cap. So what's the problem?' I say, 'Well, the next day you put out regulations that effectively have *a cap*.' He goes, 'But I told them there's no cap.' 'But you put out regulations that have a cap.' We did this for about three minutes back and forth."

It is a dramatic rendering, complete with voices, the point of which is to describe the obstacles Feinberg is creating and the lengths to which Howard is going to break through them to get full compensation for the families.

After Howard has prepped the crowd of two hundred, he takes a short break. Feinberg arrives at eight, and before Howard ushers him into the room, Feinberg jokes about how they've both walked the plank lately. By the end of the night that line will have taken on new meaning.

When the meeting starts he takes a moment to tell the group how lucky they are to have Howard as their advocate on these issues. Now he begins addressing an assemblage gathered to hear answers, and not necessarily the ones he's about to give. The whole procedure has been anxiety-producing, because so much money is in the balance. Howard had designed the meeting so that when family members asked their questions, he could follow up with additional ones rather than letting Feinberg control the agenda.

Toward the end of the evening a woman asks him what happens in a divorce case, where her children are dependents of the man who died. But the man has remarried. The new wife has been named the executor and the sole recipient of the will.

"All to her. There's nothing I can do," Feinberg says.

"So the kids are out of luck."

"That's not what I'm saying. I'm saying there's nothing I can do. Tough luck as far as I'm concerned. That check goes to the wife. Why? Because the victim *says so*. If the kids want to file a claim in probate court about the estate as a whole, go ahead. But leave me out of that.

"Let's get another question. It's been a long day."

"Well, it's been a long *four months* for us," a woman says. "We'd like a little more compassion from the Special Master."

People start clapping, not every one, but a group of twenty or so. Feinberg hates it. It's the tabloid TV style of clapping. "I've got nothing but compassion for you," Feinberg says. "And it's not even a thimble of what you're feeling."

The main issue tonight, and in the last days, revolves around whether the fund has a cap. A formula exits for salaries up to $231,000. Anyone who earns more than that and wants a higher settlement has to argue the case before Feinberg.

"There *is* no presumption for those earning more than two hundred thirty-one thousand dollars. So . . . You've got to do a little bit more *work*," Feinberg says, his voice is raised now. "You've got to put in *not only* that you earned four or five hundred thousand dollars a year for the past three years. But you've also got to demonstrate that that would likely continue. We won't presume—"

The audience yells out objections.

"*Listen*," he shouts above the din. "We *will not presume* that that would have continued. That's the challenge. Without a presumption, there's *no cap*, but you've got to do *more work*. You've got to demonstrate that increases would have continued for the next fifteen years. You've got to do that, otherwise you won't prevail." He's beginning to wind things up, but as I scan the room the crowd looks agitated.

"You're suggesting we only got six percent raises every year," a young man says. "Is that all *you* get? I bet not. You made a lot more than two hundred thirty thousand dollars last year, right?"

"How do *you* know?

"I know. Do you think we're *stupid?*"

He says nothing—the man's tone is combative. Feinberg, I suspect, would like to bring this to a close and cut his losses.

"You say you understand, but you don't really. You didn't lose a loved one," the same man says.

More people yell things, or clap, or jeer. Feinberg has absorbed much of the rancor that early on was directed at Howard. Now it's gained volume and force, if not as much air time.

"Obviously I can't begin to put myself in your shoes." His microphone is whistling now. "But I'll give you one bit of advice for what it's worth." He waits until it's quiet.

"The reason I am so committed to the program is that whatever people tell you—*it's the only game in town.*" No one likes this one, not the phrasing nor the spirit. He is telling them they have no ground from which to bargain. They have no choice—take it or leave it.

"I will do my best to look after your interest, but there's *no future* in litigation. My answer to the person who wants to sue is 'You're out of your mind. If you want to litigate, *go ahead.*' The *real* pressure on me is *not* that people are going to walk away from this program and litigate. That's up to them. It's a *loser.*" He lowers his head and peers above his glasses.

"The real pressure on me is that since you *can't* litigate, I have got to bend over backward to make the program fair. In a way, it would be easier if people could litigate, if you didn't like what I did you could sue. It's precisely because you can't sue—and any lawyer who tells you that you can is giving bad advice—that I feel a special obligation to make the program work."

He ends by saying that the program *is* working, and still could be made better. Then he thanks Howard, thanks the crowd, says he's learned a ton, that he always learns the most from talking with audiences like these.

A man down the aisle has been irritated all evening. Now he stands and calls out, "Mr. Feinberg, Mr. Feinberg, I have one more question, Mr. Feinberg!"

Some now are legitimately applauding. Feinberg shakes Howard's hand and then walks down the aisle on his way to the door. Howard remains onstage ready to resume the meeting once Feinberg is gone. He wants to be able to frame the issues for the crowd, to let them know that there *are* options and that he will be looking into them.

"Mr. Feinberg," the man from my row yells again, and now he's in a jog to the center aisle and on a collision course with Feinberg. He is six feet three or so, and I will learn later that he lost two daughters. He stops within a foot of Feinberg.

"You could have a lot more com*passion*, Mr. Feinberg. *You* visited a construction site. For us it's our lives. In every meeting you demonstrate only callousness. Don't you see this is our life?"

A tight circle forms around the men. In the midst of this, Howard signals Tom Lavin, a former police detective, who unobtrusively steps near the men. He and Feinberg's driver escort Feinberg out. Feinberg acts unfazed. He shakes hands and answers more questions as he leaves the conference room. At the door he's greeted by more parents and spouses, and another circle forms around him. A tiny gray-haired woman, who I will later learn is from Romania, the mother of a twenty-seven-year-old who died in the attacks, steps forward and begins shouting.

"You—cannot—pay my pain! This is not a flea market! I will not negotiate my son's life. Why are you making me *negotiate* his life?"

Then she repeats what she's said. *"This is not a flea market. You cannot pay my pain."*

Feinberg, stunned, just listens, as the same things are said again.

It is a moment of sharp, unbridled pain, like Danielle's at Doug's service, or Howard's on the *Larry King* show, or Edie's the night she was planning Gary's service and everyone started talking about why the buildings fell.

"I'm not trying to pay your pain," he says quietly.

Allison stands next to the woman and puts her arms around her. This is what's left behind, people trying to do well by one another, yelling at one another, attempting to find outlets, or measures of what they've been through. There are no numbers to quantify the sadness, the rage, or the emptiness.

Just after the anniversary of the attacks, Stephen Merkel and the firm's lawyers and economists will submit to the Department of Justice an eighty-page brief, called "The Book," on behalf of all of the families. The document will challenge Feinberg's regulations and the methodology he has used to interpret the Victim Compensation Fund and reduce the awards given to each of the World Trade Center victim's families.

H UNDREDS OF DETECTIVES in white space suits and face masks sift through the thousands of tons of debris trucked in every day from the Trade Center. After the concrete blocks and iron beams are removed they begin to find personal effects of the victims: watches, pens, ID cards, wedding rings, wallets, photographs, bracelets, pins. The effects are placed in boxes and will ultimately be returned to the families. Among the artifacts, detectives find pieces of bone, which will be DNA-tested to determine the identity of the person. Later an officer will visit a home somewhere in Long Island or New Jersey, Connecticut, or the Upper West Side of Manhattan. Increasingly the families we see at the meetings have been receiving these visits. Sometimes the knock on the door comes late at night. One woman says she'd gone to bed when an officer arrived and told her that they'd found parts of her husband. She didn't sleep for two days after receiving the news, and yet she says she's relieved that this period—the time of waiting—is over.

The newspapers feature pictures of shelves cluttered with watches and jewelry. A number of people will comment that these keepsakes remind them of items salvaged from the Holocaust. This is what remains of the human cataclysm that for so long was buried beneath the smoldering ruins and twisted metal of Wall Street. A few sculptures from Bernie's prized Rodin collection have been located, feet and heads missing. They are grim reminders of a lost age—the age of proud opulence.

Many, though, have yet to be found, and rumors abound that the Rodins have been stolen, that somewhere there is a recovery worker with *The Thinker* sitting in his basement.

Amy Nauiokas and Hank Morris, Howard's adviser and friend, are sitting around the oval table in Howard's office prepping him for *Larry King*. It has been a good week. Earnings were announced on Wednesday, and there's been good press ever since. Howard gave Diana Henriques of the *New York Times* the first crack at the story, and she ran a rave in the business section. The next day the *Wall Street Journal* and other newspapers published similar articles.

Cantor had turned a profit in the quarter starting October 1st and had earned 19.7 million dollars. In terms of the 25 percent plan, this meant 4.9 million dollars would be paid out to the families in the form of health care and cash. In addition, eSpeed had, in fact, had its first profitable quarter ever, earning almost 8 million dollars. Many of the major news organizations pick up the story, although some, like CNN, remind the audience that Cantor was the company who'd been criticized earlier "for its insensitivity."

Hank Morris tells him, "What you should try to do essentially is let people know you're a *mensch*. So that people will think, *I'd love to work for him*." Morris is wearing a dark red sweater over a blue shirt. He has thin metal-framed glasses, gray hair, and a smart, reassuring presence.

The last time Howard went on *Larry King* was five months ago to announce the plan to give a quarter of the firm's profits to the families. It was an emotionally raw performance, at the center of a tumultuous time.

"They're very happy to have you again," Amy says of the *Larry King* show.

"Larry King is not a bad guy," Hank says. "He's not going to go after you."

"He's going to ask you about the salaries," Amy says.

"'Howard, why'd you cut off the salaries?'" In her white cowl-neck sweater and gray skirt, Amy doesn't much resemble Larry King, but she does her best. He begins to talk about the mind-set back then. "We could not do more at the time. We could do more over time. It's exactly what we said and it's exactly what we did."

Amy and Hank are nodding. "Right?" Howard says. "Over time people will stop focusing on September 11, but one firm will always be there, because they're our family and our friends."

"'Why do you think people were criticizing you?'" Amy asks.

"It was a moment in time when for whatever reason you became a lightning rod," Hank suggests.

Howard stops Morris for a moment. "I think I can be even more sympathetic to the people who attacked me," Howard says. "I know how they feel. I lost family too. It was a scary and confusing time." There are usually a dozen true answers to any question about what was going on in the early days and what he was thinking. It's hard to give a simple one-sentence response.

Howard moves on to other topics. He says Lee Amaitis and the rest of the Cantor office should be covered in medals. "There were two hours when I was lost. I was hiding under a car, and then walking through the smoke, and these guys never went into hibernation. They weren't thinking about how many of their friends they lost. They were thinking of keeping the business alive."

Amy asks him about the relief fund.

Howard says his sister's been amazing. That she'd put together a team of volunteers shortly after the attacks, and now, five months later, they'd given out more than eighteen million dollars. "The fund didn't even exist until September 14, and now its their hub. When the families need information, they go to the relief fund website. It's how they keep in touch with each other. This is Edie's life now, it's her mission."

"Does it seem like five months ago?"

"It feels like five months since September 11th. But it feels like a lifetime since September 10th."

"'Howard, the last time you were in here you were very emotional, and you've taken some criticism for it. How would you respond to that criticism?'"

"I honestly didn't expect to be so emotional, but you can't lose everyone you worked with and your brother and not be. If someone can't understand that, then I hope they never do really understand it, because no one should go through what we went through."

7:05 P.M.

At home, Joel and Geri Lambert and Allison greet Howard at the kitchen door. Allison is holding Casey, who's dressed in pink-and-white pajamas. The boys start performing for him and talking over one another. They have too much to say and I have the sense they feel there's a clock going. They know he'll be heading out soon, and they want to take advantage of the few minutes they have. Howard goes downstairs to change, and Brandon, in front of his sprinkle-covered cupcake, is miserable until his father returns.

The winter Olympics are on the kitchen TV and everyone's talking about the ice skating controversy. The Canadians have been awarded the second gold medal. Karen gives Howard a once-over with a little makeup. Joel wears an American flag pin.

As Jimmy drives us downtown, Howard's going over again what he might be asked and how he might respond. He's talking about Allison. He wants to remember to thank his wife along with everyone else. He's said this several times today, "My wife is fantastic." Allison has been hosting support groups for the victims' wives who've just had babies, and for the fiancées. Howard can't remember how many there are, so he calls Allison on the cell.

"Thirty-eight women were pregnant on September 11; fourteen of them for the first time," he relays to us. It is a depressing statistic.

We pass Madison Square Garden and turn onto Eighth Avenue in front of the CNN building. Teresa Curly, a CNN producer, greets us in the lobby. We're taken to the floor for *Larry King*, a green room for CNN interviewees. A man in a black turtleneck heads off to tape an interview; a short bookish-looking man in a worn brown sports jacket waits to take his spot on *Crossfire*.

On the television, there's a report on Iraq, and the possibility of a U.S. offensive there. Howard fixes his glare on Saddam Hussein and comments on his berets. Then he glances over to the man on the couch.

"Hi," he says. "I'm Howard Lutnick."

The man introduces himself as an expert on surveillance issues for the ACLU. This will be his second time on *Crossfire* in a week. He doesn't recognize Howard by face or by name.

"What do *you* do?" he asks.

"I'm the chairman of Cantor Fitzgerald," he says.

"Oh, oh, yes of course," he says, chastened. "I'm so sorry about what you've gone through. You've been through quite a lot?"

"That's the understatement of the year," Howard says not antagonistically.

He asks the man about his stance on surveillance, and then they're into a conversation about the proliferation of overhead cameras in England. He's trying to stay loose here.

At 7:27 we walk by equipment and editing rooms, passing a group of technicians watching an episode of *The Simpsons*, and Howard approximates the accent of one of the characters. The studio for the *Larry King* show is a black-walled cave of a room with the familiar red, white, and blue map of the U.S. behind a table where the guest sits. Teresa Curly attaches a microphone to Howard and gives him his earpiece. We go back to watch in the green room, so we can hear the questions as well as the answers. Amy settles in. She's as nervous as a mother watching her son in the school play.

"United Flight 175 hit the South Tower," Larry King says, "where nearly seven hundred Cantor Fitzgerald employees were working." Someone has fed him the wrong information—wrong flight and tower—but Howard responds without wincing or correcting him.

Larry asks him where he was, and he has to tell the first-day-of-kinder-garten story again. Looking at the burning buildings, could he have imagined how many lives would be lost? Howard says he knew it would be bad.

Then come the questions he's been anticipating. Larry asks why he went on television, and about the criticism he received over the salary issue. He answers that he wanted to tell the world that the company was still there, still open for business, and that the families are together, and will be taken care of. His voice is scratchy, his tone earnest. There is one emotional pitch here—it is that Cantor Fitzgerald is a business miracle, and that everyone has pulled together to make it happen.

After the break, Larry says, "You've been described as a hard-nosed guy, Howard. Do you think your competitors were surprised at how you responded to the tragedy?" He deflects the question and once again praises the men and women who feverishly worked to save the firm. He is magnanimous by intention and in effect.

Larry, visibly moved, tells Howard that he salutes him. And then it's done. Seventeen minutes.

On his way out, Howard thinks aloud of the people he didn't thank. "My customers. I should have said we really have fantastic customers." And then he realizes he hasn't thanked Allison or Edie.

Amy says, "You did great, Howard. It went really well."

But he's focused still on what he didn't do.

In a month or so, Howard will be back in the CNN building to report eSpeed's latest earnings. After the interview, he'll share an elevator with former New York mayor Ed Koch.

"I'm Howard Lutnick from Cantor Fitzgerald," Howard says by way of introduction, though he's fairly certain Koch knows who he is.

"Cantor Fitzgerald . . ." Koch says. "What happened with that guy? How did he screw things up so much? I mean, he's doing much better now, but why'd he screw up like that?"

Howard at first assumes it's a joke, but as the seconds pass he realizes it isn't. Koch doesn't know who he's talking to.

"*I'm* that guy," Howard says. "I'm the chairman of the Cantor Fitzgerald."

Without missing a beat, Koch says, "Why'd you screw up like that?"

Howard takes him through the short version of what he was up against. As they leave the building, Koch shakes his hand. The incident will stay with Howard for a few days. It bothers him some but it makes him laugh, and he knows that's a good thing, a step in the right direction.

THE PEOPLE I WORKED WITH at Cantor were people I respected and liked. I had recruited and promoted them, become part of their lives. We built a place that was bound tightly together. And in many ways the 1993 bombing was the catalyst for that. We emerged from that crisis stronger, closer.

In the early fall I was talking to one of our widows about how she could let her inlaws play a role in her child's life. And it made me think of Michael and Julia Gardner. I started what we now call "Men's Night Out." Every Thursday, no matter what's happening at work, I take off early to visit with Julia and then take Michael out with my boys in their pajamas to an arcade or to Dylan's, a candy and ice cream store with every kind of flavored sprinkle in the world. I want to be someone Doug's kids can count on.

On my way home from "Men's Night Out" with Doug's five-year old son, Michael, I talked to him about his dad. I said, "You know I'm bigger than your dad, right, Michael?"

"No way," he said. "My dad was so much bigger than you."

I teased him also that I was a better basketball player than his father—an even bigger lie. When he said his dad was better, I fell backward as though he had wounded me. Then he told me his dad was better than me at tennis, and when he did, I told him this time he'd crossed the line. I said, "Listen, he was not a better tennis player. Your dad never beat me, never once." And Michael fell backward, into the seat of my car.

What I've learned in these months is that it's security people crave now that they've lost so much. It's hard not to feel responsible for what happened, to come to peace with the fact that, as Stephen said, "They were there and we were not there."

Policemen and firemen—as awful as the thought is—begin their days

knowing there's a chance they might not make it home at night. Their oc-
cupation is built upon bravery, and, by definition, puts them in harm's
way. My men and women never told their spouses "Today I'm going to
work, and tonight I might not make it out." Because for them, they were
just going to the office.

I'm often asked when this will be over, and I can't really say. Cantor,
the company, these families, are my life. I don't want it to be over—not if
that means we'll be cast apart from one another.

March 10–17

LaChanze and I are talking on the phone about Calvin and all the plans
they'd had.

"We were just about to get a house. We were looking in Riverdale,
because it had taken us so long to figure out where we wanted to live.
He wanted to live in New Jersey—get a little house in Montclair—but
I didn't want to. He didn't want to go to Westchester, so we decided on
Riverdale. We were saving our money. We were going to put our girls in
private school. We were just looking forward to having a family."

LaChanze was worried that Calvin would be a strict parent because
his own father had been strict. "He said, 'I'm glad we're together because you won't let that happen.'"

Calvin would come home, read Celia a story, give her a bottle, and
then put her to bed.

"One thing I loved is that if my patience was running out, I wouldn't
have to say my patience is running out. He understood," LaChanze
says. "Calvin and I were getting to the point in our marriage where we
were letting go of the reins. We were just getting comfortable with our
lives."

She describes the moment she knew she'd marry him as a moment
of complete comfort—a recognition.

"He made me much more trusting. He gave me the ability to depend on someone else. To let someone love me."

She says after six months she still doesn't think about the terrorists,
about Osama bin Laden.

"I know that they did it and I know they're the reason my husband isn't here. But it doesn't do me any good to be mad at them. I just know that he'll get his due, either now or later. I'm a true believer that you reap what you sow. But I'm just more upset that my husband's gone. I don't have any room to be upset about anything else. I'm more lonely really. I've always missed him. Before I cried every day and now it's every other day. I think of vacations. I'm not excited about going to Ghana or Rome, or all the places we'd talked about going. I can't imagine going to those places without Calvin. And you know people say to me, 'Oh, LaChanze, you're young. You'll find another man, you'll get married again.' That's a whole other aspect of this that really pisses me off. Because telling me to find another man minimizes what Calvin was to me. They say, 'You'll fall in love again.' I don't want to fall in love with someone. I don't want to go through meeting someone and having them love my daughters. I just want my husband. I vowed that my daughters would be raised in a traditional home, whatever that means. That was one of my dreams, and they just completely destroyed that."

Nancy Shea says the wives she talks to have been simultaneously following the news and trying to avoid it. "There's some anger toward the media," she says when I talk to her just after the Memorial Day spate of shows and newspaper reports about the attacks. "Because the families feel they've been used in a ratings game and our children have been subjected gratuitously to the image of the buildings falling, and the constant mention of 9/11. We'll be out somewhere and CNN will be on. Or I'll be driving with my kids and the car next to us will have a sign that says, 'WE WILL NEVER FORGET.' As though anyone would forget. I think it's hardest on my kids when they're at school. Someone will bring it up and then the whole class will turn and look at them. I hate that that happens."

Lately, Nancy says she's been trying to keep her fury in check, and her sadness about the mistakes the government, and specifically the FBI and CIA, made prior to 9/11, the possibility that all this might not have happened if the authorities had pieced the clues together earlier. News of those failures has only added to the reluctance many families have toward signing on for the Federal Victim Compensation Fund.

"Then when two fifteen comes around I put it all aside. Because I've got math homework and baseball practice, soccer games, and dinner to make. I need to have a good face for them, and for Joe."

A burden for many of the families is that their grief is a part of a national story that won't go away. Somewhere there's a balance between the country's desire to understand what's happened and the families' need to get on with their lives. But in order to reengage within their communities, the families may have to accept that their personal loss is, and will always be, part of a collective loss, that all the flags, bumper stickers, T-shirts, all the money mailed in, all the teddy bears, quilts, and toys, are gifts of the heart, symbols of a vast and profound empathy that still has trouble finding adequate expression.

Years from now the young children left behind by the terror attacks will be reading about the events of last fall in textbooks. They'll be called on in class to recite a fact, or offer their opinion on the government's response, and they'll either tell everyone who they are or more likely they won't. They'll feel proud or sad, or a little of both. Maybe they will find comfort in the distance they've traveled.

S TUART FRASER is talking about his mental state eight months after the cataclysm at his firm.

"What helps is that I can see other people through this. My friends' wives, my wife, my in-laws, Howard. There are the big people you were closest to, but then sometimes you start thinking about the hundreds of other people you knew, who you'd drop in on and talk to certain times of the week or month." Stuart has been thinking a lot lately about Carlton Bartels, his friend from a wilderness camp they both attended. "He was working for a power company. He and I wanted to begin an environmental brokerage business. I told Howard about him. I said he was one of the smartest guys I know. Of course, Howard hired him, and he was great for us. His funeral was a real watershed for me. I went to between sixty and seventy, but I only spoke at about three of them. Each one was worse than the next until Carlton's. The hard thing about Carlton's was, it was the first time I was going to see my camp family, about fifty people. I was nervous because I knew them very well. But people were really sweet to me it turned out."

He takes a sip of water. "You know we went to a medium. It was a pretty wild experience. My wife, Elise, was with me, and so we talked about Eric." Eric Sand is Elise's brother.

"Elise says, 'Oh yeah, the medium says Eric has the best seats in the house. He can go anywhere he wants. No one's in front of him. He can see everything.' I tell the medium he just got Jets tickets last year. He waited seven years on the list and he was really looking forward to taking his dad to a game. Eric's instructing her to tell us we should take his dad to a game, don't sell the tickets, tell his father *hot dogs,* hot dogs will convince him. I'm thinking to myself, *Okay, we're gonna be at a game and a hot-dog guy is going to trip and fall into us.* So that night Elise called her father and she tells him what happened, and Elise says, 'The medium said we should mention hot dogs.' He starts crying. Eric and his dad had gone to a game and Eric bought them hot dogs, and that was the big joke. 'The first meal my son ever bought me.'" He laughs.

"Then the other thing the medium said is, 'He wants you to know that he sees everything. He is still there with his son and he is watching him. His son is jumping up and down on something.' The medium's looking off in the distance. She says, 'This is very strange. He is jumping up and down on a *waffle.*' This is where she's lost me. A *waffle*? So we call up Eric's wife, Michelle and mention it to her, and she says that about two weeks ago a new mall opened up and we took him. There is a whole play area in the middle, soft plastic things kids can jump on, and his favorite thing in it was the waffle."

Stuart shrugs.

"Unbelievable, right?" he says. "So we keep talking, and eventually she asks, 'Who's Doug? Dougie?' she says. She's getting this from Eric apparently. Now no one called him 'Dougie' but me that I knew about, so that was kind of weird. We talked about Doug. She says, 'Who's Jennifer?' I say, 'Doug's wife.' She says, 'Jennifer is having a hard time. She keeps dreaming about him dying in terrible ways. Tell her that he didn't. Tell her it went fast.' You know, tell her this and that. She says, 'She won't see him. He's there. He's kissing her.'"

"Doug's kissing Jennifer?"

"'Yeah,' and then she goes, 'Who's Freddie? Freddie wants to know why no one has asked for him yet.'

"She says, 'Fred seems pretty impressed with his hair. Doug says it's not fair, it's hereditary.' How would she know Doug's hair was thinning?

"And then we asked for Carlton. And so I don't say a word. Elise says we want to talk to Carlton Bartels. The medium says, 'Give him a minute. He wants to come in differently from everyone else.' She says, 'I hear music.' And I am sure it was a Grateful Dead song because he is a Dead Head. And she says, 'He's showing me a boat in a lake, rowing across the lake. He's showing me a fire, a campfire burning.' How did she get Carlton right? She says he's smoking, and Carlton's the only one of these guys who'd be smoking.

"We asked for Bernie. She says he wasn't up there. 'He died five years ago.'

"'There are too many people,' she said. I said, 'Is there anybody that needs to talk to me?'

"She says, 'Who is Stanley?'

"I say, 'Stanley, the shoeshine guy.'

"She describes him as a large slow-moving man. Stanley is six feet five. Seventy-something years old. He spent thirty-five years in the army, a master sergeant in India, a former sparring partner to Joe Louis. A really nice guy. I always invited him to parties with his wife.

"I go, 'Shit! He was a good man.'

"She says, 'No, he says *you* were a good man. He wants you to know that all the little things you do are remembered up here.'"

There is more that she knew. What's most significant is how Stuart and Elise drew comfort from their experience. Many of the living talk of dreams they have had where they've talked to friends, seen them at work. Stephen Merkel saw David Weiss floating by their Trade Center office. Tim Grazioso's daughter saw her father in the kitchen of their Florida home a day after the attacks. Tim O'Brien's daughter saw her father lying in bed next to her mother one Sunday morning. In nearly all of the conversations, it is the dead comforting the living, and not the reverse. They are powerful moments of passage for the grieving. They are forgiven for their sins, real or imagined. But there is much more to it. Some talk of the instant of seeing a husband or father or

brother or friend as confirmation of what they had been suspecting—
that none of this had actually happened. They had finally woken up
from the nightmare.

And then they are gone all over again, and the loss moves to another, deeper level of certainty.

Acknowledgments

There is no way in one book to capture the extent of what happened to Cantor Fitzgerald on September 11 and in the subsequent weeks and months. *On Top of the World* is not meant to be an exhaustive study, but rather a glimpse of a community under tremendous stress in the wake of a national tragedy. For every story included here there are a hundred left out.

There are many on whom I've depended during the writing of this book. I want to especially thank Howard for calling me in September and asking me to begin this project, for granting me unlimited access, and for having the wisdom to know that Cantor Fitzgerald's story was one that needed to be told.

I am indebted as well to the surviving employees of Cantor Fitzgerald for allowing me in their midst and for the generous time they spent talking about their experiences. Lee Amaitis, Paul Pion, Karen Weinberg, Lynne Granat, Joe Asher, Amy Nauiokas, Phil Ginsberg, Tom Trillo, Bill Rice, Stuart Fraser, Kent Karosen, Phil Marber, Diny Ajamian, Stephen Merkel, Chris Sorenson, Frank Walczak, John Law, David Kravette, Joe Noviello, Matt Claus, Clive Triance, Jim Johnson,

Shaun Lynn, Steve Williams, and Gerald Levy were among many Cantor employees and friends who were of great help.

I am especially appreciative of Allison Lutnick, Edie Lutnick, and Lewis Ameri; and of the Gardner family: Jennifer, Charlotte, Joe, and Danielle for their friendship, warmth, and insight. Maryann Burns was a perceptive and unwaveringly honest guide to the world of Cantor Fitzgerald.

I want to thank Jane Friedman and Cathy Hemming for recognizing the importance of the story, and placing their faith behind it. Susan Weinberg oversaw the process with wit and wisdom. I want to thank as well Carie Freimuth, Patti Kelly, Cindy Achar, John Jusino, Elliott Beard, Roberto de Vicq de Cumptich, Georgia Morrissey, Jennifer Swihart, and Brian DeLeeuw for their hard work and kind words.

David Hirshey and Jeff Kellogg worked indefatigably on all matters editorial, and their intelligence, good humor, and gift for the sentence was enormously appreciated. They labored many long days and nights to make this a better book. I want to thank Ellen Levine who worked tirelessly on behalf of this project and who found for it such an apt home. Louise Quayle, Emily Haynes, and Jean Lum Hoy offered needed insight and assistance. And thanks to Hans Gerhardt, who lost his son Ralph, for suggesting the title of this book. My stepmother, Carol Lamberg, kept a roof over my head in New York and was as always a fabulous friend and adviser.

Finally, I want to thank my wife, Hilary Beggs, for her patience, love, and everything else through so many long weeks apart.